MEDIC
DHARMA REIKI

A FULL CIRCLE BOOK

MEDICINE
DHARMA REIKI

Medicine Dharma Reiki

An Introduction to the Secret Inner Practices

With Extensive Excerpts from *Dr. Usui's Journals*

Lama Yeshe

Foreword by *Paula Horan*

FULL
CIRCLE

MEDICINE DHARMA REIKI
© All Rights Reserved 2000

First Indian Paperback Edition, 2000
ISBN 81-7621-081-1

Published by FULL CIRCLE PUBLISHING
Head Office: 18-19, Dilshad Garden, G.T. Road, Delhi-110 095
Tel: 228 2467, 229 7792 • Fax: 228 2332 • e-mail: gbp@del2.vsnl.net.in
Editorial Office: J-40, Jorbagh Lane, New Delhi-110 003
Tel: 462 0063, 461 5138 • Fax: 464 5795

Print & Production: SCANSET

18-19 Dilshad Garden, G.T. Road, Delhi-110 095
Tel: 228 2467, 229 7792   Fax: 228 2332

Printed at Imprint Solutions, Delhi-110095

PRINTED IN INDIA

TABLE OF CONTENTS

PART IV

Appendices

NOTICE

Men Chhos Rei Kei© and Medicine Dharma Rei Kei© are registered Trademarks of the Rei Kei system of healing. The system is based on the 'Tantra of the Lightning Flash', and the notes and other papers of Dr. Usui Mikao and Dr. Watanabe Kioshi Itami. The author's father purchased these papers in Japan in 1946. They are now placed in the custodianship of the 'Dharma Society of the Glorious White Peacock'.

The term Reiki or Rei Kei was coined by Dr. Usui in his notes. The Tibetan syllables 'Men' (medicine) and 'Chhos' (Dharma) were added by the author as an expression of his gratitude to the country and the Lama-physicians of Tibet. They are also a pointer to the fact that an emissary sent by Dr. Usui found a copy of the 'Tantra of the Lighting Flash' and related commentaries at the famous Medical College of Chagpori Ling near Lhasa. These Tibetan manuscripts came in as a great help when Dr. Usui reconstructed some of the parts of the 'Tantra' that were missing in the Chinese and Japanese versions of the text.

Throughout the book, the term 'Medicine Dharma Reiki' was substituted as it is the spelling common today.

Only teachers who have received proper authorization from the Spiritual Director of the western branch of the 'Dharma

ACKNOWLEDGMENTS

First and foremost I wish to express my gratitude to Mil Jernigan without whose untiring help and work at her computer this book would not have been possible.

I am also grateful to Ms. Hanne Strong, Director and Founder of the Manitou Foundation, Standing White Buffalo Woman, and Tsunmo (Tibetan: 'Noble Queen') of the Baca Grande, who a number of years ago impressed on me the need for me to give public teachings, and whose efforts for the preservation and propagation of healing disciplines I believe is unequaled by any person in our time.

Mr. Gary Leikas, who has been instrumental in getting the ball rolling for *Medicine Dharma Reiki*.

Furthermore I owe a deep debt of gratitude to all the teachers of *Medicine Dharma Reiki* for their support and work in spreading the teachings.

I especially wish to acknowledge Dr. Paula Horan and Matthias Dehne for their help in editing the manuscript, and without whose insistence and inspiration I never would have started writing. Their persistence also brought me together with my publisher.

Finally I gladly thank Shekhar and Poonam Malhotra of Full Circle Publishing, New Delhi, without whose encouragement and willingness to publish, this project would have never been feasible.

FOREWORD

An Encounter with the Ancient Lineage of Reiki

Hasten back to your country; offer these things to the court,
and spread the teachings throughout your country to increase
the happiness of the people. Then the land will know peace
and people everywhere will be content.
In that way, you will return thanks to the Buddha and to your teacher.
That is also the way to show your devotion to your family. —

Hui-ko's final instruction to Kukai

It gives me great joy to have the privilege of writing this
short introductory essay on the ancient lineage of Reiki. I am sure
the revelations in the following pages will be exciting reading for
anyone seriously interested in the Usui Method of Natural Healing. More than any other book, *Medicine Dharma Reiki* connects
us with the historical roots of Reiki. It is, therefore, probably the
most important publication among the many that have been re-
leased on this ancient Japanese system of spiritual and self-healing. The author places Reiki in the context of an age-old transmission, going back all the way to the time of the Buddha. He does
so, not by conjecture or hindsight, but by presenting as evidence
Dr. Usui's own words, the man who rediscovered Reiki a little
over a hundred years ago.

A Groundbreaking Contribution to the
Understanding of Reiki

In fact, excerpts from Dr. Usui's journals and notes make-up a good two-thirds of the text, while the author contents himself with the role of a commentator. Dr. Usui's writings are the flesh and bones of this book. Lama Yeshe merely points out some of their ramifications, elucidating the particular features that any reader, unfamiliar with Shingon (Japanese Tantric) Buddhism, would overlook or misinterpret. The fact that there is a written transmission for the entire Reiki system is in itself groundbreaking. It will change forever the way Reiki is received. The source for this written tradition is the "Tantra of the Lightning Flash That Heals the Body and Illumines the Mind".

The book is groundbreaking in yet another way, as it serves as an introduction to the entire system of esoteric practices from which Reiki is derived. A system which is more far reaching and far more complex than what we presently know about Reiki. The small part of Reiki that to date is known to most of the millions of practitioners around the globe, is the lay form of Reiki. Dr. Usui referred to this simplified lay form of the teachings, which he himself devised, as the 'pacification', or the 'soothing hands'. As Dr. Usui states, hands-on Reiki 'heals indirectly, by calming the mind and raising the Life Force Energy'. It is extremely beneficial in stress release and as a tool for the gradual elimination of many of the psychosomatic causes of discomfort and disease. However, it is only a fraction of the techniques, that Dr. Usui applied in his own medical practice.

As a second great boon, *Medicine Dharma Reiki* introduces us to the complete picture of Reiki as practiced by Dr. Usui himself. It allows us to get a glimpse of the complete system of Medicine Dharma or Men Chhos Reiki, which is precisely the form of Reiki that Dr. Usui taught to a small group of his heart students.

These teachings had been lost for over forty years because of the ravages of World War II. They only resurfaced in 1994, when Lama Yeshe happened upon Dr. Usui''s notes and journals. The author describes how a whole chain of synchronicities finally led to the discovery of Dr. Usui's writings, and the subsequent reconstruction of his teachings from the very same source, which Usui had used, the "Tantra of the Lightning Flash That Heals the Body And Illumines the Mind".

Dr. Usui and the "Tantra of the Lightning Flash"

This scripture came to Japan in the eighth century. Kukai (774-835 C.E.), also known as the 'Kobo Daishi', brought the manuscript from Mainland China where he had studied the text and its practices under the guidance of master Hui-ko (746-805 C.E.). Many illustrious teachers have been part of this lineage before and after Kukai, for example Mahacharya Nagarjuna, the famous practitioner of non-duality, Tantric adept, and master of the alchemical Siddha tradition, as well as several Chinese and Japanese Emperors. At some point, the lineage vanished into the great unknown. There seemed to be no more living masters, carrying the transmission.

This is when Dr. Usui came into the picture. According to his own statement, he found an ancient manuscript, the "Tantra of the Lightning Flash" in a used bookstore in Kyoto in 1896. It 'set his heart and mind on fire'. It was such a revelation to him that he was immediately motivated to study the text and to work with the practices until he had mastered them. He then applied them in his medical practice whenever it was appropriate, and gathered serious students around him to whom he would transmit the teachings. In this way, the lineage was revitalized.

However, the more Dr. Usui worked with the material that he had taken from the ancient manuscript, the more he clearly saw that the demands the Tantra made on the practitioner were far too strenuous and exacting for the average man or woman. He was, thus, inspired to devise a simplified form of hands-on healing, based on the essence of the teachings. This simplified system he called 'Reiki'.

The Tradition of the 'Hidden Treasures'

At around the same time that Kukai introduced Tantric Buddhism to Japan, calling it Shingon ('True Word') in reference to the chanting of certain key seed mantras, Padmasambhava also introduced Vajrayana or Tantric Buddhism in Tibet.

Especially in the Tibetan Nyingma school of Vajrayana Buddhism there is the tradition of the so-called 'Hidden Treasures'. These are scriptures, ritual items or works of religious art, which were completed and then concealed by Padmasambhava, the founder of Tibetan Buddhism, to be rediscovered in the future by a specific person at a specific time when their presence would be needed to transform certain negative energies. In Tibetan, these 'Hidden Treasures' are called Terma. The most famous example of a Terma is the well-known Tibetan Book of the Dead. This text was dictated by Padmasambhava to his consort the Lady Yeshe Tsogyal in the late eighth century. As predicted, Karma Lingpa then rediscovered it in a cave on Gampo Dar Mountain in Central Tibet, in the fourteenth century.

Taking the Tibetan Terma tradition as a basis for comparison, the way Dr. Usui 'found' a copy of the Tantra of the Lightning Flash in an antique bookstore could well qualify him as a 'Treasure Finder', and the manuscript itself as a 'Hidden Treasure'. The way Dr. Usui stresses the particular relevance of these teachings for our times also points in the same direction.

Similarities and Differences between the Lay Form of Reiki and Medicine Dharma Reiki

Both the lay practice of Reiki and Medicine Dharma Reiki use mystical empowerments to help the practitioner attune to and, thus, more easily discover their innate abilities to draw on certain energies. Each one focuses on healing as a tool to calm the mind and raise one's Life Force Energy. Both also need to be practiced regularly to have the desired effect. Finally both evoke the greater awareness that leads to peace and ultimately, to enlightenment.

Where they differ, really lies in the more intense commitment which is needed to practice and realize the benefits of Medicine Dharma Reiki. In the lay practice of Reiki, you only need to spend fifteen to thirty minutes of laying on of hands each evening and morning. The first level of Medicine Dharma Reiki, however, requires the additional follow through on a sadhana (spiritual practice) that minimally takes thirty to forty-five minutes on a daily basis. It requires this added time in order to charge water for healing with the energy of the five elements, and to generate oneself as various Tantric deities (archetypal manifestations, each representing a specific energy matrix). To learn to generate oneself as various energy manifestations takes consistent follow through, with the bottom line being a total dedication to full self-realization in one lifetime, on the Vajrayana path. At the Second Level, a whole pharmacopoeia is learned in addition to special visualizations and fire ceremonies to dispel negative energies in whole areas. The most recent translations have brought to light certain practices to regenerate whole environments where destruction has occurred. Again, to generate such energy, even more time and more consistent practice are essential to remove all doubt in the practitioner as well as the karmic obstacles, which invariably cross one's path.

Ultimately, Medicine Dharma Reiki is only suited to a person who is interested in the healing path as a vehicle to full awakening and is, thus, dedicated to transcending all suffering for the benefit of self and others.

A Meeting of Mind Streams

In Tantric Buddhism the meeting of teacher and student in the moment of true initiation is called the meeting of two mind streams. When the student is ready, so will be the teacher and the teachings. This is a good way to describe my own first encounter with the Usui story as told in his own words, and the teachings of the Tantra of the Lightning Flash.

It happened almost three years ago, in November 1997. Together with Narayan I was taking a break from India, visiting the US in order to take care of the final arrangements for the sale of a piece of property we still owned in the Pacific Northwest. We had flown into San Francisco to be with my sister in Northern California for a few days when I called Judith, a Reiki friend from Baltimore. As we hadn't talked for a while, we started to exchange news and I told her about our plans of drive up North on I-5. At that point she cut in excitedly, 'In that case, you have to stop on the way to meet Lama Yeshe on the California Oregon border. He has found Usui's notes and diaries, and can give you a whole new perspective on Reiki.' Great, I thought to myself, may be he'll even share a few quotes for my new book, and then asked her for the phone number and address.

A few days later we were on our way. We stopped near Cave Junction to visit this mysterious man. Our plan was to stay for at the most an hour or two, and exchange pleasantries over a cup of tea, and then head on. At 4:00 p.m. sharp, we arrived at the Lama's 'Hermitage of the White Peacock', actually a chalet on the premises of a Motel near a town so small that I have already forgotten its name.

Two hours passed, then four, then ten, then twelve. We left Lama Yeshe's house at exactly 4:00 a.m. the next morning absolutely inspired, transported and transformed. There was no doubt left in our minds that we had met the 'real thing', an authentic spiritual teacher of an authentic lineage, offering authentic teachings. It felt so wonderful, we were bursting at the seams. The twelve hours had gone by in a flash. Actually, the sense of time passing had been completely suspended. We both appreciated that we had just reconnected with a Dharma brother whom we had known for many lifetimes.

As an interesting coincidence, we found out that Lama Yeshe's root teacher, H.H. Khamtrul Rinpoche VIII, was also one of the first living Buddhas Narayan had met on his earlier visits to India in the mid-seventies. The similarities in my own life with Lama Yeshe's were uncanny: we both have a doctorate in psychology, and were brought up around the military, moving every three years. We listened to excerpts from Usui's diaries, and were blessed by a White Mahakala ceremony that Lama Yeshe conducted for our benefit. It was all so incredible that with deeper reflection we decided to participate in a series of Medicine Dharma Reiki teachings and empowerments to be held the following summer in July 1998. It felt like something that needed to happen, a logical next step on the Reiki path.

I was so surprised by this strange turn of events because at that particular point in time the last thing on my mind had been to seek out another teacher or set of spiritual practices. My own Satguru Papaji had just passed away in September that same year, and I felt completely saturated with His incomparable Grace. When a being like Papaji, a living Buddha so vast and loving, leaves his or her body, a spark is ignited in their devotees that carries the seed essence of realization. My main impulse at that time was to simply sit quietly with this overpowering Grace, and allow it to engulf me. As we connected so deeply with Lama Yeshe and Usui's lineage of the Tantra of the Lightning Flash, I concluded that my Satguru must have lead me to Lama's doorstep. When a diamond falls into your lap you don't hesitate, but gratefully accept it.

Therefore, both Narayan and I, together with three of our students, attended the 3-week Medicine Dharma Reiki retreat in Oregon in July 1998, and we both were initiated into the master level of the system. Since that time my daily Mizu-Hari practice as well as a few others I have since been given by another Tibetan master, have become the focus point of my life. Somehow for me, these daily practices have created a matrix for the release of many vasanas or karmic obscurations, and help to keep me in touch with the gift of Silence that I received from Papaji. Both Narayan and I love to share Medicine Dharma Reiki with others, whenever the occasion arises.

How Usui's Diaries and Medicine Dharma Reiki
Support the Understanding Of the Lay Practice of Reiki

According to my own experience, the practice of Medicine Dharma Reiki and the reading of Usui's written heritage are a great support for the teaching and practice of the lay form or Three Degrees of hands-on Reiki. With the introduction of Usui's own unique personality and his inspiring words, they enrich it beyond imagination. As a matter of fact, before encountering Lama Yeshe I wrote only two books on the lay practice of Reiki in eight years. After having been exposed to Dr. Usui's material and the steady focus provided by the daily generation of certain energies, I have completed three more books in only two years. Somehow the reverberation of my Master's death, the completion of almost fifteen years of the lay practice of Reiki, and the richness imparted by what feels like a homecoming to the heart essence of a lineage, have all coalesced to a virtual fountain of inspiration. Together with Narayan, I am now happily working on several writing projects. Thus, there has been an incredible boost in creativity, and a more focused embodiment of the teaching.

Furthermore, the existence of Medicine Dharma Reiki does not render superfluous the need for the lay form of Reiki. As stated above, the Medicine Dharma teachings are too demanding for most people. First and Second Degree of hands-on Reiki will therefore always be needed to 'calm the mind and raise the Life Force Energy'. Thus, the excerpts from Usui's writings as presented by Lama Yeshe in no way contradict the Reiki we have known. How could they? After all, in the Tantra of the Lightning Flash they share the same source. Medicine Dharma Reiki and the lay practice of Reiki also have the same founder: Dr. Mikao Usui.

Lama Yeshe's book is a great gift to the Reiki community. It helps to sensitize the reader's awareness to the highly spiritual and ethical principles inherent in the Usui System of Natural Healing. It will also fire the hearts of some of its readers with a new appreciation for the great depth of this teaching. The lay practitioner may find inspiration in its august lineage of realized masters, reaching back in time to Shakyamuni Buddha. Most of all, may it inspire the few who really feel called upon to seek initiation into the lineage of the Tantra of the Lightning Flash. So they may join in to help generate a positive change at this crucial time when a much needed energy shift on the earth hangs in the balance.

It is my sincere hope that it will do so.

Paula Horan

Jnanasagara Dvipa,
Full Moon of the Seventh Month
Iron Dragon Year

September 13th, 2000

INTRODUCTION

Where Does Medicine Dharma Reiki Come From?

In order to answer this question, we must look into the teachings of Shakyamuni Buddha, and in particular at the Mahayana teachings that urge us to benefit others in whatever activities we perform. From the earliest times, the practitioners of the Dharma aided their fellow countrymen by practicing the healing arts. The theoretical concept of Buddhist healing originated with Shakyamuni Buddha in that all of his teachings were aimed at eliminating human suffering in all of its aspects.

If it has a choice, no being wishes to suffer and experience pain. All beings wish to experience enjoyment of life and happiness. It is the primary and only goal of the Buddha to aid humankind in a positive way, teaching them the doctrine of karmic cause and effect, the means to overcome suffering, and the methodology for gaining enlightenment. The path of Mahayana Buddhism teaches us that by aiding others we can aid ourselves, and at last gain the total victory of full and complete enlightenment.

What better way is there to aid other beings than by eliminating the suffering caused by illness? And instructing beings on both the mundane and spiritual level of how to maintain bodily health and spiritual well-being at the same time?

Lord Shakyamuni Buddha taught us that in a different world era and a different time a physician with right motivation and compassion gained enlightenment and became a Buddha. This Buddha is known by various names, such as Medicine King Buddha or the Lord of the 'Lapis Lazuli Light'.

Shakyamuni Buddha also taught us that when properly invoked, Medicine King Buddha could grant supernatural healing and also empower the healer to carry on this supreme work on the physical plane.

Reiki

A Japanese physician, Dr. Usui Mikao, in the late 1800s and early 1900s after assiduously studying Buddhism, developed a hands-on healing system that was able to tap into the divine healing energies of Medicine King Buddha and apply these energies to the patient with whom he was working. Not wanting to limit it only to Buddhists, by the use of symbols and invocations, he created a simple lay practice available to everyone, regardless of religious or philosophical persuasion.

From Dr. Usui's efforts and the teaching that he gave, Reiki has evolved today into one of the most popular nonsectarian healing system practiced worldwide.

How Do Reiki and Medicine Dharma Reiki Differ?

The only way in which Medicine Dharma Reiki differs from the teaching and methodology of Reiki, is a matter of degree. It was Dr. Usui's intention that all of the components of the Buddhist healing techniques which could be used by non-Buddhists should be incorporated into a system of healing and that this system could be taught to benefit mankind. Medicine Dharma Reiki is the totality of that system of which Reiki is a part.

In order to practice Medicine Dharma Reiki, however, it is necessary for the practitioner to be a practicing Buddhist and to have received the necessary empowerments and instructions. The source of our information on Medicine Dharma Reiki is taken from the Tantra of the Lightning Flash and notes and various papers by Dr. Usui and Dr. Watanabe Kioshi Itami. They were found contained within the case in which the text of the Tantra was kept.

This material sets out a complete healing system according to traditional Buddhist methodology, and also includes the methodology for utilizing the divine healing that is somewhat parallel to both the Indian Ayurvedic system and Chinese Medicine. Since this information is found generally in the commentary it is considered additional to the basic cannon, occurring over a period of over 2500 years, although within the cannon of the Tantra itself, a great many parallels to Ayurvedic medicine can be found.

What Is the Meaning of the Words Men Chhos or Medicine Dharma?

Due to an incredible synchronicity of events, my father purchased the Tantra, its commentaries and Dr. Usui's notes in 1946. It seems fated that I with my parallel Shingon background (to Dr. Usui) and my current status as a recognized Vajrayana Buddhist Lama and a member of the Drugpa Kargyu Order of Bhutan, became the overseer of these teachings. I chose the words Men Chhos, Tibetan for "medicine" or "healing", and "supreme teaching", because they clearly describe the essence of the texts. Thus, in English, the phrase Medicine Dharma Reiki was coined.

Since much of the material contained within the Tantra is of early Indian Mahayana and Vajrayana origin and since a great deal of this teaching has been preserved by the Tibetans, it seemed appropriate that this material be also given a Tibetan name. The

Sanskrit would be Bhaishajya Dharma, which simply means "medicine doctrine".

The Theory of Buddhist Healing

Buddhism teaches us that all suffering is brought on by our past negative actions and is a result of the harm caused to others and ourselves by those actions. The actions could either have been performed in this life or many previous lives. In order, therefore, for an illness to be truly healed, the causative karma of which the illness is the result, must be pacified.

There are many methodologies taught in Buddhism to bring about this condition. Medicine Dharma Reiki teaches us that as well as physical, spiritual remedies must also be applied. The Tantra teaches us those remedies and also the means by which we may attune ourselves to the healing energies of universal benefit, happily and freely dispensed by Medicine King Buddha.

It demonstrates to us at the same time how we can alter our lives, that we may benefit all other sentient beings and ourselves.

The 'Dharma Society of the Glorious White Peacock'

Because Medicine Dharma Reiki is a Buddhist teaching with a direct lineage going back to Shakyamuni Buddha, it is important that a master of substance guides its dissemination in the world. Sponsoring the Medicine Dharma Reiki Foundation is the Dharma Society of the Glorious White Peacock, organized in 1931 by Tisien Wakhyo and carried on by his son, Tsien Tsei Mya Rinpoche, a Chinese Vajrayana Lama and member of the Drugpa Kargyu Lineage of Bhutan, who presently resides in Taiwan. The purpose of the Dharma Society of the Glorious White Peacock is to promulgate the beneficial teachings of the Buddha throughout the world. The peacock, which in Buddhist iconography represents the ability to transform poison for the benefit of others, is an appropriate symbol for the re-introduction of this ancient healing system to the world.

Tsien Tsei Mya Rinpoche considers both the Reiki and the Medicine Dharma Reiki teaching to be supremely beneficial for the well being of all sentient beings. He considers it to be extremely important for all people during this dark time of the Kali Yuga, when new diseases are appearing in the world and both human and environmental resources are being strained to the extreme.

At this time when the stress and tension placed on human beings is so great by virtue of cultural imperatives, Rinpoche feels that a return to the traditional methods of healing, ethics, and teaching relating to human conduct, are a necessity if civilization is to survive and become stabilized. Rinpoche feels that Medicine Dharma Reiki is one tool to assist in accomplishing this desired end.

In short, we believe the ancient and traditional healing systems contained in traditional Reiki as taught worldwide by Mrs. Takata and the teachers in her lineage and the more complex Medicine Dharma Reiki teaching can only benefit all beings and assist in alleviating suffering caused by accident, illness and disease.

As I was raised and grew up as a Buddhist, I encountered a number of different schools of Buddhism. As a Shingon Buddhist, literally from birth, I was well trained in the liturgies of Shingon Buddhism.

In my teens and twenties I became familiar with the liturgies of the Pure Land School and of Tendai, due to my devotion to Buddha Amitabha. After meeting Kun Chab Si Chu Rinpoche, I became familiar with the liturgies and devotional practices of the four major Tibetan Buddhist schools and that of the Chinese liturgy of the Za Ming School.

My father had purchased several lacquer boxes of Japanese texts in 1946 in Japan, and in 1994 during a conversation with my father it was discovered that one of these boxes contained information on Reiki. I have discussed with Kun Chab Si Chu Rinpoche the application of these teachings to the current usage of Buddhism in the West and it was decided that these texts are in conformity with the best traditions of Mahayana Buddhism and leave no necessary form of worship, devotion or activity out of the lineage as being taught in the West.

Both Chinese and Japanese Buddhism emphasize the well-being of society and spotlight the activities which an individual can perform while on this earth, in this human body, for the benefit of sentient beings. Japanese Buddhism, surprising to some, emphasizes the aspect of the Buddhist path that is enlightenment through service to others, not departing from the traditional North Indian format for Mahayana Buddhist practice, and taking into consideration that at that early time in Buddhism's development there was no definitive line drawn between Sutra and Tantra for the general public in devotion and sadhana practice.

Following advice and prayers given in the notes of Dr. Mikao Usui, and following the form given in both the Sutras and Tantras, yet not neglecting Western thought and mindset, we are establishing an explanation, teaching, and practice principally for use in Medicine Dharma Reiki. The lineage and practice of these teachings that reflect Mahayana thought would be beneficial for any serious student of Dharma practice who has been given proper introduction to the texts (empowerment or initiation, and instruction in practice).

As I hold both the Vajrayana Buddhist (Drugpa Kargyu Order of Bhutan) and since a child, the Japanese Shingon empowerments, pith teachings, and instructions in Shingon practice of the deities invoked in these practices, and since I have the full papers, teachings and instructions of Dr. Usui and Dr. Watanabe, and since I have had the intensive training, retreats, empowerments and instructions of a Lama (minister, priest) I do not consider it presumptuous on my part to prepare the Medicine Dharma Reiki teachings to carry on the lineage of Dr. Usui's work to help where healing is needed in this world.

Lama Drugpa Yeshe Thrinley Odzer, *The Ninth Drugmar Rinpoche, Drugpa Kargyu Order of Bhutan*

Spiritual Director, *Men Chhos Rei Kei©, Medicine Dharma Reiki* (Written at the Vernal Equinox, 30 March 1997, at the Hermitage of the Blue Peacocks.)

Part I

The History and Background of Buddhist Healing

1

THE JOURNEY BEGINS

The Synchronicity of Events Leading to the Reconstruction of Medicine Dharma Reiki

There are various times in a person's life when a beginning or new direction occurs. When I decided to write this book I began to reflect on the one point that started me on my journey toward Dr. Usui, Medicine Dharma Reiki, and this book.

I was born in Japan, the son of an American military officer, and a Carolina housewife. Two years previous to my birth, my father had converted from Unitarianism to Shingon Buddhism, so I was actually born a Buddhist. Other than the one major difference of being a Buddhist, I was raised as a middle class American. My father chose to remain in the military, and by the time we returned to America in 1952, he had ascended the ladder to the rank of Major, so I was raised as a 'military brat', and spent a good part of my life on military bases.

Our family Buddhism at that time was very much like the average Christian or Jew and only came up on specific occasions, such as Buddha's birthday or his Parinirvana. Shingon Buddhism in America, which I found when we moved to Silver Springs, Maryland, was 'a Sunday thing'. There we attended temple on Sunday with a few military people who had accepted Buddhism, a few Western civilians, and a large number of Japanese who were attached to the various missions, such as Embassy and Consulate in Washington, D.C.

We would go in and sit for an hour, sing the Japanese liturgy and the Bonze (priest) would preach a sermon, courteously in English, as there were Westerners present. At home every evening before dinner my father would read from a small book of readings published by the International Buddhist Society, and then we would say a few evening prayers, as set forth in the same book.

I attended private school in England and kept up my prayers and readings and then chose to attend university in Canada. After the first year of university my roommate was the son of a Japanese Consular official and so we had our devotions together, although he was not Shingon, but Shinran.

It is important to mention that Buddha Amitabha, the Lord of Boundless Light, was one of the principal Buddhas worshipped by both of our schools of Buddhism. In our lineage of Shingon, he was most important for lay people, and I had chanted his prayers for as long as I could remember.

After university, I followed my father's footsteps into the military, and because of my Buddhism was assigned as intelligence liaison to a Thai Ranger Unit. When the Bhutanese Vajrayana Lama, Kon Chab Si Chu Rinpoche, came from Nepal to purify and reconsecrate a small Vajrayana temple which had been desecrated by a Khmer Rouge incursion across the border, I went to meet him and found one of my teachers.

I was invited to visit him in Kathmandu, Nepal, after I left the military. I did so and became a Vajrayana Buddhist with the Drugpa Kargyu Order of Bhutan. I was then sent by him to receive empowerments by His Holiness Dudjom Rinpoche (Nyingmapa), His Holiness the Gyalwa Karmapa (Karma Kagyu), His Holiness the Dalai Lama (Gelugpa), and finally my root Lama, the Khamtrul Rinpoche (Drugpa Kargyu).

Upon reflection, any of these events would have served as a beginning of my journey, but on further reflection, I found they were not. Upon looking back over my life I believe there was one pivotal point that you might say was the beginning of all this: and that happened about three weeks before my return to the United States. That was the year 1975 in Kathmandu, Nepal.

I had rented a small house in Kathmandu as I like my privacy and the life at Rinpoche's temple was busy, to say the least. The monsoon had begun and I was reading a text by Chogyam Trungpa when my maid announced someone was there to see me.

It turned out to be Katherine Sutherland, an English Dharma practitioner, and student of His Holiness the Dalai Lama. I had met her on my visit to Dharamsala, and we had become friends and saw each other occasionally here and there in Kathmandu. The monsoon was in full force and Kathy was wet and bedraggled and had come to ask a favor of me.

It seems that a Karma Kargyu Lama, Lama Karma Yonten, was visiting from Bhutan and was planning to give a Medicine Buddha empowerment, but because of the weather and the appearance of Urgyen Tulku in Kathmandu to give teachings and empowerments, the attendance at Lama Yonten's empowerment was expected to be scanty. She also indicated that Lama Yonten was short of funds and had hoped for some support because of the empowerment. I agreed to attend and make a small donation. After feeding Kathy a large bowl of warm dal, partaking of one myself along with a number of cups of tea, we departed for Lama Yonten's empowerment.

The empowerment was taking place at the home of a Hindu merchant living in Kathmandu, a Mr. Ramananda, whose wife was ill and who had asked that the empowerment be given at his home. Upon entering I was introduced to Lama Karma Yonten, who was a jolly, round Bhutanese. Unfortunately the only thing I really remember about him is his winning smile, which displayed several gold teeth.

There was a small group present, some of Mr. Ramananda's friends, a couple of Tibetan refugees and their wives and children, and a few Western students. The empowerment given was that of Medicine King Buddha, Lord of the Lapis Lazuli Light, according to the lineage of Mingyur Dorje and Karma Chagme. Lama Karma Yonten spoke no English at all but fortunately an English speaking Sherpa was present, Mr. Rinchen Sherpa, who acted as translator for the talk.

I had received empowerments previously, in Kathmandu, Sikkim, Dharamsala, and of course from my root Lama, the Khamtrul Rinpoche. These had been rather grand affairs with incarnate Lamas present and much pomp, circumstance, and ceremony. Here, on the other hand I was experiencing more of 'the peoples' tradition', and as things progressed I became very moved. Lama Yonten, not even a Rinpoche, spoke for about two hours and told the story of Medicine King Buddha.

He particularly emphasized Medicine Buddha's great compassionate mind, its vast love with equanimity for all beings, and imparted to all of his hearers and particularly to myself the concept of the unwavering flow of compassion and healing energy that flowed from the heart of the Lord of the Lapis Lazuli Light.

He then very quietly and simply gave the empowerment and I believe that everyone present, for a while, was transported to a Pure Land, where no imperfections exist, and which is governed by infinite compassion. I do not believe that anyone left that Newari home that night without experiencing a real taste of the meaning of an enlightened mind.

Later on I received many empowerments, some grand and some small. I even went on a Lama retreat, was officially fully ordained as a Tibetan Vajrayana Buddhist master, and subsequently was recognized as an incarnate Lama, the Ninth Drugmar Rinpoche of the Drugpa Kargyu lineage of Bhutan. Then the Japanese texts that my father purchased in 1946 came to me, which events I will describe in a later part of this chapter. But it was that evening and night in Kathmandu, I believe that pointed me in the direction that would eventually lead me to writing this book and becoming a teacher of the Medicine Dharma Reiki discipline.

The Journey Continues

After completing my Lama retreat, I returned to the United States and began to teach traditional Vajrayana Buddhism. While visiting at the Baca Grande Ranch near Crestone, Colorado, I encountered Reiki for the first time. Out of charity I will not describe my initial reaction, but suffice it to say that I was neither impressed with the system, nor with the people from Boulder who were "marketing" it; to call what they did "teaching" would be an insult to any authentic form of spiritual discipline. Consequently, at the time I rather dismissed Reiki.

In 1990, I decided that I would pursue my Dharma teaching in Oregon and finally in 1992 settled for a while in Portland. I announced the opening of our center and that I would be giving a Medicine King Buddha empowerment. The very first student to attend was Gary Leikas; he received the empowerment and we established a close relationship. It was through Gary that I became familiar with what Reiki actually was, and because of Gary's compassion toward his patients and his work with hospice, I became impressed with the system.

At this point, it is important to mention that in 1989, prior to our move West, I had visited an old acquaintance, Dr. Ajari Werrick in San Francisco. It was important in the sense that Dr. Ajari was a practitioner of both Tibetan Buddhism with Shakyapa, Nyingmapa, and Shangpa Kargyu connections, as well as a fully ordained Japanese Shingon Buddhist priest (Bonze). He felt at the time, that since I have previously been (since birth) a Shingon practitioner, I should receive from him the transmissions of the Shingon priesthood. He told me I would 'probably need it sometime', and although I really did not agree back then, in order to repay his kindness and hospitality, and because he had become a close friend and I did not wish to offend him or hurt his feelings, I agreed.

Subsequently the ordinations were bestowed upon me and I was given the text and detailed instructions concerning the performance of the Shingon Fire Offering, the Saito Goma. Later, I was to reflect back and conclude that it had been a major turning point on the journey.

In late 1992, Gary, my Aunt Mildred Jernigan and I decided to share a house in Portland. I became more familiar with Reiki practice, and on communicating by telephone with my father, then in Belgium, I mentioned that our housemate, Gary, was a Reiki practitioner and now due to my teaching, a practicing Vajrayana Buddhist.

The Mysterious Lacquer Boxes

To continue this narrative to the present, we must return to 1946 and the islands of Japan. My father, a very junior officer in the American occupational forces, had become friendly with one of the officials in the new Japanese government. He had subsequently learned of Shingon Buddhism and decided that it was what had been missing in his life. With the minister acting as translator, he began to take instruction in Shingon Buddhism.

One evening while visiting the Temple and receiving his instruction, a small group of Shingon monks had arrived from the Northern Prefecture of Tokyo. During the fire bombing of Tokyo, they had suffered the loss of their Temple and their livelihood. Fortunately as the great firestorm was approaching their Temple, they carried numerous of their texts to safety, many of their ritual implements, small statues and other Dharma items. When faced with desperation and starvation, they had sorted through the scant remains of their religious establishment, deciding to sell some of the items that they considered unnecessary for their practice in order to raise money for shelter, food and clothing.

Among these were four lacquer boxes that contained folio sheets of religious texts. After having thoroughly examined them, they concluded that these were unnecessary for the practice of their form of Buddhism or were duplicates of texts they already possessed. It is necessary to mention here that the major texts of Shingon Buddhism brought by Kukai, the Kobo Daishi, from China to Japan in 805 CE were the Mahavariochana Tantra. In one of the lacquer boxes a duplicate of this text was found, and it was explained to my father that the other three contained various commentaries, instruction manuals, and so on.

The monks fortuitously arrived while my father was taking instruction and attempted to sell the texts to the Osaka Temple. In the economic devastation as an aftermath of the war, the Osaka Temple had almost no money and was unable to purchase the texts.

My father, with the usual fervor of a recent convert to a religious system, and as he had just been paid, agreed to purchase the texts. He had intended to present them to the Temple at Osaka, but the local priest seemed rather disinterested and so my father decided to keep them, as a connection to the past of the religious system that he had recently embraced.

While I was growing up, these four mysterious lacquer boxes had reposed on a high shelf in my father's study, along with statues of Mahavairochana, Fudo, Amida and Kannon. It was not until late 1993 that we realized the significance of one of the boxes.

As I mentioned earlier, I had communicated to my father about my student's Reiki practice. He then to my surprise informed me that he had had the cover sheets of the texts translated from the Japanese and that one of them referred to Reiki. Noting my interest he agreed to dispatch the box to me.

The Texts Arrive

On a dreary winter day in early 1994, a messenger from McChord Air Force Base brought me a real surprise. One of the four mysterious lacquer boxes had arrived in Portland.

My Japanese, of course, is strictly limited to the part of the spoken language I picked up as a child. I contacted a friend of mine from my former life in the military who had taught Japanese at the Monterey Language School. He referred me to a woman translator who he knew personally and who was connected with a midwestern university. I contacted her and my aunt and I made a hasty trip to Kinko's copy service in Portland. Throughout that night we carefully photocopied the texts. The copies were then sent off to the translator and a month and a half later a parcel arrived that was somewhat like a small nuclear bomb exploding in our living room after we had listened to the tapes of the translation of a portion of the material.

Our translator had carefully prepared an index list of the material contained, though she had only actually translated a small portion of the vast contents of texts, assorted papers, lecture notes, correspondence, patient records, etc. Here is a brief summary of the four basic divisions of the contents:

1. The Tantra of the Lightning Flash, a Tantra dictated by Shakyamuni Buddha to a contemporary householder and physician in Varanasi, India.

2. Chinese and Japanese commentaries on the Tantra.

3. Notes by Dr. Usui Mikao, somewhat of an autobiography, on how he came to possess the Tantra, how it brought a change in his life, and the system of healing he developed from that Tantra, along with musings and lecture notes, correspondence, notations on patients he treated, comments on the life and times in which he lived, etc.

4. Commentary both on the Tantra and the life of Dr. Usui by his chief student, Dr. Watanabe Kioshi Itami, and a small Buddhist sadhana which Dr. Watanabe wrote to his master, Dr. Usui, on the day after Dr. Usui's death.

Fortunately much pertinent information has been translated to date (just over half of the material) and using that knowledge and my knowledge of Buddhist practice, I have been able to put together a syllabus for Medicine Dharma Reiki, levels 1, 2, and 3.

Now I must digress a little bit and say that even though I had no question as to the authenticity of the material, and even though I am trained in esoteric Vajrayana Buddhism, at the time, there were still serious questions in my mind about the usefulness of the system for present day application. Lama or not, I am still a pretty pragmatic Westerner, educated in a scientific skeptical discipline of hard science. Being such, I truly wondered if I had an authentic system of Buddhist healing, or simply the musings of a middle aged Japanese physician with somewhat of a spiritual bent.

Having had thorough instruction on Medicine King Buddha by my Tibetan teachers, I realized that the material contained in the Tantra was valid and did not deviate on important points from the instructions I had received. At the same time new material had been given and the new material was generally in accord and followed the spirit of Medicine Buddha's teaching. Yet still I had some doubts.

In 1986, even though at the time not an extensive practitioner of Medicine Buddha, I had had an experience that confirmed somewhat in my mind the validity of the practice. One of my students in Albuquerque, New Mexico, had sustained an injury and asked me to lay my hands on the afflicted part and recite the mantra, as he had heard Tibetan lamas did. He had sustained in my presence a seriously sprained ankle. In order to humor him I did as he asked and was absolutely amazed and somewhat taken aback when the swelling almost instantly abated and he informed me the pain was gone. If I had not seen the considerable swelling subside in a matter of a few minutes I would not myself have believed what occurred. The treatment was apparently effective, as in a few minutes he was back up on the ladder from which he had fallen and was continuing his work.

After reviewing the material that had been translated, I was still somewhat undecided as to my course of action. Upon Gary's and my aunt's urgings I gave a small seminar in late

1994 in Portland which was attended by only eight people, two of whom, other than Gary, were Reiki masters from the San Francisco Bay area. One had been a practitioner for over 20 years and the other had practiced as a master for five or six years. They were both somewhat favorably impressed and upon their recommendations and further urgings from Gary and my aunt, I chose to give another seminar in November of 1995. This was rather well attended and Reiki practitioners and masters from both Europe and the American East Coast attended.

When one of the very mature masters and his wife told me later that, by using the system described in Dr. Usui's notes, it seemed that the energy level of their application had increased immeasurably until 'it was like my Reiki had been increased to the fifth power', I felt this confirmed in my mind the validity of the system. The position taken and the results of my student were confirmed by everyone· else to a greater or lesser degree, who had participated in the seminar.

I then decided that the system was not some flighty New Age invention, but something valid. As I had grown up in a household where my mother was humorously described by my father as 'a charter member of the religion of the month club', and since during my childhood an entire array of mystics, mediums, medicine men, gurus, and even at one point Dr. Norman Vincent Peal, had unendingly paraded through our house, I could not be blamed for a certain skepticism about various 'new' spiritual systems. Yet from the time that I read Dr. Usui's notes, I did feel that there was something different here.

Being a Tibetan Buddhist Lama and having lived in America during the 80s and 90s, I had encountered people with some rather bizarre belief systems. I had been thoroughly trained, basically all my life, in a traditional form of Buddhism, which, when I had come to understand it, made rational and perfect sense. The fact that the material contained in the Tantra and

Dr. Usui's notes was undoubtedly part of this system and sprang from both a venerable tradition and from a rather ancient and authentic text, supported in my mind its validity.

That coupled with some of the results I had seen, particularly two people (both Gary's patients) who were terminally ill and had basically been revitalized and their conditions, one a spinal cancer and the other lupus, going totally into remission, had convinced me of the validity and benefit of the system.

Thus, I decided to embark upon the authorship of this book. In it I hope to set forth the system in an understandable manner. This will be a difficult task, as from my experience with my students, I feel it necessary for my readers' comprehension to explain in some detail the history of Buddhist healing practices, and at the same time explain a bit of the philosophical concepts of Buddhism. In order to understand the material contained in the Tantra, the commentaries, and the writings of Dr. Usui and Dr. Watanabe, it is necessary to also understand the view that they held of illness, karma, and healing.

In the West we are strongly influenced by two somewhat opposing systems of belief; on one hand we have Christianity and on the other the 'religion' of science.

Both Dr. Usui and Dr. Watanabe, not to mention the authors of the Tantra and its commentaries, were the products of a different belief and value system and a totally different and somewhat alien cultural background. What might seem ordinary and commonplace to them might seem extraordinary and somewhat bizarre to us, and vice versa.

As an example, in the late Victorian times in which Dr. Usui lived, Victorian Westerners had a fear of bathing and water. Most Victorians believed that bathing, and especially frequent bathing, could lead to disease, debilitation and even death. On the other hand, natives of Japan felt that NOT bathing at least once daily might lead to disease, debilitation and death, but even that aside, would certainly lead to social censure and rejection by their friends and other members of their society as a matter of course.

Furthermore, in the West we appear to subscribe to two opposing but nevertheless interlocking belief systems about disease: the first very traditional Christian view is that somehow God is punishing us for something we have done in this life, or perhaps because of the sins of our ancestors. The other is that through no fault of our own, but due to mindless circumstance, we have encountered a germ, possess a defective gene, or were crossing the street at a bad moment when that semi-truck just happened by and ran us down. On the other hand Orientals are convinced it is our own actions in this or a previous life that bring about the occasion for illness, accident, or a defective gene.

In order for us to understand the philosophy contained in the Tantra and in the writings of Dr. Usui and Dr. Watanabe, I shall first attempt to give an understandable explanation of the cultural views and philosophy contained within the Tantra, the commentaries, and then the writing of Dr. Usui and Dr. Watanabe.

It is not my intention, nor is the scope of this book, to present a long dissertation on Buddhist philosophy or healing practices, but rather to elucidate the system of Medicine Dharma Reiki. For further information about Buddhist philosophy and healing and its history and the civilization in Japan, China, and India, I refer my readers to the bibliography at the end of the book. So with that in mind let us begin our own journey from ancient India to the present day, following the course of the development of the system of Men Chhos Reiki.

2

THE RELIGIOUS BACKGROUND
IN INDIA AT THE TIME
OF THE BUDDHA

In order to understand the basis of Medicine Dharma Reiki,
one must look to the origins of both the philosophical view
and applied techniques of Indian medicine at the time of
Shakyamuni Buddha, circa 563-483 BCE.

Buddhism was first taught in India and many of its elements had their origin in the ancient Hindu belief system present
at that time in India. However, even in the Buddha's time, two
very different religious systems were co-existent and had to a
certain degree even merged. Before understanding religious
and philosophical views of that era it is therefore necessary to
comprehend what these two systems were, how they differed,
and where they overlapped.

The Indigenous Indian Religion and The Religion
of the Aryan Invaders

Prior to the Aryan migrations from the Caucasus Mountain region into India, a well developed culture and society with its own religious system had existed for ages in India. This system recognized a male deity usually shown with his arms entwined with snakes. This was the deity that was later to be worshipped as Shiva. His equal and consort was the great Mother Goddess (in Hinduism later known as Parvati and other forms of the Goddess), and their son was Ganesh (Ganapati), the "Elephant-Headed One". This belief system has come down to us almost unchanged and is widespread in India today, although for many the Goddess isn't considered equal to Her consort and mate any more. Equality between the sexes for both deities and human beings were one of the most striking features of this ancient indigenous Indian culture of the Mohenjo Daro and Harrappan age.

I have in my home a small murti (religious statue) that represents Shiva, his consort Parvati (or Shakti), and Ganapati as a child complete with elephant's head. I humorously refer to it as 'The Holy Family', for that is exactly what it is. As far as we can tell, the ancient system made use of yogic techniques and meditation and its goal was a personal unity with the Divine or Universal Mind, represented by the Goddess and by Shiva and their son Ganesh, or Ganapati.

The central concept of this religion seemed to be, as it is today, a recognition of one's own self-nature as divine. Solitude, meditation, and the various yogic techniques were the tools provided to gain this realization. It seemed that man did not recognize himself as separate from the godhead, but as an expression of the godhead, manifesting in physical form.

The idea of the Divine manifesting in the physical was actually the original view and realization of the ancients in Europe, in the Middle East and on the Indian sub-continent. It was only later replaced by the idea that God (or the different male gods of different cultures such as in Mesopotamia, Greece

16 Medicine Dharma Reiki

and Rome) were little more than deified parent figures blown up out of proportion who demanded obedience from their 'children', and if they disobeyed, punishment was the result.

We have carried this latter concept over to today in the West. Note such phrases as 'the children of God', and of course, 'Our Father Who Art In Heaven'. This child/parent relationship between an almighty and vengeful God (generally male) and its followers has been extremely prevalent since the late Bronze Age and has led to numerous wars, conflicts, both spiritual and physical. Crusades, "holy wars", religious discord and so forth are the most consistent element in history, as we know it. The same is still going on today, for example between the Israelis and the Arabs or the Catholics and Protestants in Ireland, who each have conceptualized a different father deity and are in conflict, which brings to mind echoes of two small boys standing out on a sidewalk, fists knotted, and belligerent expressions on their faces, each proclaiming until they are blue in the face: 'MY DAD IS A LOT BIGGER THAN YOUR DAD AND HE CAN WHIP YOUR DAD!'

When the Aryans arrived in India they brought this 'father' system of religion to the Indian sub-continent. On the one hand we have a group of people native to the area proclaiming 'God is Divine Self, permeating all existence, and manifest in all beings.' Then we have the warlike newcomers proclaiming 'Our God is in Heaven and He is the Father of His people, and His name is Indra'.

Now when you are aware that Godhead is within you and everyone else, and not riding on a cloud or enthroned upon a mountain at the center of the universe, then your approach to the Divine would take a different form. Instead of looking externally, one would look internally. Not so with the 'children' of a divine parent.

The children of a divine parent, like any child, have a love/hate relationship going and also a fear/dependency relationship at the same time. For example, I might have loving parents but they set down particular rules for me to obey. I know that if I sneak down and steal cookies from the cookie jar, I will likely be punished. Perhaps I will be sent to my room to ponder my sins, perhaps I will be spanked, or perhaps I will be deprived of cookies. Or perhaps my parents will no longer love me and maybe abandon me in the woods, in the desert, or on a street corner. Since I am dependent upon my parents for food, clothing, shelter and protection, this could have tragic results if I am only seven years old. Therefore, I walk under a cloud of fear and attempt to do all I possibly can to please my parents, or at least to hide my sins from them.

Does this sound familiar? Any child has been through it and any believer in a parental style god lives with these same fears every day of his or her life. How many times have we heard the preacher say, 'God will punish you!'? And how many times has the adherent of such a religion prayed: 'God forgive us our sins!'

Now when one has a parental god (or goddess) and is dependent upon them for survival, then one walks in fear of displeasing that deity. For instance, if one is a hunter and it gets angry with you, there will be no game. If one is a farmer, there will not be enough rain, too much rain, or hail may destroy one's crops, and therefore one would presumably starve, because most likely if the parental deity is angry with you and if you tried to make war on the neighboring tribe to steal his food, you would lose because your deity would not be with you.

Therefore, you would try to get back into your deity's good graces, and how would you do this? Well, the system that seems to have developed among the Aryans and in the ancient Middle East was animal and even sometimes human sacrifice, as well as material possessions. We even see vestiges of this in our present day society with 'Thanksgiving Day', which of course, no matter what our legends say about Indians, corn, and turkeys, is a vestigial survival of the ancient festivals of thanksgiving by agrarian people for a good harvest.

When the Aryans arrived in India they brought this system intact. The Vedic gods each had prescribed ceremonies for offering and an intact code of conduct to be carefully followed by their devotees. If the sacrifices were not performed in the prescribed manner it was believed that divine retribution would follow. As the Aryans became settled and established on the subcontinent, so did their religion. And in many parts of India it is practiced today in exactly the same manner that it was practiced 3000 years ago. Throughout India today, the smell of burning ghee (clarified butter) permeates the atmosphere as the priests of Agni make the divine fire sacrifice to the Vedic gods.

Now you may ask what all this has to do with Medicine Dharma Reiki and healing, and why would this book begin in this manner? To understand the causes of illness and their actual origin, we must understand our own human nature and our own human condition. Up until the early 20th century, and even remaining today in the West, there is the concept that illness is a divine punishment meted out by a parental style god for one's own misconduct, and in most cases is probably deserved, as no one is perfect and everyone has probably at one time or another broken some of god's rules. If one entertains this erroneous view, then it is a major obstacle to the healing of self and others.

It is also necessary to understand the religious concepts of Buddha's time in order to understand his message and the healing methodology that he taught. Existing side by side and slightly interpenetrating each other at his time were the two systems mentioned above. The concepts of parental style gods and of the divine presence within all manifestation had both rather universal influence on his society and part of his mission clearly, as stated by himself, was to liberate men from the bondage of dependence upon a sacrificial religion for their salvation. With these concepts in mind let us examine briefly Buddha's life and teaching.

3

THE LIFE AND TEACHINGS OF SHAKYAMUNI BUDDHA

In 563 BCE at Kapilavastu in the north of India or very south of Nepal, in the district of Gorakhpur near the modern day Paderia, was the seat of the noble house of the Shakyas. There ruled King Shuddhodana and his wife Queen Maya, the daughter of Suprabuddha. Maya had recently traveled to visit her sister Prajapati. She was returning to Kapilavastu to give birth to her child. However, at the Grove of Lumbini nearby, her labor came upon her and she gave birth to a son.

Legend tells us that immediately upon birth, the child spoke and took seven steps. Legend also tells us that at the time, the Vedic gods headed by Indra also known as Shakra made obeisance to him. To mark this most sacred spot which was sanctified by the birth of the Buddha, the Emperor Ashoka erected in 239 BCE a pillar inscribed with the simple statement, 'Here was born the Enlightened One'.

Before the birth of the Buddha, a prophecy was made to his father by a peripatetic Brahman that the child would either become a 'universal king' or gain enlightenment. His father, like any other politician, past, present or future, had his own agenda. The idea of his son becoming a 'universal monarch' and the honor of being the father of a 'universal monarch' filled him with great joy and apparently a certain amount of ambition. This led him to isolate Siddhartha in a cocoon of luxury.

As Siddhartha's mother had died seven days after his birth, a not uncommon occurrence in those days most likely due to childbed fever, his maternal aunt, Prajapati, raised him. When he had reached 16 years of age, as was traditional, he was married. His parents, according to custom, had previously arranged the marriage.

His spouse was Yashodhara, his cousin, and the daughter of the Raja or King of the Koli clan. After thirteen years of marriage, she gave birth to his son, Rahula.

From his birth until he had reached the age of 29 years, Siddhartha was surrounded only by great luxury, fine food, music and dancing. Finally, history tells us that one day he ventured forth from the palace and first encountered the real world. He saw a woman giving birth; he saw an individual suffering; he saw an aged person; and horror of horrors: a dead body. Moved by this experience, he developed compassion and empathy for the sufferings of humankind.

Finally, he resolved to set forth to find the origins and the cure for human suffering. Renouncing the luxury of the palace, the opulent prison his father had constructed for him, he resolved to wander about in the world. One night a heavy sleep fell upon all who dwelt in the palace, from the king himself down to the lowliest soldier. Siddhartha was then able to set forth on his quest.

First he placed himself under the tutelage of the two famous Brahman gurus, Arada Kalama, and Udraka Ramaputra, who dwelt at Vaishali. He was dissatisfied with their teachings and then went to the Brahmans and pujaris at various temples to see if he could find truth and, thus, gain knowledge of the origin of human suffering. There he only saw the wanton murder of animals in expiation for human misdeeds.

The Sutras tell us that their suffering revolted him, and he actually lectured the pujaris on the complete futility of taking life for the expiation of human sin. He also attempted to teach them, without results, that by taking the precious life of innocent animals and birds, they were creating loads of negative karma for themselves.

Leaving Vaishali in disgust, Siddhartha wandered into the jungle of Uruvila, near Gaya in Magadha. There he encountered a settlement of five of the pupils of Udraka, lead by Kaundinya. They were submitting themselves to the most austere practices in order to train their senses and gain control over their passions. For six years he stayed with them, eating nothing but roots, seeds, and sometimes even bird droppings. His body became completely debilitated and shrunken.

One day while bathing in the river Nairanjana he tried to return to the bank but was unable to. If Sujata, the daughter of a herdsman living nearby, hadn't helped him from the water, had not given him some rice cooked in milk, he would most likely have died.

Once revived, he concluded that the severe ascetic practices that he had performed for six years, rather than being a means to gain enlightenment, only led to the destruction of his mind and body. He therefore resolved that he would sit under a Bodhi tree until he became aware of the true meaning, cause, and means to overcome the suffering of sentient beings.

One night while sitting in deep meditation, he realized the cause of suffering and the means by which suffering might be escaped. He perceived that mankind grasped at worldly possessions and sought for pleasure, that although inherent within human nature was the knowledge and virtue that could lead them to the understanding of true reality, they yet remained in mental darkness deceived, ensnared by their own passions and, thus, given over to ignorance. He understood that they did not comprehend karma and the law of cause and effect.

At first he hesitated to go out and share his insights with others, as they were hard to grasp. Instead, he decided that he would remain a peaceful recluse. Only when the gods asked him to consider that there might be a few rare beings, able to understand the subtle teaching of the Awakened One, did the Buddha set forth and follow the fire of his inspiration to teach these doctrines to those who suffer. He taught that all self-grasping needs to be let go off, and that compassion for all sentient beings needs to be awakened. He taught that there is only one helpful desire: the desire to free oneself and others from the tumultuous ocean of suffering that all of Samsara is.

And what better way to assist them, what greater life could he lead than to go forth and teach to all who would listen, the means of liberation which he himself had discovered under the Bodhi tree, that they too might gain the knowledge that was his. When that night had ended and dawn streaked the eastern sky, a truly new day had dawned for mankind in this world era. Prince Siddhartha, son of king Shuddhodana, had become the Buddha, the truly Awakened One. He would teach mankind about suffering, the cause of suffering, universal compassion and liberation from suffering. He would teach them the path to a special kind of happiness that is not subject to change, never turning into misery again.

Firmly resolved to pursue his endeavor, he set forth for the city of Varanasi. On his way he encountered a naked Jain monk, Upaka, who was awe struck by the Buddha's appearance, and the joy that he seemed to radiate. Upaka inquired of him as to his teacher. The Buddha replied: "I have no master. I have no equal. I am the Perfectly Enlightened One. I am the Buddha. I have gained Peace. I have obtained Nirvana. To establish the righteous teachings I am journeying to Varanasi. There shall I light the Lamp of Life for those who are covered by the darkness of suffering and death."

Outside Varanasi at Deer Park, he encountered his former companions, Kaundinya and the four ascetics. When he approached them, they agreed among themselves to give him no recognition, or refreshment, for it was obvious for all to see that he had given up his practice of austerities. Yet, the Buddha's kindness was irresistible. They could not help but listen when he explained to them the Four Noble Truths and the Noble Eight-Fold Path, which was the famous first sermon that he taught.

Almost immediately thereafter, the Buddha met Yakas, the son of a wealthy merchant from Varanasi, who was acting the part of a madman because he was so greatly disturbed by the sufferings of mankind. Thus, he drowned his sorrow in alcohol. The Buddha comforted him with his teachings, showing him the blessed path of the Dharma, and made him a disciple. Seeing that Yakas had become a follower of the Buddha, his fifty-four close friends and associates in dissipation (in other words: his drinking buddies) also became students of the Tathagata.

He then sent sixty students forth in the eight directions of the world to proclaim his Dharma teaching. Buddha then gained a thousand new disciples when on a hill near Gaya, after preaching a sermon on the futility of the fire sacrifice, he converted the three leading proponents of fire sacrifice: the three brothers Uruvilva Kashyapa, Nadi Kashyapa, Gaya Kashyapa, and all of their disciples.

From Gaya, accompanied by all of his students, the Buddha traveled to Rajagriha, the capital of Magadha. At Rajagriha, King Bimbisara, accompanied by his retinue, generals, ministers, and many of the Brahmans, set forth to hear the Lord speak. On hearing his sermon, the King and many of his retinue became followers of the Lord Buddha, members of his Sangha, or assembly.

After entertaining the Lord and his students, the King presented them with his pleasure garden, the Venuvana Grove in Magadha. At the same time, during the Lord's stay in Magadha, Shariputra and Maudgalyayana and Mahakashyapa became his students.

During his life and travels, the Buddha gained many disciples, high caste and low caste, Brahmans, pujaris, householders, robbers, assassins, wealthy nobles, and poor beggars, both men and women. Among his converts were King Prasenajit, King Udayana of Kaushambi, Angulimala the bandit and assassin, Upali the barber, Sunita the rag picker, and Alavaka the cannibal. Many of his relatives also became his followers. His father became a lay disciple and his son a bhikshu or monk, his wife and aunt were the first two members of his group of nuns. Most important, his cousin Ananda the famous scribe to whom we owe all but one account of Buddha's teachings, became his close and constant companion and personal servant.

On the other hand, Devadatta, another cousin of his, plotted many times to take the life of the Buddha, yet all the assassins sent to take the Lord's life were immediately converted upon coming into his presence. Once, Devadatta hurled a rock down from the Gridhrakuta Mountain in order to crush the Master. It immediately broke in two and passed him by without harm. On another occasion, a drunken elephant was let loose on the road when Buddha passed by. The Lord calmed it and sent it peacefully on its way. Leaders of the other sects, moved by their jealousy at the popularity of Buddha's teachings, persuaded the nun Chincha to accuse the Master before the Sangha and the elders of adultery with her. Her lies were duly exposed. At another time, Sundari was bribed to say that she had lain with the Lord. She was later assassinated and her body placed in the underbrush near the Jetavana Grove. The crime was exposed and the King ordered both the assassins and the plotters to be put to death.

At another time, Shrigupta attempted to take the life of the Buddha by poisoning him and pushing him into a pit of fire. He was converted by the Buddha and became his disciple.

In 483 BCE, when the Buddha was eighty years old, during his last travels and teaching mission in the town of Pava in Kushinagara he inadvertently was served poisonous food and attained to Parinirvana. His last words to his disciples were:

"All composite things are impermanent. Seek after wisdom and strive for liberation".

The Basic Teachings of Shakyamuni Buddha

The first and most fundamental teaching of Shakyamuni Buddha is the doctrine of the 'Four Noble Truths'; they are: 'The truth of suffering; the origin of suffering; the extinction of suffering, and the path that leads to the extinction of suffering'.

Buddha went on to elucidate these truths, pointing out that birth itself is suffering; the slow road of the maturation of sickness and old age, finally leading to death is suffering; not having one's desires or wishes fulfilled is suffering; loss of a loved one, friend or relative is suffering. All beings must be born. This of course is an absolute truth in itself. The Western mystic Blake pointed out that the moment after we are born we begin to die. Likewise, Chandrakiriti, the great Indian Buddhist master of the Mahayana or Greater Vehicle tells us, 'at the moment of birth we begin the journey of our life, which leads over many obstacles and with numerous twisting and turnings to the moment of our death.'

Now to some this would seem a most depressing, morbid, and hopeless view. It would seem to teach that there is no reason for life, and perhaps that a person as soon as they reached enough maturity to be able to wield a knife or a gun or throw themselves from a precipice should do so. Because if all that man is able to face before him is pain, sorrow, and suffering, would it not be better to simply be dead?

Well, this perhaps would be true if we had only one life to live, but the Buddha and many others have taught that this life is only one link in a chain of many lives. These many lives are the 'turning wheel' of Samsaric existence, the wheel to which our passions, desires, and ignorance have bound us, the vast ocean of suffering wherein beings are tossed by the waves of sickness, suffering, old age, and death, moved by the result of our own karmic actions. We are moved up and down in this ocean by currents we cannot comprehend. We are tossed around like shipwrecked sailors in a storm. Our ordinary minds do not comprehend, nor can they understand why this is so, or the forces that have led to this end.

The Awakened Ones like Buddha Shakyamuni do understand the reason, as they are able to clearly discern the origin of suffering. Thus, the Second Noble Truth is that of the "origin of suffering". Through our own actions and cravings, we ourselves, with these fetters, have bound ourselves to the wheel of rebirth. It is our own actions that have cast us into this tumultuous ocean and they are the currents that move us. Then, is there no escape? Is there no liberation from this ocean of pain?

Yes, there is liberation. This is the Third Noble Truth. Detaching ourselves from our cravings and desires, looking to the welfare of others, following a way of peace; this is the way we may extinguish our suffering, for the Enlightened One taught that suffering may be extinguished. Which brings us to the Fourth Noble Truth, the Path that leads to the extinction of suffering. And what is this path? It is the way of the Noble Eight-Fold Path.

The Noble Eight-Fold Path

One: *Right Understanding*

Right understanding is simply the ability to fully comprehend the Four Noble Truths.

Two: *Right Mindfulness*

Since the very things that have brought on suffering arise from our own mind, it is very necessary to free our minds from the passions that have brought suffering to us and to others. And what are these? Craving, hatred, and cruelty. Therefore, if we are to free ourselves from suffering we must free ourselves from these three.

Three: *Right Speech*

Speech can cause harm. Speech can cause dissension and fighting and bring sorrow to others. Therefore, the essence of right speech is to cause no harm by things that are said. One does not lie; proclaim only true answers. One avoids gossip for it can do untold harm, particularly if coupled with lying. One avoids harsh and abusive language, because it can only generate anger. And one avoids vain talk for it wastes time, effort and energy.

Four: *Right Action*

This is the core of the Noble Eight-Fold Path. One strives not to kill any living being. One avoids stealing and one abstains from sexual intercourse in situations when sex is harmful to self and others.

Five: *Right Living*

Right living is simply making one's livelihood by actions that in no way harm another being. Some of the ways that are distinctly prohibited in later scriptures are robbery, butchering of animals, extortion, and kidnapping for ransom. This should be plain to everyone that one should not engage in a profession that in any way harms others.

Six: *Right Effort*

Right effort is to engage in and direct one's energy toward the quest for enlightenment. It is to watch one's mind, keeping it in check, and in no way allowing it to stray to, thoughts which would cause harm to oneself or others. The Lord divided right effort into four categories:

First, the effort to avoid. One avoids the arising of evil or negative thoughts or actions in one's mind stream.

Second, the effort to overcome. One attempts to overcome the evils and negativities that have already arisen in one's action or mind stream.

Third, the effort to develop. One attempts to develop within oneself the good and the positive, such as detachment from worldly things, and compassion toward all beings.

 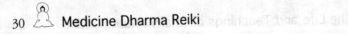

Fourth, the effort to maintain. One has developed positive and good thoughts and actions, and one strives to maintain them.

Seven: *Right Attentiveness*

Right attentiveness refers to the power of awareness: to be fully aware of all of the manifestations of one's body, speech and mind, as they arise. In other words, Right Attentiveness is the ability to notice what is happening in the moment and not being carried away by it.

Eight: *Right Concentration*

Right concentration is a method to train one's mind to concentrate one-pointedly on a given subject. The Buddha found this to be necessary for one to train the mind in this way, to overcome the vain wanderings and fancies of the mind which lead to grasping and negative actions. For developing one-pointed concentration it is advantageous to rely on the guidance of an experienced meditator. It is also helpful to read the sutras to understand the different forms of concentration elucidated by the Buddha which all serve a particular purpose on the path.

Now what is the purpose of the Eight-Fold Path? And of the teachings of the Lord Buddha? How can it be summarized, and what is its value?

As the path of liberation from suffering and the liberation from the wheel of cyclic existence, its value is inestimable. It can be summarized in this way: No being wishes to suffer, or to experience pain or loss. All beings seek to obtain happiness and pleasure. This of course includes us. Any action we commit that causes suffering for ourselves or for another is wrong. Any action we commit that alleviates the suffering of another being or assists them in achieving pleasure or happiness is a correct action. Wrong actions cast us deeper into Samsara and increase our suffering in this life and in subsequent lives. Positive action brings others and us happiness and leads us closer to liberation from the cycle of samsaric existence. This is the path that the Buddha taught.

Nowhere in all the Sutras and Tantras does the Buddha state that he will deliver us from our sins, or if you will, from our negative karma. In fact, he said that as much as he would like to deliver us, he could not. He did NOT come to take our sins upon himself, but he came to show us how to take responsibility for them and to eradicate them by our own efforts.

He himself was not the path other than by example, and by example he showed us the path we should follow. This is the path that leads to happiness, liberation, and peace and to final liberation. He did not come to liberate us. He came to show us how to liberate ourselves. He came to show us that it would be our own effort that would liberate us. He came to teach us that we are responsible for our own actions, and it is not his actions, but our own actions that bring us suffering, or peace and liberation.

The Enlightened One taught that all sickness and disease are not just coincidental occurrence, but are due to our own past actions, and that in order to overcome them, we must ourselves expiate by positive actions the negative karma we have accumulated in this and in previous lifetimes.

It is only by taking upon ourselves our own responsibility for our negative acts, and overcoming them, that we can gain liberation.

4

UNDERSTANDING
THE NATURE OF A BUDDHA

Shakyamuni Buddha himself stated that there were many other Buddhas and in numerous of the Mahayana Sutras, he taught of their nature and actions. First of all, he taught that a Buddha is a perfectly and completely enlightened individual, having purified his Mind Stream to such an extent that there are no cravings, passions, nor ignorance. Having thus purified his mind, one of the results is that complete and total compassion for the suffering, pain and distress of all beings has perfectly developed.

This compassion is not dispensed to selected beings who have been chosen by the Buddha, who are making offerings to him, who are his particular people, those who have built him a temple, and so on. But this compassion extends to all sentient beings, no matter what their religion, race, color, culture, political system, or species are concerned.

Yes, the animal kingdom is also viewed as 'beings' and Buddha's compassion extends from the highest intellectual and spiritual being down to the smallest worm wriggling its way through the earth. Since a Buddha has banished anger from his mind, as well as hatred and ill will in a perfect way, he does not become 'angry' with beings and seek to punish them for their misdeeds, knowing full well that they are punishing themselves more than sufficiently.

Each of us carries within our own mind stream, because of our past karmic actions, our punishments and our rewards. When Buddha sees us suffering, his compassion freely flows and if we allow him to, he will lead us by what measure our karma permits. This love and infinite compassion is a true characteristic of a Buddha, and as a Buddha has perfected him or herself in all ways, it is perfect. If it were not, then he or she would not be called a "Buddha".

Buddhas other than Shakyamuni Buddha have lived in past world eras in different places in our 'Three Thousand-Fold Universe', and as they have proclaimed their specific teachings, they have aided beings.

The compassion that is inherent in a Buddha strives tirelessly to aid suffering sentient beings. Why? Because it is the nature of the enlightened mind which the Buddha possesses to do so. The enlightened mind sees and empathizes with the suffering it perceives around it. Moved by that terrible suffering, it can in no way refuse to give aid and succor.

Each of us at one or more times in our lives has been moved by the suffering of another being, a dying friend or relative, someone afflicted with a terrible or incurable illness, starving and mistreated children at home or abroad, a sick or wounded animal, or a lost puppy on a storm-swept street corner howling into the darkness and rain. And we have been moved, hopefully, to alleviate that suffering. This is the action of our own intrinsic mind, the Buddha nature within us.

If our own imperfect compassion can impel us to take action to alleviate the suffering we encounter, how much more so does the compassion of a totally perfected, enlightened mind move that being to aid the suffering of humankind, and to do all within its power to alleviate that suffering. And since that mind is purified of all desires for self, all cravings, hatred, ill-will, negative discrimination, or any self-motivation, and since the possessor of that mind because of its perfection has gained supernatural powers and abilities, how much more effective will its remedies be!

These concepts will give you only a small inkling of the infinite powers, utter clarity of mind, and potential for positive action that a Buddha can and will achieve. Then you may ask an age-old question, which is the same that Christian sophists ask about the Christian God: If God (or Buddha) is all powerful, why does he not simply raise his hand and end all suffering?

I will attempt to answer this question: Buddha has purified him or herself, and has gained control over all phenomena that affect him or herself, but the universal law of karma still binds all samsaric beings. The Buddha is powerless to save US even though he has saved himself. He is NOT powerless; however, in teaching us the methodology needed to save ourselves. We must take the first steps, and then he will respond and show us the means by which we can relieve our suffering and the suffering of all other sentient beings

This is the essence of the 'Great Vehicle', the Mahayana, and this is also the essence of the teachings and practices put forth by Medicine Dharma Reiki.

As stated above, the Mahayana doctrine recognizes that Shakyamuni Buddha was not the only Buddha. In world eras past, in our own world era after Shakyamuni Buddha, and in times to come, many individuals following the path of the Dharma teaching have gained, are now gaining, and will gain enlightenment. Shakyamuni Buddha was the first to gain enlightenment in our present world era. Others, such as Guru Padmasambhava, sometimes called the Second Buddha, Marpa and Milarepa, the Kobo Daishi, the First Shingon Patriarch, and many others have reached the enlightened state following specifically the teachings of Shakyamuni, our First Teacher.

Prior to Shakyamuni, no Buddha came in this world era that we presently exist in, also called the "fortunate eon" as one thousand Buddhas will appear. However, countless Buddhas came in different world eras and in different streams of existence. Buddhism calls our universe 'three-thousand fold', and though not specifically mentioned, it is clear that Buddhism, recognizing the diversity of physical existence, recognizes also, the existence of life elsewhere in our galaxy. There are thousands of references in the vast collection of Sutras to different world systems and even mention of the inhabitants who are considerably different from the ordinary humans.

Just about every Sutra of the Mahayana elucidates a different world system or 'pure realm' ruled by enlightened beings, whether they exist on different planets or in a different realm of reality than ours is immaterial. They do exist, have been perceived by holy men or psychic yogis, some have even been visited in the physical form.

An example of this is the yogi Namkhai Jigme. Wishing to gain enlightenment and knowledge, the yogi invoked a number of dakinis or goddesses of initiation and a text was revealed to him containing instructions for the fire offering ceremony, called Riwo Sancho. He was told that if he followed the instructions of the text assiduously he would be able to pass into secret lands physically. He did the practice and gained this ability. It was he who brought Buddhism to the land of

Sikkim and his fire offering, the Riwo Sancho, is a common practice used by Lamas of many lineages.

It is also said that Buddha Padmasambhava, through his practice and abilities visited many other realms and even established one of his own known as the Glorious Copper Colored Mountain, where he abides as master over many faithful disciples. In the lineage of Vajrayana Buddhism that I practice, the Drugpa Kargyu, there are a number of practices which if done by a properly initiated and committed yogi will guarantee rebirth there in Buddha Padma's presence.

Here it is very important to mention the most universally accepted, known, revered and widely practiced Buddha, who gained enlightenment in a previous world era, in every country and every place where the Mahayana doctrine has been taught and practiced, and even in a number of other places where the Theravadin way of Buddhism predominates, is the Buddha Amitabha, or the Lord of Boundless Light. No Buddha, not even Shakyamuni or Guru Padmasambhava is more beloved or popular than Buddha Amitabha. He is truly the Lord of Light and one of the greatest of the protectors of humanity and benefactors of all beings. The story of Amitabha is as follows:

In a different world era than ours, a yogi whose name was Ch^kyi Jungne (meaning "One Born of Dharma Teaching") was faithfully, devotedly and vigorously practicing the teachings. He looked around him at his world system, which does not seem to have been very different from ours. Wars were being fought, sickness and suffering abounded, there was poverty also and for some people food, housing and the necessities of survival were either lacking or extremely difficult to obtain. Most people did not have leisure to better themselves or to practice a spiritual path. Too many were caught up in the conduct of every day business, amassing wealth at the expense of others, distracted by the quest for gratification and pleasure, or working long hours to put one bowl of rice on the table for their families.

Others were starving, others afflicted by disease, others were engaged in warfare either defending what they considered to be theirs, or taking from other people what they wanted to be theirs and considered it their just due. Sound familiar?

Things haven't changed much since Ch^kyi Jungne's world era apparently. With the pristine clarity gained from his practices, Ch^kyi Jungne considered this and thought: 'Would it not be wonderful if such a place existed where none of these distractions were present? Where there were no wars, fighting, where sickness and suffering were not words which were even heard, where the necessities of life were readily available for everyone, where greed, hatred and ignorance found no place?'

He then resolved that 'when I gain Buddhahood I resolve to create such a place, as I will then have the power to do so. I also resolve that whosoever calls upon my name with faith I will grant them the ability to be reborn there. Under my tutelage and that of my advanced students, especially Avalokiteshvara (Chenrezig) and Vajrapani, they will be able to practice Dharma without distraction; through my supernatural power as a Buddha, when they wish food or shelter or even water for a bath, clothing, companionship or any such thing, it will immediately be manifested. Also if they wish to travel to visit other Buddhas, this ability will be granted, and on the day that they travel, they will be able to return home before dark.'

Now this last boon may sound a little silly to us, but in past times it was not. When a Buddha, Bodhisattva, or other great teacher was giving a teaching some distance from you, traveling there might be at great expense and could place oneself in considerable danger, especially if one had to camp out

in the middle of nowhere in the night. Robbers, thugs, canni-
bals, roving non-attached soldiers, not to mention snakes and
wild animals, could end one's life very quickly, so to some
people, returning home before evening from a teaching would
be a great blessing. And to be able to effortlessly travel to such
a place would be a wonderful, miraculous activity.

But we digress. After this resolution, and because of it,
Ch^kyi Jungne gained enlightenment in the presence of his master,
Jigten Wangchuk Gyalpo ("Powerful Lord of the Ten Directions")
and Ch^kyi Jungne became the enlightened Buddha, and he
kept his vow, making it possible for any Dharma practitioner,
whether accomplished or not, who would call upon his name to
be reborn in Mahasukhavati or the Land of Great Bliss.

One simply has to refrain from causing harm; this is done
by the observance of the Five Shila Ordinances, they are: to
refrain from killing, stealing, lying or spreading malicious gossip, sexual misconduct, and the use of intoxicants. In those
days the intoxicant referred to was alcohol, but my teachers
agree that today this would include any drug not used for a
medicinal purpose. Basically the final ordinance indicated that
to use any material that would cloud the mind stream of a
being and perhaps lift inhibitions which might lead to wrong
conduct would be inappropriate behavior.

Our Kargyu Lamas tell a story to emphasize this. It goes:
There once was a yogi who was practicing Dharma in the
mountains. A farmer's daughter from the fields below dispatched
by the people in the valley would bring him food, clothing,
and fuel for his fire and warmth. One day she appeared carrying a bottle of chang (a very intoxicating Tibetan liquor), and
leading a goat. She told him that she would kill herself if he
didn't do one of three things: lay with her, drink the chang or
kill and cook the goat.

The yogi thought it would be terrible if she killed herself, but that if he lay with her, he would break his vow of celibacy; if he killed the goat, he would take a precious life and that would be very wrong. He felt that if he drank the chang it would be a far lesser breach of conduct, so he drank the chang.

He immediately after finishing had sex with the woman, and when he had finished, both were hungry, so he slaughtered the goat and cooked it for their dinner.

This is a simple teaching story for the instruction of simple people, but it does indicate that alcohol and other intoxicants lead to acts that we can regret later. For instance, who would willfully run down a child with an automobile or kill an entire family if their judgement were not impaired?

When I was employed as a substance abuse and mental health professional, I worked with a number of these people on a daily basis. The drunk driver when he starts our never intends to drive drunk or injure anyone, but after a few drinks his perception is so impaired that such things no longer matter. This of course was perceived by Buddha Amitabha and wisely written as the fifth ordinance.

In order to be reborn in the Land of Great Bliss, one must also have faith in the Dharma teaching and in Buddha Amitabha. If one takes refuge in him, cleans up one's life by observing the ordinances, thus, eradicating negative karma, and if it is one's intent, one is reborn in his Pure Realm and without obstacle can receive his teaching and practice one's spiritual path unhindered.

There are many other Pure Lands, in fact as many as there are enlightened Buddhas in our Three-Thousand Fold Universe. Chenrezig, the Lord of Infinite Compassion, has established his paradise of Potala. Greatly powerful Vajrapani and Hayagriva, two wrathful Buddhas, have established respectively Changlo Chen and Dagan Wangthrab. The great protector

Mahakala rules over the "Cemetery of the Shady Grove of the Single Sandalwood Tree" and the Glorious Goddess over the "Heavenly Tent Abode". Mahavairochana is Lord of the "Flower Bank World" and Buddha Ratnasambhava is over the "Land of the Piles of Many Jewels".

These places are not imaginary, but real, established by Buddhas who have in the past gained enlightenment and committed themselves to aid sentient beings in our vast Three-Thousand Fold Universe. Though many in number and diverse in character they all possess the same enlightened mind as Shakyamuni and the other Buddhas, and their enlightenment is the same enlightened mind, the heart of compassion that we too can possess should we strive do to so.

5

MEDICINE KING BUDDHA:
Lord of the Lapis Lazuli Light

According to the scriptures, the Land of Great Bliss of Buddha Amitabha is located in the western direction of our world system. Medicine King Buddha's Pure Land, called that of the "Lapis Lazuli Light" is to the East. The story of Medicine Buddha and his enlightenment begins like most of the biographies of the Buddhas and Bodhisattvas. In a past lifetime when he was a simple human being, he made the commitment to give rise to the enlightened mind, to aid and help all beings disengage from what produces suffering and cultivate what brings about happiness.

In the biography of Shakyamuni Buddha, his previous lifetimes are also mentioned pointing out that through his own effort and striving, Shakyamuni, as all other Buddhas, was able to perfect his human state. Shakyamuni was not always a Buddha, but at one time a mere weak, suffering human exactly like ourselves, who was able to perfect his humanity into the final stage of spiritual evolution, that of a Buddha, a fully enlightened being. From the cocoon of human form through his own efforts and strivings, he emerged as the divine Enlightened Being.

Medicine King Buddha's own story begins when he and his younger brother were wealthy laymen living in a fortunate time and a fortunate place. There came to their country a peripatetic teacher and monk known as "Matrix of the Sun". He gave Dharma teaching in that place and, on hearing it, the two laymen awakened in themselves the enlightened mind. They made generous gifts of medicine which not only healed the 404 physical ailments and emotional disturbances, but also went far in assisting the individual who ingested the medicine to cut off the karmic causes of the illness, the 'three poisons': anger, lust, and greed and, thus, become purified.

The great Sangha then bestowed the appellations "Medicine King" on the older brother whose previous name had been "Starlight" and "Supreme Physician" on the younger brother, "Brilliant Lightning", or "Lightning Flash". As you will come to understand later in the text, all of these names, especially the last one, have an important connection with the transmission of Reiki through the ages.

Both brothers apparently gained enlightenment and the older brother, Medicine King, established the Pure Land in the eastern direction, of "Lapis Lazuli Radiance". Having made the basic vow in his previous lifetime to heal all beings of all illnesses, he now set forth to accomplish this end.

He took the following twelve vows:

1. May brilliant rays of light shine forth from my body after I am enlightened, bringing light to uncountable world systems. May all beings manifest in a perfected physical form like unto my own.

2. May my form be like unto pure and luminous lapis

lazuli, shining with a light brighter than the sun and moon, lighting the way for all who journey in darkness, showing them the path they should walk.

3. By my wisdom and skillful means never to be exhausted, may I aid all beings to obtain the necessities of life.

4. May I expound to all beings the teaching of the enlightened way, and may all who practice lesser vehicles come to be established in the practice of the Great Way.

5. May I aid all beings to follow proper moral conduct. At the mere mention of my name may those who have transgressed the precepts be re-established in proper conduct and not fall into lower existences.

6. By the mere mention of my name may those who are handicapped or deformed be restored to a perfect form.

7. At the mere mention of my name may all who suffer sickness or are afflicted by illness be restored to health.

8. May all women who seek to be reborn as men in their next life accomplish their wish. (Keep in mind, due to the repression of women, it was difficult as a woman in previous times to be able to pursue enlightenment.)

9. May all who are under sentence for punishment by the civil authorities be delivered from this affliction.

11. May the hungry be provided food, and may they finally come to partake of the supreme Dharma teachings.

12. By the mere recalling of my name, may those who are destitute of clothing and shelter have all their needs supplied.

We see that his mind, being moved to compassion besides wishing to heal all beings of their afflictions, Medicine King Buddha, much like Buddha Amitabha, has vowed in a very specific way to aid sentient beings. Not only does he wish to heal the physical afflictions, but he also wishes to alleviate the suffering inherent in worldly (or samsaric) existence. Such things as hunger and destitution apparently existed in his time as they do in ours. Things don't seem to have changed very much.

If we take a close look at our condition, we must admit that even now, at the beginning of the twenty-first century, we wander about in mental darkness, still seeking a light to guide us on our path. We see greed, malice, and hatred about us and ask many questions as to why. Even though modern science has made many strides, we still see crippled, handicapped, and deformed individuals and sickness, suffering, old age, and death are ever reminders that all of us are tossed about in the turbulent ocean of samsaric existence.

But because of the actions and striving of Starlight, the layman physician who by his compassion and empathy was led to relieve suffering and aid all beings, there is available a sure help if we but call on him from our states of woe. This is the essence of the doctrine of Medicine King Buddha and this is the essence proclaimed in Buddhism, which is set forth in the Healing or Medicine Dharma, called in Tibetan, Men Chhos.

Shown in most depictions of Medicine Buddha are seven other Buddhas surrounding him. Supreme among these and crowning his head is Buddha Shakyamuni. Also depicted are the Healing Buddhas: "Excellent Name", "Precious Moon", "Golden Medicinal Spice", "Free From Suffering", "Proclaimed Dharma", "Vast Ocean", and "Dharma Conscious". In many Tibetan texts, though not in Men Chhos Reiki, they each have their own mantras, and sometimes special invocations for specific purposes. Generally, however, in China, Tibet, and Japan the commentaries state that they are invoked simultaneously and perform their specific healing function when invoked by either the Medicine Buddha mantra or the Long Dharani mantra. In fact, in the long dharani (long form of the mantra), the Sapta Tathagata, or seven Buddhas, are specifically invoked and mentioned.

Surrounding the seven Buddhas in an outer circle are the sixteen Great Bodhisattvas of the Mahayana School; among them are all generous Samantabhadra; all wise Manjushri; greatly compassionate Chenrezig (Avalokiteshvara); Saye Nyingpo or "Earth Store Bodhisattva" who even extends the compassion of the Buddhas to the Hell Realms; and very important to the practice of Medicine Dharma Reiki: Vajrapani, containing within himself the great intrinsic magical power of all the Buddhas and the keeper of the Secret Doctrine. Mahayana tradition tells us that all the Tantras and healing teachings were entrusted to the keeping of Vajrapani. The following story from Buddhist tradition tells us why:

Vajrapani was formerly the great god Indra, King of the Gods and Undefeatable Warrior. In the battle against evil and negative forces, he rode forth on the 100-tusked white elephant to do battle against the forces that would cause harm. But he has another aspect as well, that of the sage and meditator, who sought to understand the nature of existence and, of course, his own nature.

It was this that most likely prompted him to be among the first gods who paid homage at Shakyamuni Buddha's birth. Later he became a disciple of Shakyamuni and was given the name Vajrapani and the title "Guardian of the Secret Doctrine". In this capacity, Vajrapani is the protector of the Tantras.

When Buddha Shakyamuni was on the earth and was

being served by his new and very fervently devoted disciple, Vajrapani, it became necessary for Shakyamuni to dispatch a message to Varuna, King of the Nagas. He was seeking about for a messenger when Vajrapani, filled with that sáme kind of willing devotion many new students display, volunteered to act as messenger.

Buddha pondered the matter and before agreeing to allow Vajrapani to do him this service, warned Vajrapani that the Naga King Varuna was an exceedingly powerful monarch and was not very tolerant of arrogance in others, and considering that this was one of Vajrapani's traits, for after all, he had been King of the Gods and that Vajrapani should act very humbly and tread carefully in the presence of the great Naga Lord. Vajrapani agreed that he would follow the Sage's advice.

He traveled to the palace of Varuna, where he was met by Varuna's chamberlain. Vajrapani was told that Lord Varuna was conducting business and would be with him after a while. After what seemed to Vajrapani a long time had passed, he called upon the chamberlain, only to be told that Varuna was at dinner and would be with him after a while.

After many more hours seemed to have passed, he called on the chamberlain, only to be told that Varuna was with his wives and would be with him after a while. He was kept waiting and Vajrapani again called on the chamberlain, asking when he could see Varuna. He was told that having sported with his wives, Varuna the Great One was napping.

A few more hours slowly passed and Vajrapani became increasingly irritated. Eventually, he once more inquired of the chamberlain as to when the interview would be bestowed and was told that the Lord of the Nagas was bathing and would soon be ready to receive him. Finally, the audience was granted and Vajrapani, furious at the delays, immediately upon entering the throne room arrogantly threatened and berated the Naga King; whereupon Varuna struck Vajrapani with leprosy for his folly.

It is said in the tradition that it was a severe case and those parts of Vajrapani's anatomy immediately began to separate from his body and fall off. Vajrapani, horrified by his affliction, swiftly returned to Shakyamuni, who basically said in so many words, 'I told you so'.

Vajrapani begged Shakyamuni to heal him, who then said he was unable to do so, but perhaps another great deity, Hayagriva, would assist. Subsequently Hayagriva was summoned and he called upon Garuda, the Eagle of the Gods, to assist.

It is said that then the Garuda seized the Naga King and flew high above the earth, threatening to drop him if he did not reveal the mantra that would heal the leprosy and also other afflictions, such as insanity, epilepsy, swellings caused by water, rheumatism, arthritis, dropsy, etc. The mantra was revealed and the affliction of Vajrapani cured.

Because Vajrapani was a divine being who was unacquainted with suffering, yet had suffered a serious and debilitating physical illness brought on by his own pride and arrogance, and therefore could empathize with those who were similarly afflicted by disease, Shakyamuni entrusted him with the keeping of all secrets of healing knowledge. He is, thus, closely associated with Medicine King Buddha, and in the practice of Medicine Dharma Reiki is frequently and effectively invoked to cure serious illnesses that respond to no other treatment.

Surrounding Medicine Buddha in an outer circle are the 'Twelve Yaksha Generals' who guard and protect the Medicine King's teachings and the practitioners thereof. They are said to each command 7,000 soldiers, retainers, and so on, bound to their service. In ancient India, a Yaksha was a wild forest spirit who sometimes could bring harm. They could also, however, bring good fortune and were invoked as a protective deity, for property, livestock and so on and as bringers of wealth.

The great deity of Indian origin, and direction protector Vaishravana, a yaksha himself, is viewed as the "Supreme Lord of Wealth" and the "King of the Yakshas". He is closely associated with Vajrapani, as shown by the fact they share the same Pure Land of Changlo Chen.

Further information about the origin of Medicine King Buddha and his retinue can be found in the following Sutras:

1. Sutra Spoken by the Buddha on the "Contemplation of the Two Bodhisattvas, King of Healing and Supreme Healer".

2. Preface to the Sutra on the "Merits of the Fundamental Vows of the Master of Healing Tathagata".

3. Sutra on the "Merits of the Fundamental Vows of the Master of Healing, the Lapis Lazuli Radiance Tathagata".

4. Sutra on the "Merits of the Fundamental Vows of the Seven Buddhas of Lapis Lazuli Radiance, the Masters of Healing".

All of these are available in English translation in Raoul Birnbaum's book, *The Healing Buddha*, first published in 1979. This book can still be purchased in a print on demand edition and contains the above mentioned sutras, but also excerpts from other Buddhist sources and a thorough and scholarly discourse on Medicine King Buddha and the associated practices and rituals. I highly recommend it for constant use by any practitioner of the healing arts.

6

THE BUDDHIST PERSPECTIVE
ON DISEASE AND HEALING

The Buddhist view of illness, its causes and cures, is based on the insight that all suffering which any being experiences is due to karma and the consequences generated from past actions.

Some people may feel this is an overly simplified view and may even dismiss it as a guilt producing religious trap. However, you only need to take pause and observe more closely. In everyday life, the applicability of the law of cause and effect on human suffering becomes quite obvious. A man robs a bank, is tried and convicted and imprisoned. An athlete overextends his body while young and suffers consequences in middle age. A person with a little bit of wealth eats large quantities of rich food, smokes cigars, and stresses himself at amassing more money, and dies with a heart attack at 50. A child refuses to brush its teeth and suffers cavities in its 20s, and so on.

Furthermore, there is not just one life but many, like beads on a string, and misconduct in one life is not cancelled by death, but the consequences are carried on in the never-ending mind stream through all subsequent lives until it has ripened into suffering.

Buddha taught that all suffering is the result of our own actions and that the end of suffering is the purification of our mind stream and elimination of the karma that has led to our suffering. In Mahayana Buddhist thought, the teaching of Shakyamuni Buddha, the Dharma itself, is the medicine that heals all suffering and leads to lasting happiness.

Since the Buddhas can work only for the welfare and good of beings, they seek to alleviate suffering by teaching the methodology and applying their supernatural powers when called upon to do so. The source of all medical knowledge, whether allopathic, naturopathic, spiritual, or of whatever other modality, originates in the incomprehensibly compassionate mind of Medicine King Buddha and is given freely to all living beings when the beings' karma permits it and the situation requires it.

This is truly the meaning of universal compassion. If we are able to utilize the knowledge or energy, then it is available for us. If we cannot use it or are unable to, the Buddhas and Bodhisattvas will assist us by instructing us through their teaching to prepare ourselves.

Now, to return to karma and the cause of illness: Sometimes it is difficult for us to understand how something we could have done a hundred or a thousand or ten thousand years ago could affect us now. Or why a god would punish us for something so long past. The simple answer is that god (God) does not punish us; we punish ourselves. How can this be? It is quite simple. It is based on the Buddha's teaching of interdependent origination.

The Concept of Interdependent Origination

Philosophers and scholars have written volumes over the past 2500 years on the concept of 'interdependent origination'. Learned explanations by Nagarjuna, Atisha, and Taranatha are filled with detailed examples that illustrate this principle.

The doctrine of interdependent origination is Newton's Third Law of Motion applied to the human condition. For every action there is an equal and opposite reaction. Interdependent origination states that no effect can occur unless there is a previous cause. So, if you are suddenly faced with a problem or challenge, there is definitely a good reason.

As a modern Buddhist, I do not believe that there are 'Lords of Karma' in iridescent white robes recording in a book all my actions, or that the Secretary of Yama, the "Lord of Death", is keeping track of my right and wrongs. I know, however, and beyond doubt that they are not, but that I am. Let's examine this for a moment.

When I was a child, as are all children, I was taught certain things by my parents and later by my peer group. For example, my parents taught me that I couldn't void my bladder or empty my bowels at any time and any place. I would soil my clothes or my bedding, or cause a public embarrassment. I still carry that training with me today and at least most of the time search for a small room with the proper plumbing to do what I need to do.

Now, some children are taught prejudice. For instance, that black people are evil and criminal; women are stupid and weak; and that Jewish people are deceitful and money grabbing; that Orientals are cunning; that Germans are brutal; that the French are immoral; the Italians and Greeks are dirty in their bodily habits; that Swedes, Norwegians, and Danes (my family is of Swedish origin, by the way) are kind of dumb and slow. And what is interesting, is that many people I talk to, who are well-educated, modern, and liberal, still carry some vestiges of this type of programming; even though we know it is not true, we still believe it, even if on a subconscious level.

Furthermore, as a psychologist I have encountered many individuals who believe it is quite all right to steal or to gossip and lie about their neighbors, or to force themselves on women in a sexual manner, because they are convinced 'the women really want it'. I have encountered men who truly believe that if gay women ever had 'a real man' they would change their sexual orientation. But in all fairness to my gender, I must add that I have also met a number of women who believe that if they ever got a gay man in bed and he experienced their charms, he would never look at another man in a sexual way again.

I am using these really extreme illustrations to make a point, and I think that all of us realize that these are reinforced myths that many in our society hold to. Examine yourself and look for the ones that you hold. Things that have happened to us in the past influence us all, and we conform our behavior, more or less, to social norm. We have all heard the expression that man is a creature of habit or the expression 'by force of habit'. Our views which lead to our actions are very much a part of our conditioning and difficult to change. Our opinions and previous experiences in this life have vast influence on our views, but particularly to our reaction in a given situation. I am going to share a very sad story now, based on the experience of one of my patients, as an example.

Mary's Night of Terror

While I was visiting a friend of mine who was a prominent psychiatrist in Marin County, California, and enjoying a leisurely dinner at a lovely French restaurant, his pager went off indicating one of his patients (whom I shall call Mary) had been brought in to a local emergency room and his presence was required. We quickly finished dinner and I accompanied him to the Emergency Room.

I must digress here for a moment for those who do not know anything about the place in question. Marin is a county of California located across the Golden Gate Bridge, north of San Francisco. It is unique in the sense that it is one of the five wealthiest counties in terms of per capita income in the United States, with a population whose average educational level is that of at least a B.A./B.Sc. It is at least one of the most liberal counties, maybe even the most liberal county in the entire United States. Its inhabitants are probably the most tolerant and spiritually aware people in the country.

Mary was an accountant, a CPA, but also had a Masters in Business Administration and was the administrator of a major medical center across the Bay in San Francisco. Mary was also a Zen Buddhist, her husband a medical doctor. She was active in numerous civic endeavors; a card-carrying member of both the Sierra Club and Green Peace and life was very meaningful for her. But this one evening a sequence of events occurred which required four days of hospitalization.

While driving back from a Women's Club meeting in Stinson Beach to her home in Mill Valley, her Mercedes stopped on a lonely stretch of Highway 1 and would no longer function. After a few minutes, a BMW pulled up behind her and three men got out to offer their assistance.

They were black! Mary went into a total panic, which soon led to hysteria. She bolted from her car and ran blindly down the road. The black men took out after her. She then, in panic, tried to run into the roadside brush and fell into a 10-foot ravine, breaking her ankle. She began to scream.

Two of the black men went down through the brush into the ravine whereupon in total hysteria, she knocked one of them out with a rock. Fortunately for Mary and her victim, the BMW was equipped with a car telephone and the third man called the police and an ambulance.

The men she believed to be her assailants were a local doctor, a male nurse, and a member of the City Council in a small Marin County town.

After being interviewed by my friend and myself in the hospital and realizing that they were indeed not assailants but three good Samaritans, one of whom was a nurse that she had given a concussion and a permanent scar on the side of his forehead, she was horrified at her actions. But she said that when she saw three black men approaching her car, she had 'totally lost it'. Intellectually, she understood the motivations that had compelled her actions, but she could not control her emotions in that situation.

It is interesting to note that she had never had a negative experience with an African-American person, male or female, nor had she been sexually or otherwise assaulted by anyone in any way. She indicated that she worked daily with African-Americans and had numerous African-American friends, but her programming as a child in Chicago and parental warnings and peer group myths had led to her hysterical reaction. She admitted that these prejudices which had long been buried had surfaced and had compelled her actions that night on the lonely deserted stretch of Highway 1.

Fortunately, the three men understood how such things could happen and pitied and empathized with her. Her assault victim refused to press charges and did not run to a phone to call his lawyer. After all, he was one of those tolerant, liberal people: a Marin County humanist.

Of course, this is rather an extreme example, but it is a true story and perfectly illustrates how the conditioned residues within our mind stream or continuum can lead to an extreme form of behavior, a compulsion if you will, that could have led even to Mary's death had it been a steep cliff, many of which exist on that stretch of Highway 1.

Past Karma and Present Results

Experiences that we have had in previous lives are still carried about in our Mind Stream and form our actions and proclivities in this life. They leave us open to accident and disease, irrational actions, shortening our life span and causing our sufferings and misery.

The Buddha taught that there cannot be an effect without a cause, and if there is no apparent cause in this life, then the cause must be from a previous life. Many western religious teachers say that deformed or diseased children are born in such a state because of the 'original sin' committed by Adam and Eve. This gross misinterpretation of the story of Adam and Eve which promotes a blaming mentality, makes no sense, but the teaching of the Buddha that we carry the results of our own actions within us in our mind stream through many lifetimes, is a logical explanation which becomes apparent if you only examine your present life.

Now, you might say to me, 'Lama Yeshe, you are straining my credulity. How can I believe that the cold or flu from which I am now suffering has a past karmic cause?' Well, let me give you this humorous example:

Thirteen lifetimes ago when you were a Bohemian peasant, knowing that you should practice generosity and hospitality, you did not. A traveler came to your door to shelter from the storm and by turning him away, he got a terrible cold which he had for at least two weeks and throughout your other twelve lifetimes you have managed to generate other karma of this or that type that would lead to a 'karmic concurrence' in this lifetime.

You are sitting at home on a cold, rainy, windy night by your fire, or you are snuggled warmly in bed reading a novel or perhaps hopefully a book on the Dharma, when your telephone rings. It is your sister telling you that your brother-in-law is passed out in Joe's Happy Time Tavern and that the publican who owns Joe's is about to call the cops, and that she desperately needs you to baby-sit for her eleven children while she takes a taxi over to collect hubby and the family car which happens to be parked in a No Parking zone and will most likely be impounded.

To get the point, you must remember that some time in the past you generated the positive karma that allowed you to be warm and cozy, perhaps reading a Dharma book, and also the negative karma that saddled you with such an idiot sister who would be stupid enough to marry such a loser as your brother-in-law. We now have a confluence of causes. The effect is about to occur.

Your generosity coupled with your love for your sister, your sense of social responsibility, and your knowledge that you would probably have to loan your sister money to get your brother-in-law out of jail so he might continue his chosen profession as rag-picker, and your sister's car out of the impound lot, you hurry out the door into the rain without your raincoat and get thoroughly soaked.

Then of course, when you arrive at your sister's and she leaves, you become stressed out when your oldest niece tells you she is pregnant and she is not sure which boyfriend it was, your oldest nephew tells you he is gay and his boyfriend has AIDS, the next three children in line are fighting over who gets to play with 'The Game Boy', and the other children are screaming, and you discover the 7-month old has a severe case of diarrhea and the household is out of Pampers. At the moment of discovery, the 6-years old tells you the baby has just swallowed a piece of his Erector set and he wants it back. Shortly after that your sister and hubby arrive having a serious family altercation.

You immediately extricate yourself from the situation, rushing home in a downpour of rain. A couple of days later you aren't 'feeling well' and you know that you really should have sheltered that poor traveler thirteen lifetimes ago.

An illness is due to some karmic cause, which can vary greatly. Some can cause emotional problems and others, varying degrees of physical illness. Simply because the common cold is caused by a virus and sinusitis by a bacterium, does not mean that their occurrences are random. Within the coherent, discrete field that is the individual, the cause which allows the invasion of that bacterium or virus, or the mutation of the cell that leads to cancer, must be present for the illness to develop and to run its course. We also must consider that positive karmic causes in the past have been generated and are preset within us as well. Therefore, one gets a bacterial infection caused by negative karma. One has the positive karma to be living in a stable financial situation, have medical insurance, and encounter a good physician, and be prescribed the specific remedy for the infection.

One says then, 'If I have this good karma, why did I get sick in the first place?'

The answer, of course is, 'you had bad karma as well.' Remember bad karma and good karma do not cancel themselves out in the mind stream. They cancel themselves out in your physician's office, instead. You ask then how can we cancel out bad karma?

The Functions of Medicine King Buddha

The first step is to be mindful, conduct oneself as a Bodhisattva and, therefore, not create the bad karma. The second is to practice kindness, generosity, and the other perfections, so that it is not created in the first place. And the third is to invoke the Buddhas and Bodhisattvas and ask their aid and assistance. In the case of illness or physical injury, Medicine King Buddha and his associated Buddhas and Bodhisattvas would, of course, be the most appropriate. Since the fully enlightened Buddha could only work for the benefit and welfare of humankind, and never cause harm or suffering, it is only logical that he would be willing to assist and help humankind in the eradication of illness as well as other human sufferings. Since the practice of medicine is one of the ways by which suffering is alleviated, Medicine King Buddha, the divine and perfect physician, should be invoked.

Sitting enthroned in the East in his domain called "Lapis Lazuli Radiance", he is willing to grant aid to anyone who calls upon his name. From his compassionate mind alone and his enlightened intention all healing wisdom and knowledge springs, both mundane and supra mundane.

However, just because we have invoked Medicine King Buddha does not mean that an instant ray of spiritual healing is going to cure all of our woes. It could and has happened, but also one could be brought together with a fine naturopathic, allopathic, or chiropractic physician who would in his or her knowledge have the specific cure for the specific problem from which you are suffering. If we believe that all healing knowledge and methodology issues from the mind of the Divine Physician, Medicine King Buddha, then the knowledge possessed by the naturopathic, allopathic, or chiropractic physician has also originated in the mind of Medicine King Buddha.

Today, many people disdain the efforts of Western physicians, malign drug companies for the development and sale of chemical drugs, and turn to entirely naturopathic-homeopathic healers for their health needs.

True, there are many materialistic and greedy allopathic physicians and in view of the manipulation and machinations of their political action committees, most drug companies are somewhat suspect. But we must remember that their healing knowledge and modalities are nevertheless from the mind of Medicine King Buddha. A certain group of people wish to paint allopathic physicians and drug companies in the blackest colors, not realizing that within the field of alternative healers there also exist greedy charlatans who promise miraculous cures and only cause the death of their patients.

In both the established and alternative fields of medicine, there exist the good and the bad, the kind and the greedy, and it is foolish to reject one system or the other simply because of the morality of some of its practitioners. Thousands of people died in the influenza epidemic of 1917 for want of antibiotics. Up until the discovery of penicillin, a cut, a scratch, a broken blister or simply a bad cold with complications could lead to death. Nowadays the simple administration of an antibiotic can save lives and end a particular suffering.

According to Buddhist tradition all medical knowledge originates in the compassionate wisdom mind of Medicine King Buddha. This is not a discussion as to the merits or failings of one system or the other, but simply the statement of the historical view in Buddhism as to the source of healing knowledge.

In every country influenced by the Mahayana, the concept of Medicine King Buddha has shaped the outlook and view of the causes and corrections of human illness. However, nowhere in the Buddhist canon of scriptures is it taught that Buddhists should rely exclusively on spiritual modalities of healing. The health prescriptions and pharmacopoeia and nutritional advice given in the guidelines for the early monks and nuns are absolute proof of this. If the bhikshus in the times of the Buddha, and shortly thereafter, were to rely solely on spiritual means for their physical health and well being, then the prescriptions would not have been given, nor dietary instructions and other so-called 'mundane' health advice.

Rather than excluding the physical universe, Buddhism teaches us to view the spiritual and physical as one, not simply two interdependent halves of our being. In that sense a dose of a medicinal tincture or tablet of penicillin share the same so-called spirituality, and are part of the Mandala of healing that, in all its aspects, is regarded as Medicine King Buddha's physical emanation. And we may carry this even one step further and notice that they are part of that same physical/spiritual universe that all of the teachings of the Medicine King Buddha are part of.

From this holistic perspective, spiritual healing and physical healing are the same because the physicians and spiritual healers themselves are a non-dual unity, and we are part of that same unity. Although the reality which we experience is illusory and there is apparent separation, this apparent separation is also illusory and is merely a result of our incorrect view of absolute reality.

As is stated at many places in the Buddhist liturgy, the offering, the offerer, and the object of offering are not separate entities — and neither are the healer, the healee and the medicine. This is, of course, the view at the level of ultimate reality. But looking at healing in this way, we see that no matter what the treatment or the person who administers the treatment, as long as it is beneficial, it is not to be rejected because of our own personal preferences or prejudices.

According to this purely pragmatic approach, whether a person is healed by supernatural waves of spiritual blessing which issue from the heart of Medicine King Buddha; or by an injection of penicillin ordered by an allopathic physician and administered with a sharp pointed instrument by a smiling nurse who says, 'This is not going to hurt us very much'; or by an herbal decoction administered by a gentleman dressed in feathers while beating a drum; if the cure is affected and suffering is alleviated, the healing came from the same source, the compassionate wisdom mind of Medicine King Buddha. In other words: From an all-pervasive energy that is the base for all healing.

I know it is a concept hard to accept that there is no difference between a so-called miraculous healing and an injection of penicillin, but that is a reality. Let's look at this from another point of view. I basically was raised as a Westerner and have great reverence for the drug penicillin. I know what it can do.

When penicillin first came on the market our, parents and grandparents in their generation commonly referred to it as the 'wonder-drug' or the "miracle pill". To fully comprehend the miraculous powers of antibiotics we would have had to have lived in our parents' and our grandparents' generation to appreciate the great change that antibiotic drugs brought to the lives of many other people around them.

Or we will learn to appreciate them again in the coming post-antibiotic age. According to a recent statement of the World Health Organization, this is just around the corner due to a serious misuse of these powerful agents, which for decades now, have been prescribed even for a common cold. This misuse has made many pathogens resistant to their influence, and as a result there are, for example, new strains of tuberculosis that do not respond to antibiotics.

Penicillin was discovered before I was born; yet I can say that I have had first hand experience of its power. During my stretch of military service (1969-74) I was privileged to serve in Northern Thailand. Accompanying me was a platoon of Marine Reconnaissance men complete with an FCM Medic or, if you prefer, corpsman. The people whom we lived and worked among had never experienced modern medicine and the results of our corpsman administering the simple drug penicillin and tetracycline was the stuff of which miracles were made.

Children who had no hope of survival or whose affliction would have caused eventual blindness were cured within hours. Adults who would have developed septicemia and would have died leaving their children orphaned recovered in a short time to again take up their job of living.

Later after my discharge, when I visited Nepal and traveled about the country I carried with me a supply of penicillin and tetracycline and with the little knowledge that I had gleaned from our corpsman and the fact of living for five years in a country without a doctor, I believe I wisely administered these medications.

In fact, just before my long-term retreat in Mustang, my little First Aid medical knowledge saved the life and leg of His Royal Highness the King of Mustang. I find the cures that my wee particle of medical knowledge brought about were indisputably in my mind miraculous. And the local people who viewed these events came close to deifying me. This was somewhat frightening, but at the same time, it really hammered home that 'miracles' need not be brought about by prayer and invocation, but that a small pill can sometimes work more magic than the prayers of a saint.

Now, some people would think this would lead a person to reject the concept of divinity and begin worship at the temple of medical science. Not so. The miraculous activity brought about by the little white pill has the same origin as miraculous cures used by lamas (and I have seen many!). They all originate — the pill and the puja — from the same source: the compassionate mind of Medicine King Buddha.

What I have said, please, is not to be taken as a panegyric for penicillin, Western Medicine, or any medication. I singled out antibiotics simply as an example. Many new and old medicines exist, both allopathic, naturopathic, and herbal, that work miracles and bring about the end of suffering and illness.

What I am trying to impress upon my readers is that these all issue from the same source and it is only an absolute fool that would reject one system for the other. The combined disciplines of herbal, naturopathic, homeopathic, allopathic, chiropractic (if you have ever had a vertebra seriously out of place, you know your chiropractor is a divine healer!), and spiritual healing are in reality one system, the system of alleviating the suffering of illness.

7

THE HISTORY OF BUDDHIST
HEALING AND ITS SPREAD
THROUGHOUT ASIA

The Indian Heritage

Buddhism is not alone in promulgating healing as an integral part of religious practice. From the earliest times, Hindu Brahmin priests recognized the karmic origin of illness and administered treatments either by offering sacrifice, by use of magical incantations from the Vedas, by the direct administration of herbs, by the manufacture and use of unguents and salves, or by the actual performance of surgery in some cases.

Early historical records dating from the Ninth Century BCE indicate that early Indian physicians performed bladder surgery for the removal of bladder stones. Some early texts list the protocol for surgical removal of bladder stones and other good post-operative treatment profiles. Although there is no mention of it in the texts, archeological remains indicate that trepanning was a common treatment of head injury, and that the operations were obviously successful due to the discovery of skulls containing healed surgical scars on the bone which indicate that the patient, for some number of years, had survived his surgery.

Archeological finds dated 700 BCE show bronze lancets, scalpels, and trephines. A rather amusing text gives the symptoms of boils and piles and the suggested treatments. Boils are brought to a head with herbal applications and lanced. It is mentioned that two sturdy physician's assistants should hold the patient immobile while the lancing is performed, lest the physician be injured by the patient during the procedure.

Piles were treated by either herbal application or by moving the patient swiftly back and forth between a hot and a cold bath. This procedure is still used today in America and was given the name 'Sitz Bath'.

A number of other texts dating from 500 BCE to 500 CE indicate a rather sophisticated knowledge of anatomy and treatment protocols. A pharmacopoeia dated at approximately 400 BCE prescribes a tea made from the rauwolfia plant as a treatment for both insanity and high blood pressure. Reserpine extracted from the rauwolfia plant was added to the Western Materia Medica in only 1942!

Numerous Indian sources indicate knowledge of asepsis and the necessity to keep the operating room clean. Highly antiseptic balsams containing benzoin, storax, clove and cinnamon were compounded by physicians and used to treat wounds caused either by accident or sustained in battle.

Naturally occurring rock alum was used to control blood flow from a wound or an abrasion and the discovery of bronze needles along with scalpels, lancets and trephines, indicates that suturing was not unknown. Decoctions of flaxseed rice bran, and antimony were used to treat constipation. Syrup of strychnine was prepared from the nux vomica apparently as a cardiac tonic, and opium mixed with sugar cane juice was used for pain control and diarrhea. One of the oldest Indian diarrhea remedies that is still current today, is the tincturing of dried poppy husks in palm wine. This is actually recommended as superior to the opium, as the decoction is not quite as stupefying as opium itself.

A Third Century BCE document in the British Museum prescribes a decoction of *cannabis Indica* for 'narrowing vision'. Although these ancient physicians probably did not understand the mechanism of Glaucoma, they understood its mode of treatment. In the same document the foxglove plant (*digitalis*) is recommended for the treatment of heart patients. The document even indicates that small doses are to be given at the beginning, slowly increased until the patient improves. Then the patient is to be maintained at that dosage.

Mention is made of mandrake as a narcotic for sleeping and the use of Asian hellebore to treat heart conditions and high blood pressure. There are clear warnings about overdosing the patient with these drugs and a clear description of the symptomatology of overdose and antidotes.

It is clear from early sources that diabetes was treated by diet, and toothache by clove oil. These treatment modalities are still used today by physicians and dentists; clove oil being available at most pharmacies in the West. Clove oil is clearly an allopathic medication. Its principal constituent, eugenol, a complex phenolic alcohol, is not only an extremely strong and effective antiseptic, it also has the ability to deaden and eventually destroy neural receptors ending the excruciating suffering of toothache.

We may therefore conclude from these sources that at the time of the Buddha (Sixth Century BCE), medical treatments in

India were well developed and the human body and medicine were looked at in a scientific way.

The Shiva Puranas examine the karmic cause of illness to a great degree and promulgate the philosophy that illnesses are caused by past karmic actions. This philosophical concept was clearly carried over into Buddhism and plays a major role in forming the Buddhist view of illness. Thus, when Buddha came into the world, the stage was set for the emergence of the Buddhist healer.

Healing in Buddhism

The early Buddhist monks were not socially or culturally isolated, but came from all walks of life in ancient India. Many were extremely well educated men and women and it is not incorrect to assume that a few were physicians. Buddha himself in the Mahayana Sutras emphasized that healing the sick was one of the ways in which universal compassion could be actively achieved.

Many texts and historical records of the time indicate that the lay and monastic communities were exceedingly active in healing endeavors. Other Mahayana texts deal specifically with healing both by spiritual and physicals means and give 'specific remedies for specific illnesses. Four points of view are clearly indicated in Buddhist texts:

1. The treatment of disease through the use of diet, herbal medicine and surgery.

2. Karmic causes of disease and prescribed spiritual treatment for these same diseases.

3. The concepts that a healing of karma not only led to spiritual growth but also to the healing of many physical ailments.

 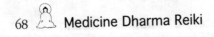

4. That due to past negative karma an individual was left open to demonic possession and afflictions by negative entities; some of these entities being the ghosts or spiritual remnants of beings killed, harmed, or afflicted in some way in previous lives by the sufferer.

Numerous texts in the early Pali canon make it clear that the four necessities for the sustenance of life are clothing, food, lodging, and medicine. Medicine was obviously viewed with great significance as the strenuous life of the early Buddhist teachers and monks required physical health and stamina.

Shakyamuni Buddha himself emphasized proper diet. A certain dish composed of rice, milk or yogurt, mixed with honey and spices revived the Buddha when he left the ascetic life, and sustained him during his meditation that led to his enlightenment under the Bodhi tree. It was one of his favorite prescriptions for others. The Buddha also proscribed against gluttony, advising the King of Shravasti that a reasonable diet would aid him in attaining a long and healthy life.

In the Vinaya Mahavagga, Section 6, is found a complete Materia Medica. Starting with the Buddha himself, Buddhist monks began both a codification of medical practice, and development of a systematic treatment modality. Although the monks were advised against the taking of alms specifically for the treatment of illnesses, it nevertheless became the general practice, since the Buddha himself had laid down specific treatment modalities and means for the monks to keep themselves healthy, so that they might, in good health with vigor and stamina, perform their meditation and teaching functions. Compassion itself, the very foundation of Buddhist teachings, led the monks to share their knowledge and abilities with the general public.

Also the monks soon found that the treatment of illness among the general public could give them an excellent opening for the promulgation and exposition of the Dharma, and also a means by which to accrue personal merit. By the Third Century BCE, Buddhist physicians were known throughout Northern India as accomplished and proficient healers, some becoming quite famous and being retained by the royal courts.

In the "Sutra of The Golden Radiance", two entire chapters are devoted to healing and medicine. In this same scripture it is also related how during a previous incarnation, Buddha Shakyamuni studied all the principles of medicine that he might instruct and assist the people of that time. The Sutra clearly establishes that the healing profession is a suitable livelihood for both monk and layman alike. In the Sutra the principles of Indian medicine are clearly and succinctly stated along with the concept of compassionate healing. This text is especially revered in Central and East Asia; not only in these areas did it lay the foundation for the establishment of the sound Buddhist medical practice, but it also led to public appreciation which even reached as high as the Court. This led of course to Buddhist physicians being entertained at the highest levels and opened the way for the promulgation and exposition of the teachings to the rulers and other notable men and women of importance.

In many cases this led to the subsequent establishment of healing and learning centers throughout Central Asia, including Tibet and Mongolia, and further east in China itself. We will examine Japan later, where again, the very same pattern was repeated.

In Central Asia at that time very little was known about the scientific treatment of disease. The normal patient would have to subject himself to the ministrations of the local shaman who depended upon his supernatural abilities to bring about a cure.

At that time as even today, for many ailments both physical and psychological this affected a cure. But when the Dharma arrived, and recognized the efficacy of the shaman, and even later adapted some of his techniques, the very fact of the recognition of his techniques and abilities and the additional knowledge which they brought, led to the quick recognition of Buddhist healers. Using their knowledge of herbal medicine, diet, and sanitation, plus surgical techniques such as the simple lancing of boils, the monk-physicians were able to effect many positive social changes.

Monk-Physicians in Mongolia

A Mongolian story, perhaps a parable but also perhaps true, tells how the Chinese monk Chiu Quan Dang delivered an entire tribe from extreme suffering due to the affliction of one Tamshar, the local King. It seems that for a period of three years, Tamshar had been afflicted by a demon. This affliction manifested as a large boil or number of boils, as some stories go, on his buttocks.

The affliction prevented His Lordship from mounting his horse, so he could not ride out on his hunt or other noble pursuits. It also seemed that his affliction, if you will excuse the pun, made him the 'butt' of many of the nobles' jokes.

Lying on his side propped up by numerous soft cushions, he would hold court and issue his edicts. It was noticed that most of the time his punishments were extremely cruel and severe; also on certain days the slightest annoyance could lead to a cascade of wrath and the deaths of numerous servants, ministers, and even a few of his wives. His entire kingdom walked or rode in fear; in fact, it is said that in the last year no one dared ride a horse near his yurt, even on the most innocent mission, since it would be taken as a direct insult to His Lordship and construed as a subtle insult to his manhood.

One day, an unfortunate Chinese monk, Chiu, was captured and brought before His Lordship. He was about to be executed when the Captain of the Guard who had captured him, intervened and indicated to all present, especially Lord Tamshar, that the man possessed great magic. It seems during the four-day journey from his place of capture that the monk had been able to completely cure a very painful eruption on the left shoulder of the Captain, where his armor had rubbed him and chaffed his skin.

The Captain, knowing the terrible demonic affliction under which Tamshar suffered, and noticing the similarity of his affliction on his shoulder to Tamshar's affliction located elsewhere on the royal body, suggested that perhaps this Chinese monk could be of some small service to Tamshar.

After dismissing all the courtiers except the Captain, two guards, and the monk, Tamshar consented to a physical examination of the afflicted area.

After conducting an examination, the monk assured Tamshar that indeed in a very short time he could exorcise the demon, but this required that he be given total authority over Tamshar for a five day period, and that also that should he affect a cure, he would be pardoned for any improprieties committed during that five day period.

Tamshar indicated that indeed he would give those orders and that if the cure was successful would grant the monk any and everything he wished. However, if the monk did not succeed in the five-day period of relieving the suffering, he would be tied between two horses and pulled apart. The monk readily agreed and began treatment immediately by applying hot and soothing herbal poultices and greatly calming the irate ruler by therapeutic massage, which is believed by many authorities to be the ancestral treatment which led to the development of Shiatsu and Acupressure. After the first four days the boil was still present though somewhat soothed, and Tamshar in a better mood. Therefore, Chiu reminded Tamshar of his agreement and indicated that for one tenth of an hour he would now totally command the fate of Tamshar, and that at the end of that period he guaranteed on his life that Tamshar would be cured.

He then ordered Tamshar to summon eight of the strongest warriors in the kingdom. By agreement, Tamshar instructed his finest warriors to do everything that the monk commanded. The monk I am sure, though quaking with fear, nevertheless tongue in cheek informed the assembled warriors and His Lordship that since it was a very powerful demon, a very powerful remedy was required. Secretly instructing the soldiers to jump upon the Lord and hold him firmly in place while exposing the afflicted area, reminding them that Tamshar had ordered them to obey his every command and assuring them that he would inflict no permanent harm on the person of Tamshar or the royal buttocks, they agreed to do what he asked.

They re-entered the yurt, the six warriors seized Tamshar who at that time was shouting contrary orders that were totally ignored, exposed the royal buttocks, whereupon taking a lancet, the monk lanced the boil and immediately applied soothing herbal poultices. In a very short time, as the story goes, the Lord calmed considerably noticing that the pain in his buttocks had rapidly diminished. Four days later with Chiu at his side, he rode forth for the first time in a number of years. He then asked Chiu to choose his reward; Chiu said that he asked only that he be able to freely give Dharma teaching in the kingdom.

Tamshar said he would do even better than that since the promulgator of this teaching had been able to rid him of his terrible demonic affliction. The teaching and knowledge of

Chiu was obviously superior to any other teaching in his kingdom as it had been able to cure his affliction, and his own shamen and wise men had not. Therefore, he personally wished to take refuge in the Three Precious Jewels and he also commanded that on pain of death every one of his subjects do exactly the same immediately.

Chiu instructed him that this was not quite the way that the Buddha had intended his teaching be spread, but that if he wished he would personally give His Majesty instruction and receive him into the Sangha. This was agreed and later the entire kingdom accepted the teachings.

This led to the establishment of the Dharma in Western Mongolia. It was Tamshar's descendent Kublai Khan who under the tutelage of the Tibetan master Phagpa, made Tantric Buddhism a powerful force in the Chinese Empire, besides the already established Ch'an tradition.

It was also said that after his healing Tamshar became a kind, gentle, just and compassionate ruler. Chiu remained at the court as Tamshar's personal physician and also his first minister and advisor.

All humor aside, it is very clear from texts and chronicles that the healing abilities of the Buddhist monks led to a general acceptance of their teaching in Western China and in Central Asia.

When Buddhist teachings and medical techniques reached the Central part of the Middle Kingdom of China, they found an already well developed and very ancient medical discipline among the Han people, and medical treatises had been found as early as 2000 BCE in the National Chronicles of Antiquity. The Buddhist Materia Medica immediately both contributed to and adopted from the Chinese healing discipline. The Buddhist concept that anything which alleviated the suffering of humankind is positive and good led to swift incorporation of Chinese techniques into the Buddhist canon of healing.

This combined with the ethics of the Buddhist physicians and their simplicity of life led to their acceptance even into the Imperial circles. By the Fourth Century CE, Buddhism was firmly established in China and healing centers existed throughout the Empire.

The Warrior Monks

As empires began to decline and periods of social unrest occurred, the great monasteries began to notice the need to defend themselves against robber barons, warlords, and the general riff raff. Since monks traveled widely and could not carry weapons, it became necessary that effective hand to hand fighting techniques be developed. According to Chinese Chronicles, the Ten Tai monastery of Shao Lin became the center of this development. At the same time, since Buddhist monks were now forced to combat in order to defend their property and lives, it became necessary for the Buddhist physicians to learn to apply techniques for the treatment of battle casualties.

At this time Buddhist military physicians, trained at the Shao Lin monastery and other martial monasteries, became attached to the Chinese Imperial Army and remained so until the time of the Republic in this present century. A vestigial remnant of this tradition and the practice of wandering physicians can be seen in the 'barefoot doctor program' promulgated by Mao Tse Tung in the People's Republic of China.

Faced with the devastating lack of trained medical personnel after World War II and the "People's Revolution", the red Chinese government established extensive training programs, giving both courses in traditional Chinese medicine and Western medical practice to a large number of intelligent young people. After their training was complete, they (these barefoot doctors) were attached to the Red Army Regiments throughout the country and sent forth throughout the general population to give very high standard medical treatment.

They did not speak of the Buddha Dharma but of the social changes necessary to establish China as a Communist nation. Instead of proclaiming the wisdom of Shakyamuni Buddha and carrying Sutras, they proclaimed the wisdom of Chairman Mao and carried small red books. Using the same techniques the Buddhist physicians used sixteen centuries before, they attempted but did not succeed in bringing about an ideological and cultural change in China.

Buddhism and Buddhist Healing Practices in Japan

Since its introduction into Japan during the Nara period (600-800 CE), Buddhism was intimately connected with healing practices.

One of the earliest stories or accounts is of how an unnamed Buddhist monk removed an arrow from the shoulder of an Emperor's younger half brother and healed him, causing the Emperor to look favorably upon Buddhist teaching. With the introduction of Tendai and Shingon Buddhism into Japan in the Ninth to Twelfth Century CE, the medicine Tantras were introduced and numerous systems of esoteric healing developed, combining the monks' esoteric knowledge and powers and allopathic healing modalities.

Numerous schools of healing and medical treatment developed throughout the country. Adopting many of the Shinto healing practices, these schools were somewhat secret in their methodology, known only to initiates who nevertheless treated the public both high and low, generally free of charge.

The Emperor himself and many of the great Lords were patrons of these schools of esoteric healing and, of course, made use of their services. During the period of the civil war and subsequent skirmishes between nobles, military medicine became most important.

Samurai warriors were even trained in basic First Aid for use on the battlefield and in simple methods for keeping themselves healthy and strong. This practice became so widespread that a small medicine case became part of the Samurai's actual attire. It was in fact a personal First Aid kit, containing bandages, ointments, and herbal remedies which were used in the treatment of many things from serious wounds on the battlefield to a hangover produced by too much sake the night before.

When nobles or men of high social standing traveled, a large medicine case and either a servant trained in its use or an actual physician-monk accompanied them. It is a surprising thought to Westerners that, in the Twelfth Century CE, Samurai warriors believed by some to be the most fierce in the world were so concerned with their health and well-being that a First Aid kit was actually a necessary part of their attire.

Based on Indian and Chinese medical practice, this discipline developed in Japan. When as in China, monasteries found it necessary to arm themselves and either hire Samurai or train their own monks in military strategies, this of course served them well. The social force which gave rise to the necessity of monks developing the martial arts to a fine degree, gave impetus to the development of the healing arts.

During the Eighteenth and Nineteenth Centuries CE, Western medical practices and modalities were imported and became an integral part of the system. Fortunately, generally speaking, even today most Japanese physicians have not become so swallowed up in Western scientific methodology as to lose sight of the spiritual source from whence healing energy springs.

In the later Nineteenth and Twentieth Centuries, physicians such as the well-known Dr. Mikao Usui, who rediscovered the Reiki system of spiritual healing, combined both the metaphysical aspect and allopathic methodology in the treatment of diseases.

Now that Buddhism has made its entry into Western culture from all the Buddhist countries (Sri Lanka, India, Nepal, Sikkim, Bhutan, Ladakh, Thailand, Vietnam, Cambodia, Laos, Burma, Tibet, China, Malaysia, Mongolia, Manchuria, and Japan), we can only expect to see in the future, a resurgence of the spiritual element in allopathic medical practice. This is already occurring, as I am acquainted with a number of Western Buddhist physicians, all of whom possess an MD and practice in the general community. Though practicing orthodox allopathic medicine, they realize the underlying spiritual sources that lead to healing.

This is not to be viewed as a synthesis of Eastern and Western medicine, but simply a realization of the innate unity of what are apparently different systems of practice. We can only hope that these realizations will lead to the alleviation of suffering due to physical illness, which is the enlightened intent of the wise and compassionate mind of Medicine King Buddha.

8

BUDDHIST HEALING IN MODERN TIMES

History of the Tantra of the Lightning Flash

It is known from the notes left with the actual text of the Tantra by Dr. Usui and others that Dr. Usui found a copy of the text in a used bookstore in Kyoto. "His heart was set on fire", as he put it, when he discovered the teachings, and as best he could, began to trace its origins and attempt to find additional texts.

Dr. Usui was a well-known and respected physician who in his practice employed Japanese and Chinese, and some Western, techniques. He lived in the Osaka District where his family had lived for eleven generations. In his earlier years he had the thought of trying to find and put together the healing system that Shakyamuni Buddha taught in his lifetime in India. It is known from the Buddhist Sutras that Shakyamuni was a healer and that his techniques involved 'placing his hands on the patient and he was healed'. There is mention of healing in the Vinaya scriptures (guidelines for the behavior of monks and nuns), and in the two 'Medicine Buddha Sutras', as they were taught by Shakyamuni Buddha himself. There is much known in Indian Ayurvedic medicine dating from very ancient times about massage and manipulation theory, uses of elixirs, lotions, and ointments, and what is now called aromatherapy.

From the notes available, it is evident that Dr. Usui began a campaign to find more information about the text of the Tantra and about the techniques. He contacted the libraries of various monasteries in Japan, finding a few bits of information here and there. The text he had discovered in the bookstore continued to be the only one of its kind found in Japan, but a few elders, monks, and practitioners furnished tidbits of information: Some had known of the teachings, even a former Emperor and a Crown Prince had known the techniques in the historical past. The teachings had been brought to Japan several hundred years before by Kukai (also known as the Kobo Daishi), who had the text and apparently held it fairly close and shared the teachings with a few selected monks, elders, and physicians. In some monasteries there was knowledge of certain kinds of healing, in others there had been somewhat different techniques. From comparison with the text, it became apparent that full knowledge of the techniques had not been universally spread.

Dr. Usui began to use the information and techniques on his patients with great success. He found a few appropriate applicants and began to teach parts of the text in a small way. He found a likely candidate and sent him to China to search out relevant information and trace its passage through some of the major monasteries and centers of learning.

He felt there was more to be had in other Buddhist centers and sent his contact, a good linguist, into Tibet looking for further information. At Chakpori Ling, the famous medical college of Tibet, another text was found. Altogether Chinese, Sanskrit, and Tibetan translations were copied and brought back to Dr. Usui.

It was discovered that the Tibetan/Sanskrit text had two chapters the Japanese did not have, and the Japanese text had five chapters the Tibetan text did not have. He was able to correct some of the entries by comparing texts, and at last he felt that he had a complete set of techniques and information. He prepared sets of notes and codified the combination into what he felt was a complete whole. One of his students, a fine young doctor named Watanabe Kioshi Itami, received the full teachings. Others were at various stages of learning.

In the meantime, the Japanese government had sent several young Japanese medical students to the United States for training in Western style medicine, certainly one to the University of Chicago Medical School, one to Johns Hopkins and some to various hospitals in New York (Dr. Usui, an established physician in the Osaka area, was not among them; he never came to the United States). However, Dr. Usui through his association with these and various missionary doctors and their teaching in Tokyo, became very familiar with Western medical techniques and was licensed by the Emperor.

At the end of 1925, Dr. Usui knew death was imminent and retired to a meditation retreat and died on March 9, 1926. His body was cremated as is usual with Japanese customs, and his ashes are still reposing in a temple in Japan. He died as he had lived, a devout and saintly Japanese Shingon practitioner. Before he died he gave Dr. Watanabe Kioshi Itami, his chief student, the text of the "Tantra of the Lightning Flash", his notes, all his office files, and instructions to preserve them at all costs for a time to come when he foresaw their use in the world.

The day after Dr. Usui died, the grieving Watanabe wrote a sadhana (Buddhist prayer service) to Dr. Usui, his beloved Sensei (teacher/master).

In 1942, Dr. Watanabe was drafted into the Japanese Army as a Medical Officer and sent to the Philippine Islands. He knew that he would probably not come back to Japan; World War II was going on and the Battle of the Pacific was raging. Therefore, when he left Tokyo he took the lacquer box and sets of notes and texts to the monks in a little monastery that he knew in the Northern District of Tokyo for safekeeping.

In 1944, Dr. Watanabe was killed in the American battleship and plane bombardment when MacArthur's forces returned to the Philippines and retook Manila, the islands, and left the Japanese fleet sunken in Subic Bay.

The modern history of Medicine Dharma Reiki, which began with the finding of this material by my father, is now continuing. I am sure it will be well chronicled by our Medicine Dharma Reiki teachers in the future.

Before going on to Dr. Usui's autobiography and other relevant excerpts of his material, I first feel it is appropriate to share in his own words some of the philosophy and world view which is the foundation of both the teaching and methodology of Medicine Dharma Reiki. The following four chapters, thus, lay the groundwork for understanding this system.

9

THE VIBRATORY NATURE
OF THE UNIVERSE

(by Dr. Mikao Usui)

Today I will discuss the true cause of illness and how it arises from the sphere of our existence to manifest in our physical nature. I call this the 'manifestation of the inherent flaw'. This is an old Tendai phrase of definition that I will explain.

From very beginningless time, our true nature and existence, or our mind stream, is totally without fault or imperfection, perfect and complete, like a sphere of crystal, unsullied, and unblemished. However, through our own obscurations and acts of negative karma, this perfect pristine reality that is our true state, becomes smudged or obscured.

This pristine awareness is on the level of the Dharma body (ultimate reality), and it is the Dharma body that gives rise to our integrated energy body. This is called in Sanskrit our sambogha kaya. Now, truly it is on this level that we do most of our interaction with the universe around us. All things are energy, myself, this fountain pen with which I am writing, the paper on which I write, the writing stand, this house, this country of Japan, this world, this solar system, the sun — we certainly can perceive of it as energy — and this universe.

In our physical form or emanation body, in actual fact, although it may seem so, we interact very little. It is on the energy level where our Chi or Hara exists that the most interaction takes place. If our pristine Mind becomes obscured, the play of the energies will not be in total harmony and discord will occur. Discord will then affect our interaction with the other energies in the universe and also will cause our physical or emanation form to arise in an imperfect way. This arising, if serious, would cause us to manifest, if in the human form, as deformed, crippled, or mentally impaired.

Because we carry all of our karma within our mind stream, the negativity of that karma causes an imperfection in the arising of our energy field. The energy field then causes an imperfection in our physical body. This can manifest as an inherited ailment, such as hemophilia, a deformity in the body, such as hunchbacks (I am using extreme cases), or the lack of a limb, a mental aberration, or a problem in one's disposition.

Now, existing at the same time within the three thousand fold universe, are many human and non-human entities to which we have caused harm, whose houses we have burned, whose substances we have stolen, whose children and relatives we have slain, whose animals and crops we have despoiled, and so on.

These are our enemies who wish us harm and who seek vengeance on our flesh and substance. On the subtle energy level on which many of them exist, they are just wait-ing for a chance to harm us in return. They steal our life energy, cause the clarity of our mind to decay, and lead us to make wrong decisions_and take wrong actions which cause us harm and suffering. They steal and diminish our life force that then clears the road for illness and afflictions to overtake us; thus, we fall prey to physical illnesses, what-ever the cause.

Our subtle vibrational body gives forth a dissonance that carries through in an imperfect and impure manifestation, manifesting either physically or emotionally. This manifes-tation becomes apparent as an illness. Allopathic doctors are able to administer treatment, medications, and thera-pies to alleviate at least the physical manifestation. Reiki, the outpouring of the universal healing mind of Medicine King Buddha is able to correct the imbalance in our vibra-tory form; this allows the ailment to be diminished or alle-viated. But this does not correct the primary causes, which are our own karmic obscurations. These must be corrected by ourselves for the alleviation of the negative karma that we ourselves have created.

However, a correction in our more subtle vibratory body can most definitely lead to the development of a proclivity or impetus for the correction of the originative causative fault. It is a concept in Buddhism, Shintoism, and even Christianity that some sufferings result in purification of the body and mind. This can be immediately proven by the administration of antimony compound for a sluggish bowel. There is considerable suffering by cramping and abdomi-nal spasms after the compound has been administered. How-ever, relief of the condition is rather speedy and the body is purified of its malefic humors.

To proceed further, every plant and animal has a specific vibration. If we are cognizant of their specific vibrations, then we may administer that specific herb or animal extract to correct the imperfect vibration and, thus, balance the vibrations, making a specific correction within the subtle body. So whether we correct the vibration by the administration of Reiki or by the introduction of a medicine or by a conjunction of both, we cause this adjustment and if we do it properly and if the karma of the individual does not block all of our efforts, then the ailment is alleviated.

During the conflict with the Russian Imperial Army and Navy, many of our brave soldiers were wounded in one way or another. Surgical repairs could be made. However, I found that when treating such individuals, that those whom I treated with surgery and Reiki recovered at a much quicker rate, with greater alacrity, than those treated by my colleagues with simple surgery or medicine.

I believe that this proves the fact that before total healing on the physical level can occur, that our more subtle vibrational body must be put right.

To proceed further, the reason that I give Reiki attunements and have established a system to do so, and insist that those who practice the higher system receive Buddhist empowerment from Watanabe or some other Bonze, is that simply, they prepare and adjust the vibrational rate of an individual in a very specific way that sets up a matrix, if you will, so that they may draw on the healing energies prevalent and readily available from the Buddhas or Bodhisattvas and, thus, accomplish a specific given end.

Without these attunements and empowerments, it is not possible for individuals to gather or dispense these energies on their own. But once they have gained this attunement and ability, then the energies can be utilized to bring about an almost miraculous recovery in some individuals, and truly aid others in gaining healing and benefit; and this benefit is not simply limited to the mere physical and emotional states of the individual, but also plants a seed for spiritual development and the adjustment of the three levels of individual existence.

So, let us keep in mind whatever we do or whatever we administer, that we are working on a level of pure vibration and energy and not simply on a mere physical level or even solely within the realm of emotions. If we truly keep this in mind, our understanding will increase, and development on a spiritual level within ourselves will become an absolute certainty.

(End of this lecture by Dr. Usui.)

In this particular lecture, Dr. Usui gives us a clear picture of his acceptance of the vibratory and energetic nature of the universe. The view that he espouses is classically the teaching of Vajrayana Buddhism, as it is found in Shingon and Tibetan Buddhism.

I quote from the "Tantra of the Lightning Flash": *"From the vibration of the eternal echo of voidness the syllable AH within the heart of Adibuddha Samantabhadra, arises all things spiritual and physical, and into the vast abyss of voidness they return. From the bhaga of Samantrabhadra arises the realm of form, for therein are all things contained."*

The Teaching

In modern times physicists have theorized and confirmed both the Quantum Theorem and the Unified Field Theorem. This is only ancient knowledge coming back to light, since the Buddha was well aware of the nature of the universe over 2500 years ago. Dr. Einstein, one of the greatest minds in human history, in the early 1900s came to the conclusion and proved it with his famous equation $e=mc^2$, that matter and energy are the same things, only their vibrational rates are different.

The Buddha taught that all things appearing in this universe are inseparable. It is only our ignorance and delusions that prevent us from seeing and understanding this. Modern physicists tend to agree, as their own discoveries have led them to Quantum Mechanics and ultimately the Unified Field Theorem.

The following is the Unified Field Theorem in a nutshell. Measurements and experimentation by the world's leading physicists have led them to believe that the entire 'three thousand fold universe' from the largest quasar to the smallest virus is composed in its actuality of a coherent energy field, and yet, this coherent energy field is only a component of the greater energy field of the universe, and that the unity of these myriad coherent energy fields is what composes, in its entirety, this unified coherent energy field that is the universe.

Now something about Quantum Mechanics: with the technological advances that humankind has experienced over the last 75 years, it has become clearly apparent that all which exists, whether matter or energy, has a specific vibration. From the densest stone to the subtleness of visible light all things vibrate, each according to its own kind, at a specific frequency of vibration, or combination of frequencies.

Should these frequencies be changed, a transmutation of the matter or energy would take place. For example, if the frequency of light is changed, the color and relative strength changes downwards from ultra-violet, through the spectrum, to infrared. If it is further lowered, it is no longer 'light', but microwave radiation; lowered further still it then falls into the spectrum of UHF radio waves, which presently are used for television transmission.

As the frequency becomes lower we travel into the area of VHF used both for television and FM radio transmission, down through short wave, medium wave, long wave, and finally audible sound, and then according to some scientists into the exceedingly low frequency of matter itself.

Our current understanding of energy is consistent with the teachings of the Buddha and other sages, as explained in detail both by Nagarjuna (circa 500-600 CE) and later on by Taranatha. If the Buddha and modern physicists are correct, the human body in all its wonders and complexities is caused to manifest in physical form by the coherent and discrete energy field that is the mind stream.

The Energy Field or Mind Stream and The Physical Emanation Body

Our own discrete and coherent energy field which is a component (and a component of the entirety of what is known as the Dharmakaya or absolute reality, which in turn, is itself the unity and entirety that is the physical and spiritual universe) contains within itself all of the karma generated during all of the experiences of its past lifetimes. Considering that this coherent and discrete energy field is deathless, eternal, and outside of both the spheres of time and space, it, in reality, is our own past, present, and future. Or to put it in another way, it is all that we have been, all that we are, and all that we will ever be. It is our sum total, and since all beings will eventually attain enlightenment, it is already enlightened, and therefore, the Buddha. Yet, because of our own obscurations and short-sightedness caused by karmic conditions which we have generated in the past, we cannot see, understand, or comprehend this, and because of the constraints that the limiting factor of the conceptualization of time, and its illusory existence within the universe, places upon us.

Since we are bound by time, and our illusory mind must move in a linear way, we only perceive things in a linear manner. Due to this illusion we are bound in Samsara and, therefore, subject to change as well. When we have finally broken our bonds and are no longer bound by the illusions of time and space, we will then enjoy our own deathless eternity that is our own true nature, or the nature of mind. And to paraphrase a quote from the Star Wars movies, 'The Force will no longer be with us, we will not be one with the Force, but realize and actualize the pre-existing fact that we *are* the Force.'

In fact, we might consider ourselves to be like a compact disc and our present lifetime is where the dot of laser light is shining. That does not, however, in any way indicate that the remainder of the disc, a discrete and coherent unity, does not exist. Take for example a disc of Bruckner's Fourth Symphony. It is composed of almost countless notes. These have been inscribed by the vibration of light onto a plastic disc. The laser light, which we will compare to time, moves in a sequential manner across the face of the disc reading the vibrations, in the same way that time moves across the face of our perception field, illuminating only the tiny portion of what is our actual chain of existence. Just as with our present perception, if Bruckner's Fourth were played in an instant rather than in its usual 120 minutes, we would hear only a confusing cacophony. This would not be the fault of the symphony but of our limited perception.

In the same way, at the present time, if our entire existence were to occur simultaneously our perceptions would be totally unable to comprehend it, or to make sense out of it, due to the karmic obscurations which blind us to the absolute nature of the Clear Light luminosity.

Carrying this analogy further, we know that contained within the Clear Light are all other colors. Hold up to the light your laser compact disc and you will see a rainbow spectrum of colors that are absolutely exquisite in their brilliance, each a discrete frozen vibration of light, which is activated by the laser, converted into digital information and then into sound.

Were they to play simultaneously and concurrently, they would simply be a representation of their sum: Clear Light. We are the same as that disc, the sum of our experiences and actions and that sum is our enlightenment when we are capable of perceiving it. Yet again, bound by our obscurations, created by our past karmic actions, we are unable to perceive it and, therefore, require the linearity of time in order to exist in our present state of the illusory physical realm.

As each of us is a discrete coherent field, or energy form, so are the Buddhas. And in the Greater Unified Field, we are one with them. Therefore, our specific training is to teach our perceptions that this is, in fact, a reality and to reach our perceptions beyond our karmic limitations and to manifest these energies in our healing work.

The healing energy of Medicine King Buddha is vast and without bounds. When we are able to actualize the concept in ourselves that no separation exists between ourselves and Medicine King Buddha, then we are able to fully utilize this healing energy in order to benefit ourselves and others, even if we have not actualized our inherent unity, we are nevertheless, able to utilize this energy to a greater or lesser degree according to the level of our accomplishment and achieve the purpose of healing.

This is also true, in the same way, with any of the other deities whose energy we choose to utilize. It must be remembered, however, that these energies must be used with absolute discretion and only for benefit. The very nature of the mind of the Buddhas is based only on the concept of benefit, never in anger or for causing harm. Should we attempt this it would only tend to generate more karmic obscurations for ourselves and separate us further from the wellspring of life.

The Discrete Coherent Energy Form: The Body, Karma, Sickness, and Healing

Buddha's teaching of interdependent origination, or the law of cause and effect, or karma, teaches us that nothing occurs without a cause. For a negative effect such as illness, originally it was necessary that we instituted at some point in our past existence a negative cause, or colloquially, generated a negative karma, or simply stated, 'did a No-No!' This negative action or "No-No" caused harm to a sentient being or a number of sentient beings and at the same time naturally, caused harm to us by planting the seed of future retribution. This cause and eventually the conditions for its results were recorded indelibly on our own mind stream. Therefore, the seed of suffering was sown. Our future actions (from the time frame of the original actions) then led to situations that would fertilize it and bring it to fruition.

The universe is an organized and orderly place and not the chaotic and confused entity that some would have us believe it to be. Just as the motion of the stars, the propagation of light waves, and the movements of unseen energies obey physical laws, so are those beings who inhabit the universe subject to the spiritual laws which also govern that segment of the universe. Therefore, it is incumbent upon us to enact positive actions and to set aside our negative actions and intent. We do this by the practice of positive acts, such as kindness and generosity and we refrain from causing pain, unhappiness, and suffering to other beings.

Lastly, and of even more importance, is to draw on the energies of the Buddhas and Bodhisattvas who have taught us the methodology of purification and application. When working with a patient we are applying directly the healing remedy of the Buddhas and Bodhisattvas to cure a primary disease, yet we must keep in mind as we apply this energy, these vibrations if you will, in the same manner as the allopathic physicians, we are only alleviating the effect and not the cause.

We would consider an allopathic physician irresponsible if, with a patient suffering from cancer, he only prescribed a pain remedy to relieve the patient's pain and took no other measures to cure the patient. So too, we would be irresponsible if we only used our science of Medicine Dharma Reiki to heal the disease. We should work to impress upon the patient the necessity to adopt a positive life style so that he or she may maintain the good health and progress spiritually and, thus, eliminate from the mind stream the original cause of their suffering. This does not mean that we should attempt to convert them to Buddhism or 'lay a heavy trip on them', in fact, that would be wrong and might even be counterproductive, but it does mean that we should give guidance and counsel whenever necessary to plant within them a seed of positive action which could lead to the development of a more helpful, compassionate, and thus, more health-filled way of life.

This is an underlying theme in all of Dr. Usui's writings. He tells us that not only do we benefit the patient but that we benefit ourselves as well, in that we reap the virtue for the suffering we have alleviated. This is, in essence, one of the major points in his teaching. In his notes he specifically states:

'It is in teaching, living ethically, and virtuously healing others, and assisting them to live in a virtuous and positive way that Reiki itself becomes a path of self liberation, and thus the intention of Medicine King Buddha and the other Buddhas and Bodisattvas is fulfilled and accomplished.'

With that thought in mind, a brief overview of a variety of ancient healing practices can help us better understand and appreciate the principal support of Medicine Dharma Reiki practice. This is Dr. Usui's Mizu Hari or 'magic water' (water charged with the energy matrix of the Five Elements). We will also share the way in which it is utilized.

10

THE METHODOLOGIES OF VIBRATORY HEALING

From earliest times consciously or unconsciously, healers, shamen and physicians have used various vibratory methods for healing. Some of the oldest are found in the Rig-Veda and the other early Vedas that utilize the chanting of mantras composed of certain seed syllables of different vibratory frequencies to induce healing.

Moving to the West, we find in the Egyptian, Babylonian, and Hebrew systems a particular group of mantric spells, which are used to cure illness or end demonic possession. The Babylonian Talmud of the Jews gives a number of these. This carried on into early Christianity and even into medieval Christianity where Christ's name and that of the Virgin and Saints were recited over wine or water and given to the patient to drink.

Central Asian shamanism gave numerous methods of vibratory healing. To explain them all would require a book in itself. The use of drums, chants, bells, dance, and the laying on of hands constituted a few of these methods. In both Central Asian and North American shamanism, the power of the totem animal or 'helper' also entered in. We see in North American shamanism the use of the eagle feather, where the possessor, the Shaman or Medicine Man or Woman was able to partake of the power of the eagle.

Such Shamanic healers always possess a portion of the animal, feather, claw, dried heart or liver, to make a link between that animal and himself. Both in Central Asian and North American shamanism, the Shaman will 'dance his animal' or familiar and attempt to become that animal and tighten the link between that animal and himself.

In ancient cultures the priest became the god. In the more civilized countries of Egypt and Babylon, in order to assure the fertility of the land, the High Priestess or the Earth Goddess in Babylon, Ishtar, would assume the aspect of the Goddess and travel in possession to the Temple of Baal, the Heaven or Sky Father, and intercourse would take place between the two. Of course, the High Priest of Baal was manifesting that aspect as well. This ritual assured the fertility of the land and the herds if conducted properly.

In healing rituals in ancient Babylon, the priest of Ea, Lord of the Waters and Healing, would assume the aspect of the deity and perform the healing function. In many ancient cultures at the moment of the assumption of the divinity, a mask was donned by the priest or priestess. This is known generally to anthropologists and students of ancient or primitive religions as 'the assumption of the God Mask'. Preceding the assumption of the God Mask, the priest, Shaman, magician, witch doctor, or medicine man, through various means such as drumming, dancing, chanting would raise his vibrational level and even experience ecstasy and trance.

In healing ceremonies throughout the world, even to the present day, this technique is used. In present day North America, Voodoo, Santeria, and Brujeria make use of this technique where the Loah or Orisha 'mounts' the worshipper, who is sometimes referred to as 'a horse'. The worshipper then demonstrates the characteristics of the particular deity.

We see remnants of this practice also in the modern day Christian prayer meetings of the American South. If you have ever attended any of the Pentecostal or 'Holy Roller' Christian Churches, you have witnessed this phenomenon. The only question is, of course, whether the spirit possessing the worshipers is 'holy' or not. Some metaphysical theorists believe it not to be the 'spirit of God', whatever that is, but the inspiration of an ancient Cherokee-Choctaw healing deity.

As mentioned above in Chapter 8, following traditional Buddhist thought, we theorized that the universe is vibratory in nature, as are its contents including ourselves. Since we are vibratory in nature we can only conclude that our complex vibrational rates are affected and acted upon by our environment which also is vibratory in nature. Following this line of thought, it is evident that we are able to affect and act upon our own environment. If we are able to affect its vibration enough, we can bring about a physical change in our environment.

For example, if I am able to change my vibration enough in a particular direction, that vibration on the universal level will affect both my environment and the people with whom I come in contact. If I am sufficiently 'adept' at doing this and do it with sufficient power, I will affect my environment and the people whom I contact.

This is of course the nature of 'magic', and I could proclaim myself as a witch, sorcerer, Shaman, witch doctor, magician, medicine man, or Grand Master of the Temple of the

Purple Ray, should I wish to do so, and many people would accept this because I would be changing their vibrational rate and attuning it to mine when they come in contact with me.

The more adept I become at this, the greater the number of followers I could attract. Sometimes unconsciously, in fact that is mostly the case, but sometimes consciously, this technique is used by politicians, priests, revolutionaries and con men, to bring about self-aggrandizement and impose their will upon others. We have examples of this throughout history and it is clearly operating in the present day.

However, such activities bring responsibilities and if one's morals and ethics do not guide one, then one's karmic burden can become terrible. One might spend a thousand subsequent lives, for instance as a flat worm born into an unsuitable environment, or a cockroach inhabiting an insecticide plant. I am joking about this but in another sense, it is no laughing matter.

Since everything has a specific vibration, if we become cognizant of the vibration of certain substances, and further cognizant of how that vibration changes our field when it is introduced, we have the answer to all forms of medicine. Allopathic medicine can easily be observed to do this, even on a physical level.

The physiological and electro-chemical changes can actually be measured with scientific instruments such as EKGs and EEGs. The subtle vibrational body is also changed on a deeper level, which is what brings about the change on the less subtle electrical level and finally in the physical body. All synthetic and vegetable drugs work in this way. But let us move on to another subject: Homeopathic remedies.

We all know that homeopathy works. Homeopathic remedies of the standard European or Asian variety are popular throughout the world. Only tiny quantities of the vegetable or mineral drug are utilized. Rather than a direct effect on the body at the electro-chemical level, they introduce their particular vibration on the subtler field that underlies the physical.

When the vibration is introduced, a change in our field occurs which travels downward from the subtle fields to the electro-chemical and finally the physical, and the disease begins to vanish, as its underlying cause in our more subtle field is changed to a more positive level.

This of course is also why the Bach Flower Remedies are efficacious and is an explanation as well of Aromatherapy. Although aromatherapeutic agents are so potent as to directly cause effect on the electro-chemical and even physical body. However, since they are such concentrated forms of the vibratory energy of the plant from which they are extracted, they cannot help but influence and affect the underlying discrete energy field or etheric body.

Foods also affect us, but that is a subject of an entire book, and in addition we are affected by the pollutants we breathe in. Even the ionization of the atmosphere affects us and that is principally because it is a subtle vibration and acts directly on the discrete field that is ourselves. Notice how invigorating a trip to the mountains can be on a fresh spring day and how depressing it can be and even physically injurious to visit a city on a day when smog alert is occurring.

Have you ever come into a room feeling absolutely great, on top of the world, and come in contact with a person who is obviously having a 'bad hair day'. In a short time your feeling of happiness and exhilaration has vanished and you too become anxious and annoyed. Have you ever talked to a person who is terribly depressed and left the contact situation in the same state of depression? That is how others' vibrations affect our own.

Buildings and places can have vibrations of certain types and do. Visit a temple or church and piety and awe usually begins to develop. There is quite a different atmosphere between a sports arena or an animal slaughterhouse, a topless nightclub, a department store or a supermarket.

All of these examples illustrate how our universe is vibratory in nature. Police throughout the world are familiar with the mob mentality and the hysteria that results. Here are ordinary law-abiding citizens who seem to have either lost or set aside their reason and are moving almost mindlessly with a single goal. What we are witnessing is a vibratory phenomenon, when through the excitement of a situation, the vibratory rates of a number of individuals are working on a single frequency and augmenting and strengthening one another.

Panic in a building or theater is the same phenomenon. In fact, observing such a situation you can actually see the panic spreading from one point outwards in all directions, and sometimes even affecting police and firemen who are especially trained to deal with such situations. If you, like I, were alive during the 60s, just observing an escalating conflict between students and police during a campus demonstration will confirm the vibratory nature of ourselves and how our vibrations affect and can be affected by those of others.

So, what has this all to do with healing? It is the very foundation of healing science. As a Buddhist healer, I have experienced how the enlightened energies of the Buddhas and Bodhisattvas can directly affect me through my coherent energy field.

Again, because the intent of the Buddhas and Bodhisattvas is the welfare, happiness, and enlightenment of myself and all beings, I can gain only benefit from that influence, and I can pass that benefit on to others. Operating on the premise of the vibratory nature of the universe and of ourselves, if by the practice which has been set down over the centuries by Chinese and Japanese healers and Tibetan lamas I can attune myself to the frequency of these great and beneficial beings and become one with them, I can manifest their powers for good.

Medicine Dharma Reiki: Healing Through Specific Vibratory Frequencies

And, thus, we come to the essence of Medicine Dharma Reiki and the teachings and methodology that Dr. Usui has set down.

Medicine Dharma Reiki's discipline, practice and teaching instructs us on the vibratory nature of the universe and gives us a set methodology, found both in the Tantra, its commentaries, and Dr. Usui's development of this system, to accomplish this end.

A specific system is set forth, drawing from the underlying secret teaching of Tantric Buddhism and elucidating given practices to bring about healing. This healing occurs in the subtle, coherent and discrete energy field that is the underlying foundation of our very being. And, thus, the result of the healing is deep, profound, and generally permanent.

This healing is not only a healing of the body, but of the mind stream, or what in the West we would call "soul", and points us in the direction of positive action, bringing a profound and beneficial change to our lives. And once this profound and beneficial change has taken place, once we are able to assume the "god mask" of Medicine King Buddha or the other Buddhas and Bodhisattvas, we are able to pass the beneficial energies flowing through on to others, bestowing upon them aid, succor, healing, and benefit and, at the same time, accomplish our own liberation and enlightenment.

The methodologies of this system are not only limited to the spiritual but bring all forms of healing, allopathic, homeopathic, herbalism, naturopathy, massage, and acupuncture into play, for nothing which can be of benefit can be rejected, for as both Buddhism and Dr. Usui teach, all healing originates and is radiated from the compassionate mind of Medicine King Buddha.

Now, based upon this premise, which is a specific and given system and since its basis is in the vibratory universal nature, it is important to remember that although other systems are of benefit in themselves, they should be beneficial discretely within their own system, and not added to the specific system of Medicine Dharma Reiki, as its foundation of teaching is complete within itself. Therefore, it should not be mixed with other systems that operate on a different theoretical foundation.

That is not to say that those systems are not of benefit, and should not be utilized, but they should be utilized separately and discretely by the practitioner and not integrated into the Medicine Dharma Reiki system, nor should an attempt be made to integrate portions of Medicine Dharma Reiki into other systems.

Based on two very different religious and philosophical systems and widely separated by geography, North American shamanism and the Kahuna practices in Polynesia are very separate and distinct systems of healing. Both are very effective and remarkable results are obtained by their practitioners, yet are very different.

A Native American Medicine Man, a close friend of mine, visited Hawaii and even studied the Kahuna system. He was amazed by its effectiveness, and the Hawaiian practitioners were amazed at his. Yet at the end of their interaction, they agreed that the two were so very different that they could not be mixed or integrated into one system. Yet my friend was taught a number of their practices and in turn taught them a number of his. Both the Kahunas and my friend utilized each other's practices very successfully, but not as a part of their own parent system, but as another tool to achieve benefit and healing of patients.

One of my very old friends and a person very dear to my heart is an allopathic physician trained at Loma Linda University. He also extensively studied Chinese herbal medicine. He sees the benefit of those systems and also of Buddhist healing techniques. He uses all three as well as acupuncture and sometimes together on the same patient. Yet when performing surgery he does not give Chinese herbal tea by placing it in the IV bottle. Nor does he practice his acupuncture by the use of a scalpel. He agrees that all three systems are beneficial, but each is separate and discrete, at least on this physical level and that one cannot explain or be explained by the others.

So he uses them separately but equally. A saw, a hammer, and a pair of pliers are all tools which can be used to construct a house, but I have yet to see a single tool that partakes of the nature of all three. Could you imagine what a combination saw, hammer, and pliers would resemble? I am certain that the function of one tool would be impaired by the shape and form of the others. So it is with healing systems, though originating from the same source, they nevertheless should remain discrete and separate from one another.

That is not to say that any system of benefit should not be practiced, but no attempt should really be made to impose one system's discipline on another. By doing this, the purity of each system is maintained and the integrity of that system not compromised. Each one then maintains its own clear frequency, and is, thus, of greater benefit.

From all of the above it can be seen how all the phenomena we experience are simply different vibratory frequencies. Eastern and Western sciences simply approach the same subjects with different insights, yet both provide the confirmations, to support and confirm the vibratory nature of the universe and ourselves, which are the heart essence of Dr. Usui's lay practice of healing Reiki as well as the Buddhist Tantric teaching of Medicine Dharma Reiki which he rediscovered.

11

THE BUDDHIST VIEW OF
THE 'OTHER SIDE'

Before we can understand many of Dr. Usui's allusions and references, it is exceedingly important that we understand the view held generally in Japan about the 'spirit realm' or the 'other side'.

Buddhism in general recognizes "six realms of existence". They are: our human realm, the realm of animals, the realm of hungry ghosts or greedy spirits, the realm of the gods or Devas, the realm of the 'angry ones' or Asuras, and the hell realm.

Japanese Buddhist philosophy has a bit of a variant on this, because of the parallel existence of Shinto and Buddhism in Japan for well over a thousand years. This causes a certain degree of confusion to scholars from other systems of Buddhism. This same difference surprisingly is also found in Tibetan Buddhism, due to Buddhism's co-existence with Bon for about the same period of time.

In Japanese Buddhism the Japanese Lord of Death, Emma-O, became a Bodhisattva and assists the dead. His realm is not to be viewed as hell or purgatory, but in the popular religion has become a place of rest between incarnations. For convenience, the exposition I am going to give is based on a view of the other side popular for over a thousand years in Japanese Buddhism.

First, we must understand that Japanese Buddhists believe that all six realms have a point of contact. This point of contact serves as a place or gateway that inhabitants of other realms can use as a transfer point. It is also believed that just as the human and animal realms are in constant contact, so the other realms are as well, but our limited spiritual ability makes it impossible for us to perceive it.

The popular Buddhism of Japan also believes that some realms at some times manifest in our realm and exert their influence. When natural disasters occur such as tidal waves, earthquakes and typhoons, and the subsequent suffering that follows, is when the hell realms intrude into our own realm. Times of war are when the realm of the Asuras or angry ones intrudes. Times of famine and crop failure and great want are when the realm of the hungry ghosts intrudes. And times of joy, happiness, and plenty are when the god realm intrudes.

These intrusions are not accidental or random, but are controlled by the collective karma of the people in an area, province, state, or country, where the intrusion occurs. This is a very good explanation of what is happening right now in Somalia and sub-Sahara Africa, and in individual cases the manifestation of such violence in American cities and an explanation of why such individuals as John Wayne Gasey, Charles Manson, and Jeffrey Dahmer occur. The intrusion of the realm of the angry ones seems to be occurring for the last hundred years in the Middle East and generally in today's corporate world of merciless competition, while it seems on the West Coast of America, particularly in the area known as Los Angeles County, in places such as Westwood and Beverley Hills, the god realm seems to be quite active.

It is believed that each realm has graduations from gross to subtle. Our perceptions can generally only perceive the gross, so in all realms there exist beings closer to our perception and beings farther away.

Buddhism generally accepts that nagas, sadag, or "earth spirits"; yakshasas; rakshasas, and other similar entities are generally denizens of the human realm, but more subtle in their forms. Some of these in their enlightened form have the ability to manifest in all realms and it is generally accepted that the inhabitants of the god realm can manifest in whatever realm they wish. The Buddhist belief accounts for the various apparitions of devas, angels, devils, and others in our own realm.

In Japan, ghosts and Kamis are thought to be part of the human realm, just more subtle than we and experienced directly only by a few, or when the ghost or Kami chooses to manifest.

The 'other side' is believed to be inhabited by a number of beings and to be pretty much similar to our own milieu. Some spirits are very powerful, some are very weak, some are very good, and some are very bad. Some have a poor destiny, and some have an ordinary destiny, and some have a great or potent destiny. Most are kind of like us, good and bad to a greater or lesser degree, but generally trying to get along the best they can.

Some are very happy and some are very sad. Some feel left out, and others seek power. Those who are very good and have created for themselves a great and potent destiny are the Buddhas and Bodhisattvas. In our realm, they are reflected by such individuals as the Dalai Lama, Mahatma Gandhi, Albert Schweitzer and Mother Teresa.

Some are very evil and have a potent destiny and are reflected by such individuals as Saddam Hussein, Adolph Hitler, Mussolini and the people who financed them from behind the scenes. Some are very weak and evil and are reflected in our realm by such individuals as the little old man who poisons animals or Mr. Macho who enjoys hunting deer and small defenseless birds for sport, or children who enjoy mistreating small domestic animals. Those who are ordinary and good, are reflected by the little old ladies who feed stray cats and do small acts of kindness for their friends and neighbors.

Some of these weak spirits are excellent con-men and con-women, who certainly wreak havoc on truthfulness, thus, most mediums who are in contact with such personages as Abraham Lincoln, Cleopatra, Shakespeare, and your deceased mother-in-law are operating under delusion. Most positive entities have little need or desire to channel themselves through humans, so it can be frankly understood that a lot of 'channeled material from the other side' is generally suspect.

Inhabiting this same level of existence are entities we have offended in this life or in our past lives and who are able to affect our lives in an adverse way. In our uncountable past lives we have been merchants who have cheated our customers, rulers or politicians who have mistreated our constituents or subjects, we have been the wealthy who have oppressed the poor, and the poor who have fomented revolution against the wealthy. We have been soldiers who have burned the houses, destroyed the herds and crops, and who have murdered our enemies and their children. And, thus, we have created debts of karma. Now these debtors, unless they have gained enlightenment or great power for good, are our enemies and have sworn vendetta against us. They are just waiting for a good chance to wreak their vengeance on us, and they frequently do in various ways.

There are nagas, or water spirits whom we have offended in this or other of our lives by urinating in their streams or causing other water pollutions. There are mundane gods whose sacred places we have consciously or unconsciously defiled in some way. There are earth spirits whom we have offended in some way, by building things in an inappropriate place. There are forest spirits whose trees we have cut down, and so on and so forth.

These cause illness and accident and unfortunate circumstances in one's life. Traditional Buddhism and particularly Japanese Buddhism seeks to propitiate them by the use of offerings and by the application of compassion. Along with other healing tools, Medicine Dharma Reiki provides various methodologies for the propitiation of debtor spirits and the averting of their unwanted attentions. Although not relating particularly to the subject of this chapter, it is important to note that Buddhism does make recognition of negative directed energy by humans, or curses in black magic.

Dr. Usui, in his system of teaching, also provides various remedies for these unfortunate situations. In fact, the way in which Dr. Usui approaches these problems is totally and completely in line with orthodox Buddhist techniques, which have proved to be efficacious for over 2500 years.

12

DR. USUI'S 'MAGIC WATER'

From what has been covered so far, we have seen that the difference between what I will term the "lay practice" of Reiki, the first three degrees as presently taught by various other groups, and Medicine Dharma Reiki, as developed from Dr. Usui's notes and information, is the profound Buddhist connection in Medicine Dharma Reiki practices. This deep connection manifests itself in the second great difference and that is the Mizu-Hari, or 'Water of the Life Essence'.

In Tibetan Buddhism and other systems of esoteric Buddhism including Japanese Shingon, of which Dr. Usui was an adherent, and even to a lesser degree in Japanese Tendai, vases or bottles of initiation are used to bestow empowerments and other benefits on students and practitioners. The bottle that is pouring the nectar of liberation held by Kuan Yin, or Kannon (the Mahabodhisattva of compassion and mercy) is a representation of such an initiation vase.

One of the most common vases in esoteric Tibetan and Central Asian Buddhism is the tsebum or 'long life vase'. It is used in a Buddhist and somewhat shamanistic rite to retrieve the scattered elemental energies of the body and subtle body, and return and replenish them. Other such vases are used for Medicine King Buddha and many other deities for initiation or other particular purposes.

The Tibetan goddess Tara is often shown with a "long life vase" in her right hand and the great teacher Padmasambhava is frequently shown with a "long life vase" contained within the skull cup which he holds in his lap with his left hand.

The vase (Sanskrit: kalasha; Tibetan: bumpa) has for over 2000 years played a very important part in esoteric Buddhism around the world. Therefore, it is not at all surprising that the vase and its contents play an important part in the esoteric practice of Dr. Usui's system of Medicine Dharma Reiki.

Dr. Usui tells us in his notes that it is the central function of the Medicine Dharma Reiki system. He also makes it very clear that one must be a practicing Buddhist with certain initiations in order to effectively consecrate and use the 'Water of the Life Essence' or Mizu-Hari.

In order to actualize the practice one must first properly consecrate the altar and the Mizu-Hari. Of course, one must have taken refuge and the Bodhisattva vow, but further, one must be practicing Medicine King Buddha and have received the empowerment to do so and instruction into the practice in a legitimate way. The consecration depends upon the strong bond between Medicine King Buddha and the practitioner. If no bond ties the two, then the water will remain water.

One's level of practice of Medicine Buddha or Amitabha is what determines both the consecration of summoning the elements and of summoning the healing and restorative powers of the Buddhas.

I could consecrate the Mizu-Hari for them but unless they could perform the generation within themselves, it would be ineffective. It is Medicine King Buddha only that brings the lost elements and gives the empowerment to the Mizu-Hari. The other Buddhas could also come, and do, but the basis of consecration is Medicine King Buddha. Therefore, the "Tantra of the Lightning Flash" explicitly states:

'Let the yogi having received the initiation and the secret instruction from his teacher, tightly holding to his vows and diligently practicing, consecrate the sacred kalasha of healing'.

It is through the presence of the Buddha that the kalasha of healing is empowered. It should not be empowered by one weak in practice or of unstable mind, but only by one who has the intent to utilize this method for the benefit of others. We can see from both Dr. Usui and from the Tantra that one needs to be a serious practitioner of the Dharma, and since the vase or Mizu-Hari is so obviously the center of the practice, we need to speak of it at length.

Many substances, such as precious stones or objects, can be filled with energies or 'given a psychic charge'. Therefore, it is not in any way inconceivable that water which makes up both a major part of our environment and our bodies, can also be charged and empowered in a particular way. Buddhist adepts have been doing this for thousands of years. As a Vajrayana Lama and practitioner, it is very clear to me that this is of course what Dr. Usui's Mizu-Hari, or the 'magic water', is.

According to the theory of Oriental medicine, the body is composed of five elements, subjectively, rather than objectively. Furthermore, it is said that either a dissipation or predominance of the elements is the cause of disease and sickness, and eventually death, when the elements break down. Many Vajrayana Buddhist practices in Tibet and elsewhere including the "Amitayus Long Life" practice, and numerous Medicine King Buddha practices found in all the lineages, address this particular problem. Most use a vase of some kind or another to affect the restoration. It is a very common practice that when giving an initiation, the particular deity's energy is called by the Lama into the initiation vase for that purpose.

The Essence of Life Force

In Dr. Usui's system, both forms are used, but a third form is added; this is the "Essence of Life Force" within the universe and seems to be at this point, his particular and peculiar discovery and teaching. From his notes, we can glean that his theory, as taken from the "Tantra of the Lightning Flash", is that the universe abounds with this energy which is the Life Force and that by the first consecration of the water with the elemental energy and secondly with the energy of Medicine King Buddha, then the third type of energy can be summoned and consecrate the water. Further that a fourth energy appears of itself when the other energies have been invoked, and that energy is the energy of the "Universal Healing Essence". In the philosophical terms of Buddhist philosophers such as Nagarjuna and others, the presence of the previous three act as a cause for the natural manifestation of the fourth.

For example, if all the building materials and all the professionals needed to construct a house are present and the intent for the construction of a house is manifest, then the natural result would be a house. So if the dissipated elements are present, the intent which is the compassionate healing mind of Medicine King Buddha, and the "Universal Life Essence", are present in one place at one time, then the result is the manifestation of the healing energy. And when the healing energy is applied, and the intent to heal supplied by the practitioner who now applies this energy, then healing is the expected result. This, at heart, is what Medicine Dharma Reiki is all about. The rest is only commentary.

How does the Mizu-Hari work? Once the missing five elements are gathered and Medicine King Buddha is present, the intent of the practitioner directs the "Universal Life Essence" into the now charged water. He is able to actualize this, not by himself, but with the support of his practice and his intent to aid and comfort and heal sentient beings. The presence of these three then gives rise to the fourth. The Mizu-Hari is put onto the practitioner's hands and applied to the patient. The practitioner's intent is present. And that of the enlightened compassionate intent of Medicine King Buddha. The subtle elemental energies are transferred from the water to the patient. "Universal Life Essence" is applied by the intent of the practitioner, the board and the carpenter are therefore present; the directed intent creates the edifice of healing.

The elements are restored, the chi or hari is replenished, which constitute a cause; since the cause has been generated, unless specific obstacles occur, the effect or result must follow. That result or effect is healing.

So it is, if Medicine Dharma Reiki is applied correctly by a devoted practitioner who is able to generate the necessary causes and bring them together at one point in time. It is, of course, the same with our carpenter. No matter how good his intent is, and no matter how good his tools and materials, if he does not have the proper training, the result is going to be far from satisfactory. Look at many of the dwellings built by city people who fled to the country in the 1950s and tried to build without training.

So, for good results with the Medicine Reiki system, one must necessarily have the training and the tools in order to actualize the consecration of the Mizu-Hari and its subsequent utilization for healing. But just as the carpenter could not construct the house without the lumber, even if I had the intent and the training, a Medicine Dharma practitioner would be helpless without the material needed for his practice.

In the same way, Dr. Usui's and Dr. Watanabe's notes make it perfectly clear that without the physical accoutrements and the proper training and initiation, the given results will not occur. Therefore, it is most necessary to follow the instructions and utilize the Mizu-Hari.

Many objects can become consecrated, empowered or charged, but with what? Have you ever noticed that many healers after a short and illustrious career lose their abilities and become critically ill themselves? There is a simple explanation for this. They are unknowingly using their own life force to aid others, and the normal rate of life force generation by an individual is not sufficient to replenish what they have expended.

Dr. Usui's system on the other hand, both in the lay practice of Reiki and in Medicine Dharma Reiki bestows the ability to utilize and direct the Universal Life Force or Essence and the infinite healing powers of Medicine King Buddha to aid and heal beings. Therefore, one need not fear the expenditure and depletion of one's own energies in one's healing endeavors. One can rest assured that one is not endangering one's own health or depleting one's life energy no matter what level one uses of either the ordinary lay practice of Reiki or Medicine Dharma Reiki.

Like a Battery, the Specific Form as Outlined
By Dr. Usui Keeps the System Functional

Some might perceive the bottle, the water and the altar utilized in Medicine Dharma Reiki as merely symbols of a greater truth. However, symbols are important, as Carl Jung's research has shown. They are a powerful force. For instance, electricity is an energy. It is in the air around me, in the very earth, in the clouds moving overhead, and in my light socket. But how can I store it up for later use?

I can't unscrew the light bulb and turn on the switch and let it run out into a jar. I can't store it in my body by sticking my finger in the light socket because it will all flow into the ground. I can't put it in a plastic bag, in a used tea tin, or in a shoebox. There is one thing I can put it in, however, or in fact actually two: If I want to draw it out all at once, I can store it in a device called a capacitor, or I can be more conventional and store it in a battery.

Now without basic training in electronics and the guidance of a scientist or inventor before me, no matter how intuitive I am, nor how intelligent, there is no question in my mind that I would not be able to intuit how to construct, charge, and utilize a battery.

Dr. Usui, following wise instructions given in the past by Buddhist masters and his own knowledge of spiritual science and medicine, has constructed a system that works in two different segments, both of which are totally functional and by the following of specific instructions functions in a given and beneficial manner. Therefore, I can see no logical reason not to follow this system.

In the same way, if I were to add some other component to my battery or charger, it would not work. So, if we add a few feathers and crystals, ceremonial rattles, and so forth to the system we might initiate a malfunction or at best a nonfunction. Through the custodianship of some of Dr. Usui's students the lay practice of Reiki has come down in a complete and totally functional way and in no way should be tampered with by the 'intuitive' additions of others. In the same way,

Medicine Dharma Reiki has come down to me, in the form of the "Tantra of the Lightning Flash", its Japanese and Chinese commentaries, and Dr. Usui's and Dr. Watanabe's own notes. A specific system is set forth, is most functional, and should be followed without change. The central pillar upon which this edifice rests is the Mizu-Hari. The methodology for its preparation and utilization is clearly given.

Now what is the Mizu-Hari? And why did Dr. Usui consider it so important? Following traditional and very orthodox Buddhist methodology, a vase is prepared and as most of us know, the traditional shape of a vase is womb-like, a large bulge with a neck. The symbology should not escape us for within this womb or matrix represented by the vase, is contained water, the 'Water of Life Essence', in the same way that the amniotic fluid is contained within the womb of a pregnant woman.

The energies of space, time, the elements, and the power of the Buddhas cause a change within this vase. The Universal Life Essence is summoned and enters and then within this matrix, healing force grows, and with the practitioner as midwife, is given birth and takes on its independent existence for healing.

The vase acts as a battery storing the five elemental energies, the healing power of the Buddhas and the Universal Life Essence. These give rise to the Universal Healing Essence, which can then be utilized at the will of the trained practitioner.

This is the secret of Dr. Usui's specially charged water which he gleaned from the Tantra and his own unique way of using both that wisdom and methodology to bring forth the extremely potent healing forces of the Buddhas and Bodhisattvas, and of the Universal Life Essence into our world for the benefit of others.

Part II

Words of the Kind And Gentle Physician Bodhisattva

13

AN AUTOBIOGRAPHICAL SKETCH

As I stated at the beginning of this book I feel that my involvement with Dr. Usui's notes has been a journey. After the material came to me and as the translations have progressed, I have felt that I have now gained a traveling companion who himself embarked on a similar journey to the one that I have undertaken.

It is like having a guide who has traveled the same road and who can point out landmarks and points of interest. His conversations in the evening at the Inn over a long bottle of sake are both illuminating and amusing when he tells me of his experiences on the same journey, and alone in the wilderness by a campfire in the evening, shares his life views and aspirations.

I had first thought to compile a biography of Dr. Usui based on the events mentioned in his writings. Then it occurred to me that the people who actually experienced it are in a far better position to tell the story of his journey.

Therefore, I am including at this point a short piece written by Dr. Usui himself. It is not a complete autobiography, yet is sufficient in itself to demonstrate both his character and aspirations. I am also including much material translated from his notes that share his views on numerous subjects, and demonstrates his wisdom and wit.

Autobiographical Sketch and Essence of Teaching
(Translated from Dr. Usui's notes, probably dating from about 1910)

I, Usui, have decided to set down in writing my motives and aspirations and the reasons why I have introduced this new spiritual science, which in reality is a very old spiritual science, that had been lost and forgotten.

I was born the first son, the eldest of three brothers and two sisters to my father. My father was a lower level noble who in his wisdom, or perhaps cunning, had seen the handwriting on the wall concerning the old government of the military shogunate, which for the past 50 years before my birth had been toppling like a used and discarded table which finally came crashing to the floor, due to the wisdom and very well coordinated machinations of the Emperor Meiji, and his many supporters. This led to a change in the national attitude that was striking.

From the time of the Nara period or even before, until the mid-19th Century, Japan, although never admitting it, had looked toward China and in the Western direction for its inspiration and culture. This was good, for the Chinese truly possessed it. Not only did they bless Japan with the basis of art, language, writing, at least writing, the arts of calligraphy, and of course, the great gift of the Dharma, the teachings of Confucius, and the teachings of Lao Tzu. But they also implanted their penchant for the maintenance of stability and prevention of social change. This I feel, at least I felt at that time, was not good, as many young people did.

When I was 16 years old I saw my first steam engine and was moved to tears at its symmetry, perfection, elegance, beauty, and also function. Shortly thereafter there was an influx of gaijin, Western barbarians, into Japan. At first impression, they resembled the demons of legions of old. With their light hair and reddish faces, they looked to be the minions of the Lord of Death himself that had arisen from under the earth, and certainly the odor which emanated from them confirmed in most people's minds, that they had not sailed from the East to Japan, these ocean barbarians, the round-eye, but had definitely sprung from the lowest realms of the Lord of Death.

However, I met one, a Mr. Phillips, who was both a practitioner of his religion Christianity, an expounder of it, somewhat of a Bonze, something known as a 'lay preacher', and a medical doctor as well as a philosopher. As I became acquainted with him, I found him to be truly a remarkable individual who, though totally outlandish in his behavior and manners, I nevertheless recognized as a fellow human being and one of great intelligence. I felt at the time as many young people did, that I wished to learn all of this Western knowledge, and would make any sacrifice, even sitting in the room with such a fragrant individual, to absorb his knowledge.

I found him curious of our ways, and one day he asked the question that I had been waiting for; he asked why were most people revolted by foreigners. I joyfully gave him an answer that they did not bathe. This startled and amused him and he informed me that he bathed at least once a month. I informed him that most Japanese who were able, bathed at least once a day and that, unlike his folk, they suffered very little from carbuncles, boils, and other skin eruptions. This amazed him and he wished to know how we stood immersion in such cold water each day, and did it not affect our health in other adverse ways. I am afraid that I broke into laughter and explained the concept that our baths were heated. He said, yes, he had taken a few baths that were heated by pouring a pot of hot water into a copper tub.

I told him that this was not the way that a civilized person bathed and invited him to enjoy my bath. He was terribly amazed and caused me no end of amusement when he entered the hot water and turned far redder than I had ever seen any individual before. In fact, his entire white body that reminded me of the underside of an octopus' tentacle, when he emerged from the bath was a most startling shade of crimson.

However, he enjoyed the bath immensely and inquired if perhaps such a thing could be constructed for him. This was done, and it actually became a fashion among many of his friends, which was a relief to many of the students that were studying with them.

In fact, I was congratulated by the students' families and presented with a rather large sum of money, at least for an 18-year-old boy, for having introduced the gaijin to the proper civilized custom of bathing and, thus, establishing a great deal of wah ("harmony") in the community, which had formerly been upset by the remarkable and penetrating odors, these odors which seemed to be absorbed into any item they would come in contact with.

Mr. Phillips explained to me the doctrine of Christianity that rather amazed me. It seemed to me to have very many similarities to the Pure Land practice of Amida; in fact, I was finally able to understand that perhaps Mr. Jesus had learned the doctrine of the Pure Land School and then had tried to explain it to his people, who were dull of wit and they punished him by crucifying him. The principal thing I could not accept of course or at any time in the future, was that man only lived once and had to obey a rather change-able, frivolous, unkind, and vindictive god.

As a Buddhist I knew that the Buddhas were all good, but during these years from the time I was 16 until I was 27, I rejected my faith and went after the Great God Knowledge, or at least scientific knowledge which had been brought to our country by the gaijin. I studied medicine and I also studied physics and I became a medical doctor through the kind teachings of Mr. Phillips and other teachers, some from Princeton University, some from Harvard University and some from the University of Chicago.

I was granted a medical degree by decree of the Emperor and was allowed to practice with Dr. Phillips and his asso-ciate, a Dutch physician, a Dr. Kerngold. I began to learn the finer points of surgery, having mastered pharmacology and the treatment and diagnosis of disease.

At that time unfortunately, a cholera epidemic moved into Japan that afflicted our people and particularly myself. I was stricken at the age of 27. The only treatment at that time for cholera was to let small pills of rolled opium melt under the tongue. This would slow the movement of the lower intestine and the individual would not dehydrate so much. The only other thing administered was a mild mix-ture of salt water, potassium chloride, mixed with a fruit juice to prevent dehydration and expenditure of the elec-trolytes, thus, badly affecting the sodium potassium bal-ance in the body.

Now, I will say of opium that I found it at that time and later in my life a way to open the consciousness in an artificial but effective way. I learned later that I could achieve all of this simply by meditation; however, at the time it opened my mind and I am sure that the illness also had this effect upon me.

One afternoon I had sunk into unconsciousness, at least was unable to move my body in any way, when I heard Dr. Phillips sadly tell two of his Japanese associates, Tonne Dak, and I can't think of the other name, he was a nephew of Annoi Tetsuma, however, that I would not last out the night, that I was expiring and that my blood pressure was so low as to be negligible and that my heart beat was so weak that he did not expect my heart to last for the rest of the evening and into the night. This produced great sadness in the people there; it did not produce so much sadness in me.

I remembered my childhood teachings and thought of the Pure Land of Buddha Amida and that I would go there because I did have faith. In my mind I began to recite the Amida mantra, 'Namo Amida Butso, Namo Amida Butso, Namo Amida Butso', and then I fell into a deeper semiconscious reverie and then into blackness, a dreamless state, from which in the early evening I began to awake, and then notice that I was not awakening in the hospital room, but in a place filled with light, the most beautiful of golden light. And in my mind I thought to myself, I am dead and I am beholding the Assembly of the Pure Land.

Well, on both accounts I was wrong. I beheld Mahavairochana. To his right was Amida; to his left was Medicine King Buddha. Above the head of Mahavairochana was our First Teacher Shakyamuni. Countless Buddhas and Bodhisattvas and their retinues surrounded them. I immediately felt great sorrow for I remembered that I had rejected them.

Then Mahavairochana spoke to me and I beheld his face, the most kind and loving face, free from passion and attachment, yet filled with compassion for all sentient beings. And he said to me, "My poor child, you fear that because you have rejected your ancient and hereditary faith that we have rejected you. For a fully enlightened being, a Buddha, this is not possible for us to be angry or feel evil or ill thoughts toward you. We only feel compassion for you and for all beings who suffer in the churning ocean of Samsara, facing the two terrors of birth and death."

At this I was overcome with joy and happiness and at that moment understood the commitment which these supreme spiritual beings have taken upon themselves for the well being of mankind, knowing that each in the past, too, had for many kalpas possessed a human body and had undergone also untold sufferings until they were able to put their heads above the water of Samsara and step onto the dry land of Nirvana, reaching their Buddhahood, knowing all things, having experienced all things, and having developed that compassion which in any situation does not waver, but stretches onward until it is perfected in the Supreme Buddha Mind.

As I observed the Buddhas and Bodhisattvas, I felt terribly inadequate and humble before them. I prostrated many times and said to them, expressed to them, my sorrow at having turned away from their spiritual science to the physical science that had been brought to us by the Europeans and Americans.

Buddha Mahavairochana smiled and said, "But you have not turned away, my child. For all learning and knowledge which relieves suffering is from the mind of the Buddhas."

At that I was again filled with joy and yet fearful that I had not earned my place in the Pure Land among the Assembly.

At that time Medicine King Buddha spoke to me and said that I was a physician as he was, and that it would be my job, my mission, when I had recovered from my illness to work to make a synthesis of both teachings. At that time he expressed to me the age-old teaching that the spirit, the life energy, the hara, is not separate from the body and that all physical suffering first emanates from the Hara, and is due to karmic obscurations and past actions which lead to suffering; the surgeon's knife or the physician's pill can only temporarily relieve this suffering. For the individual to truly be healed, he must be healed of ignorance, hatred, and greed. He must live a moral life, walking the Middle Path and seeking enlightenment for his own self and others. That this is the only true healing, that the Dharma itself is the only balm and medicine for the suffering of all living beings.

Then when he had finished speaking, from the place at his heart came the blue light of Probassa Vaidurya, the lapis lazuli, and touched me and at that moment my mind, everything went blank and into darkness. However, the next morning I awoke. To my physician's surprise and delight, no symptom other than the weakness of my illness remained. I quickly recovered. At that time it was unheard of for a person in my condition to have recovered so completely as to have no longer any symptoms of my ailment.

I told, unfortunately, Dr. Phillips and my colleagues of my dream. They gave it the explanation of the opium which I was ingesting and the fever that I had and told me that a learned man of science could never believe such mythology and such things as were the provenance of the ignorant, unlettered peasant.

Later, about a week after I had recovered, I went to my Bonze (priest) who told me quite a different story. On hearing the dream he became angry and told me I was very arrogant; I was not a spiritual person; why would I be telling such a lie about having such a vision and so on, that not even the greatest Abbot at the greatest temples had. Why would I, a student, who was not even dressed in the traditional Japanese manner, possibly have such a dream or an experience? He called his guards; he struck me and literally threw me from the precincts of that temple.

Up to that time I had been raised as Tendai; however, almost immediately I encountered a wonderful person who was the father of the person who became my best friend. He was Watanabe, the senior. He practiced a form of Buddhism known as Shingon. I took him as my mentor and explained the dream to him.

Together we performed numerous fire offerings as a thanks giving for the particular blessing I had been given to behold the faces of the Assembly of the Buddhas. I began to meditate and study with Watanabe Bonze, and immediately my life changed. I became very calm. My desires and attachments began to break away and the obscurations which I had held in my mind since childhood began also to fall away, like clouds before the morning sun. I continued to practice and received all of the lesser and some of the greater initiations of his Shingon sect. This was a great spiritual awakening for me, and I understood that the dream within when I had encountered the Buddhas was only the beginning of the Path and was certainly not the end.

Keeping this in my heart, I practiced as a physician and became rather well known in the area around Osaka. Many people would come to me because they said I had within myself an ability to heal and that I had been born to this work. This is not uncommon among the peasantry who still have what many people refer to as superstitions, which I just a few years before had thought were silly superstitions. By this time, however, I believed were a perception and a wisdom that overcame the knowledge one learned, and a wisdom and understanding of the innate reality of things as they are that goes beyond the normal perception.

When I was 34 years old, I traveled to Kyoto and there in a bookstore I found an old lacquer casket that had the chop of the Emerji Shingon Temple. Being a devout and fervent Shingon practitioner, I felt it must contain some of the Sutras or commentaries and I immediately purchased it for a small price.

It was constructed of an outer casket of very nice teak, and the interior of camphor wood. I took it home and discovered the treasure that I had found, one that I had been seeking without knowing that I had been seeking, and one that had been entrusted to me by the kindness and compassion of the Buddhas and the Bodhisattvas of the Three Times.

It was at this time that I began to meditate on the material contained within the "Tantra of the Lightning Flash". As I read and meditated, it became very clear to me that here was a spiritual system of healing that has been revealed from the lips and tongue of Shakyamuni Buddha, and that, through the ignorance and carelessness of man, had been lost for a time. It was my decision then, that I would study and perfect this system of healing and perhaps in my old age pass it on to certain select students who would then promulgate it.

It became extremely clear in my mind at that time, that this was the mission that the Buddhas had set out for me at the time when I had the dream. That this would be the path that I was to follow and this was the way that I, Usui, would gain the level of enlightenment, by promulgating and practicing this methodology that relieved not only the external, physical sufferings, but the internal sufferings and obscurations of humankind. This would go beyond both Chinese and European medicine, it was complementary and not contradictory to either system, but was the root of both systems, for it had come from the Buddha; and as all knowledge, both the knowledge of the Chinese and the knowledge of the gaijin, it doesn't matter which, had also come from the mind of the Buddhas, particularly the healing knowledge from Medicine King Buddha, the esoteric knowledge from Manjushri Bodhisattva. So this I felt was what the dream I had experienced during my illness was concerning, and also this explained the miraculous recovery which occurred when the physicians that were attending me had said that I would not last until morning and that I would not recover.

Those were the two events that changed the path of my life and led me to the fulfillment which I now feel as I set down this writing, so that my student Watanabe, the son of my mentor Watanabe, will be able to follow, and some advice I am giving him as well concerning the conduct and concerning the way in which a physician, particularly a Buddhist physician, should comport himself in relation to others, and in the relation also to his patients. By others I mean colleagues, family, and friends.

So, I set this down now, that he may have this in order to understand my feelings, why I have initiated the system which is to be called Reiki and my feelings on the inner and outer teachings, and its applications. I have given a little history about myself and I will give a little more probably as I go on, because what being does not like to talk about his past to others. It is a common human failing that is perhaps not a failing, but perhaps is a way to share experiences which we cherish with others, to share actually our life and life events with others as a sharing, not a bestowal of knowledge as such, but a sharing on the common human condition of life, which all sentient beings that are at the human level experience, and perhaps from this commonalty of experience we can gain wisdom and understanding.

So, here is some advice and things that I would like to say. First, I want to discuss impermanence and change. I am not the same man that I was when I rose from my bed this morning, and when I rise from my bed the next morning, I will not be the same man. In fact within my body within a 24-hour period, my body is mostly water, and that water will be different water than I experienced when I rose this morning; this evening when I go to bed, most of that water will be different. In the morning when I arise, the water that was in my body yesterday will not be there, but new water will be there which I have ingested by swallowing my tea, by eating my food and by drinking water itself, or the juices from plants and so on.

The proteins in my body will be different because in many of them, the albumin will have passed through my urine and through my defecation; other proteins that I have in-gested from my noodles, from the wheat, from the fish that I eat, from the meat that I eat. These are new proteins that I introduce into myself. My skin sheds many cells. Every time I move cells fall from my skin that are dry and are replaced by new cells. My muscle tissue is replaced, and so on.

There is constant change in my body; there is constant change in everything that is around me. Now, the practitio-ner of Reiki should be aware of this, should meditate on the impermanence of himself, should view death as inevi-table, but not as a friend nor as an enemy, but as an occur-rence. I will discuss this later.

have this year — some are the same, and some are different than I had last year, and the year before, and ten years ago. And should I live another ten years, the friends I have will be different. They will not be the same people that I know now, because they too will have changed, and I will have gained new friends and have lost old friends either to simple separation or to death.

Many events occur. Impermanence is all about us, the sun rises and sets, the flower blossoms and withers, the grass grows and is cut back, the tree which has been 300 years growing is felled by the woodsman's ax. All things are impermanent and subject to change, but you know, these things are only an illusion, a shadow. They are not reality; they are only the reality that we, through our beclouded minds, perceive. They are not the true reality that really exists around us. That true reality being the mind of all the Buddhas.

So, death being an occurrence is also impermanent. Yes, death too is an illusion. Illness itself is a delusion caused by karmic obscurations; perhaps even life itself is an illusion caused by karmic obscurations. Just consider this.

And imagine that I am also a river. I flow through time. I encounter the rocks and my banks that cause my turnings. These are set before me by my karma. I flow yet around the rocks. Behind me is the mist from which I have flowed, before me is the mist into which I will flow. I am a river that flows through time. I have no beginning and I have no end and I am constantly in motion.

Death is unimportant. Life is unimportant. Life itself is a link in a chain or a ripple around the rock in the flow of my stream. For I, Usui, am a river. I flow from the past to the future, through many turnings, yet I am that same river, in the past, in the present, in the future.

Everyone is a river flowing from the past to the future. Every mind stream is unique, yet the same. The water that flows in one river is of the same substance as the water that flows in all rivers. They are not different. The formula for the water in every river is still H_2O. One might have different salts dissolved in it, and it might take on a different course; it might be wide and lazy or narrow and urgent, yet it is still water. This is the unity that all Beings share. The water in one river is the same as that in every other river.

If life is an illusion, how much more so is death an illusion? If happiness is an illusion, how much more is suffering an illusion. If love itself is an illusion, then how much more so is hatred an illusion. These things have no real existence. They are phantoms that pass through the mind. They are feathers blown in the wind. They are pebbles moving down a hillside. From vast emptiness all things have arisen and will return to that same vastness. All things keep on returning. The one permanent thing is the Mind of the Buddha, which permeates all existence.

And we are the Buddha. Truly it is only our obscurations, our clouded thoughts, our own non-understanding that separate us from total and complete enlightenment. The true practitioner of Reiki will realize this. When treating an illness he must realize the truth that illness is impermanent and is an illusion. It has arisen and it will pass. Perhaps death will occur, and that is an illusion too. And the illness will pass with the death and the river's flow will continue. Onward and onward through time. One must view things not as simply a segment or a slice. One must view things as continual and unbroken, the flow of the Mind Stream through Time, but then we must remember that Time too is an illusion, and has no real meaning or effect on us.

to me, and I know within me that they too are only illusions and impermanent. I have experienced them. Perhaps others who read my words will also experience them, but they too have no permanence. This concept of impermanence must be impressed fully on the mind of the practitioner of Reiki, the spiritual science. If it is not, then the practice is fruitless.

Before discussing the practice itself, I had wanted to say these things. They are the words of a silly old man and have no real meaning, but perhaps if they can provoke insight within you, my student Watanabe, then even though they are of little value, they will have served the purpose for which they were written.

I end this portion of the discourse now; I will continue it in the future. But remember there is no past and there is no present and there is no future, for even Time itself is an illusion and by a simple clap of the hand, it too can be returned to the void, the one experience, the timeless reality, which is the Mind of the Buddha.

14

NEUROSIS

It was inevitable that the current modern theories of psychology in Europe would make their way to Japan along with other Western innovations. Dr. Freud, in the form of his teachings arrived in Japan and was not met with cordiality by Dr. Usui. In Chapter 14, Dr. Usui gives his opinion of 'modern' psychology. He then proceeds to instruct us and dispense to us a far superior teaching. The noted Western psychologist and founder of the Esalen Institute, Fritz Perls, once commented that Shakyamuni Buddha was the first and greatest psychologist. Dr. Usui seemed to have shared his opinion.

As a clinical psychologist, I cannot help but agree with Dr. Usui's suggested methodology and I most certainly agree with his conclusions in relation to the harm that Christianity as practiced by the majority of people in the last 1500 years has caused to its adherents. The fact that reason and good sense be used in treating psychological ailments is not a radical thought in our culture. Any competent Greek or Roman physician of the ancient world would have agreed with Dr. Usui's methodology. It is really only in the last 30 to 40 years that the very methods which Dr. Usui suggested have been introduced and used in the West by such pioneers as Wilhelm Reich and Fritz Perls. I cannot help but feel that if these methodologies were widely practiced and the underlying causes were more thoroughly examined by present day psychologists practicing in this country, that greater strides would be made in the field of mental health. Dr. Usui clearly believes that self-knowledge and self-understanding are the key issues in mental health, and these concepts I believe are truly the basis of psychology.

On the "New Science" of Psychology
Translated from Dr. Usui's notes

Some Western scholars in Europe and America, particularly Dr. Freud in Austria, are trying to classify and diagnose problems in human behavior and even hinting that the mind can cause illness. What a marvelous insight for Western barbarians. Those who follow the path of Buddha and his continually revealed teachings have known this for well over 2500 years.

I am now going to talk about the so-called (I find myself laughing) 'new science' of psychology. To attribute mental disorders to the sexuality of children under four is laughable but also tragic, in that by adhering to a rather silly, pseudo scientific concept, they miss the true causative source of the problem.

But since Westerners, generally speaking, adhere to a mistaken philosophy which has its roots in a religious system which informs their adherents that they have only one chance to make good or they lose it all and are cast by a disapproving deity into eternal punishment, then how can they really understand the origins of mental disorder? If it were not so tragic and the result of their teaching so tragic, their patently ridiculous belief about sin would cause untold merriment.

Other unusual beliefs of Westerners such as wearing heavy woolen clothing including undergarments in stifling weather which, added to their fear of water, produce remarkable fragrances that in a short time can perfume an entire building, making it somewhat intolerable for civilized individuals to endure for any period of time.

The reason that I am mentioning this is that I recently visited the German Embassy and my olfactory sensorium has not yet fully recovered. In fact the odor of the building even penetrated my clothing and though fresh that morning, I have had to have it laundered twice to remove the clinging effluvia of European civilization.

It also seems that the Protestants in Europe, at least according to what I have gleaned from my readings, rebelled against civil authorities and for a period of 200 years managed to precipitate a number of major wars in Europe.

Now, to conduct war over matters of politics I can understand though not approve of. But to conduct wars and cause suffering and death over personal and family adherence to one doctrine or another I cannot comprehend. We have an example of the contention caused by this religion in our own country not even 200 years ago, when greedy court officials allowed Western merchants the right of trade with the Divine Islands, and in order to secure this allowed their missionaries to work among our people and spread their insidious doctrine of civil disobedience.

This resulted in the rebellion of a number of the great Daimyos including Satsuma against the lawfully constituted and divinely approved Emperor and Shogun. This of course, eventually led to the execution of their missionary priests and followers.

Westerners, similar to Filipinos and Koreans, have the most unusual and disgusting custom of preferring to eat meat after it has reached an unbelievable state of semi-putrefaction, and also prefer their fish to have reached a similar state before consumption. It is my belief that this custom coupled with their clothing habits and fear of water is what leads to their most interesting redolence.

But, I digress. I really must return to the science of psychology. It seems very odd to me that Japanese ladies of similar age and social status never exhibit the symptoms which Dr. Freud records concerning the young women he treats. After reading several of his writings I have come to the conclusion that the strange Western views on sexuality and the way in which children are instructed concerning the matter, seem to evolve from the Western belief that anything concerned with sexual reproduction is 'dirty, wrong, or at best somewhat shabby, and an act which is almost shameful to engage in'.

On first learning this I was struck with absolute disbelief, then when trying to solicit information about foreign sexual practices from my Western friends I had to conclude that it must be true. I could not believe that one of my foreign lady friends actually screamed and fainted in my presence when I asked her how often during a week that she had intercourse with her husband and in what manner it was accomplished.

On another occasion, I was able to solicit from a friend of mine, a foreign physician, that they performed the act in the dark while fully clothed and that in polite Western company, it was simply not discussed.

138 Medicine Dharma Reiki

Should I have asked any Japanese woman the question I asked the foreign woman, I would probably not have received a truthful answer. In order to be polite and to honor her husband, she would have probably bored me for at least half an hour with details of her husband's prowess, inventiveness, and mastery of the arts of love. His stamina and the frequency of the act would most likely have been greatly exaggerated.

In order to conduct an experiment, I asked three Japanese men and after having received the details that truly indicated superhuman endurance, I was referred to their wives for confirmation. The wives' stories were even more fantastic and I had to conclude that if they were true it would be absolutely necessary for me to hospitalize their husbands and treat them for debilitation and exhaustion.

Furthermore, during my researches in 1893, I discovered to my absolute shock that homosexual activities did not even exist in the West according to my sources, but that should they exist would be punished as the most heinous of criminal activities. This surprised me greatly because I was well aware that both their military and ship's crews practiced such activities frequently and sometimes even in a public place, disregarding the sensibilities of a Japanese passerby and disturbing the wah of an area.

During the time of the visit of the American Navy in 1895, such activities were so blatant, that civil authorities had to ban the local citizenry, particularly children, from the dock areas of Yokohama. When complaint was made to the American authorities, it was met first with disbelief, denial of such activities, and finally with the attitude that American Navy personnel were gathered from the lowest strata of society and that this was not the usual conduct of Westerners. But I pointed out that in Japan such conduct was unacceptable in public but was practiced rather openly in private, even by people of social standing. My revelation was met with disgust.

However, I later learned that the Consular Officer with whom I spoke made use for his own pleasure of young boys who rendered that service for a certain fee. I learned this when one of the lads came to me for an ointment to soothe his rectal sphincter that had become considerably irritated due to the size of the foreigner's member. The boy indicated that he was not distressed by it at all, that the particular individual was a fantastic lover, and that generally speaking the size was definitely a boon, rather than a burden.

He also indicated to me that his experience with the gentlemen who engaged in such activities did actually bathe frequently and made use of scented alcohol and were much more refined and civilized than most foreigners. In fact, one gentleman from Germany that the boy knew of actually bathed daily in the Japanese style and when in private wore far more sensible clothing. This poor chap, however, was accused by his superiors of having gone native and was ordered to return to Germany. He refused and appealed to our civil authorities concerning the matter. After deliberation by our authorities, he was compassionately allowed to remain and given a job as advisor to our foreign minister. He speaks Japanese exceedingly well and I consider him one of the most civilized of the foreigners dwelling on the Divine Islands.

But again to return to my major discourse.

I cannot help but think that this extremely unhealthy view of the human reproductive function can only lead to neurological and psychological damage in the individual. Now my assistant young Watanabe has mentioned that Buddhist monks and nuns do take a vow of celibacy, but this vow is voluntary and of course is not a requisite for the practice of Buddhism. Furthermore, it is not defining the reproductive function as 'dirty, nasty, or shabby' or any more so than any other human activity. It is taken simply to facilitate detachment from worldly matters, and we all know that a high degree of sexuality among the monks, as in the military, does exist among their conferees.

This accepted, though rather incomprehensible, at least to me, activity is simply an expression of human condition and organic need. The reproductive urge in the human being is a very strong force and its effect on the body and mind should in no way be discounted. I believe that the stifling and suppression of this urge that is practiced by most Europeans can lead to physical and mental conditions unconducive to health. I also believe it causes the various symptomatologies of hysteria and psychogenic illnesses that Dr. Freud addresses in his works.

I believe that the guilt produced by the suppression, either culturally or religiously, is the potentiator of these conditions. They are remarkably lacking in my Japanese, Korean and Chinese patients, but many of my European patients, both male and female, seem to suffer from them. As far as I can ascertain to their cause, I must attribute them to these strange religious and cultural customs which turn an everyday biological act which generally brings pleasure and joy to its participants, into an offense in the eyes of their deity.

But to address the other mental imbalances that occur in individuals, which do not have their roots in the reproductive act, and its concomitant urges.

As we have addressed elsewhere that the ultimate cause of physical illness is karmic and the resultant cure is due to the eradication either by suffering, intervention, or other means, of the karma. Once the karma is exhausted the illness disappears. So too mental imbalances, diseases of the mind, and other neuropathies, vanish when their karmic cause is eradicated. Specifically I do not profess to know the particular karmic acts that lead to the serious neuro-pathologies, such as melancholia, paranoia, manic states, and schizophrenia. I do know that it must be serious karma as treatment is most definitely difficult.

I have found that in violent or excitable individuals the administering of a combination of opium and aconite seems to have a general calming effect. And that for the melan-cholic, cocaine is sometimes beneficial. The most thera-peutic thing, however, that I have found for individuals suffering from such afflictions, is removal to a quiet coun-try setting and that alternative hot and cold baths are ben-eficial. I have found that simply talking to the individuals, though sometimes disconcerting, seems to be helpful to them. I have also found that in many of these cases, pos-session by a malevolent kami is the actual cause. Though criticized by my Western counterparts and my instructors, I have frequently and with great success made use of a Shinto medium to determine the nature of the Kami which I have usually found to be in the family of Fox kamis and, not so frequently water devils.

I have then arranged for expiatory gomas (fire ceremonies) to be performed on behalf of the individual and then an actual exorcism to be performed by a Buddhist or Shinto priest, depending upon the religious belief of the individual. Over a period of 5 years in these cases, I have found that the success rate is 87% with only 11% recidivism and recurrence of the illness. Of that 11% only two of the percentage points had a recurrence due to no external causes. The other 9 percentage points were people who persisted in engaging in negative spiritual activities that led to their repossession.

Now on to lesser imbalances:

Though I cannot say with total certainty, I do believe that most of the lesser imbalances can be attributed to the lifestyles of the individual so afflicted. When one spends all of one's energy amassing money or working tirelessly for the Government, one does create a physical and mental imbalance. Also, loss of sleep from fear of loss of one's money, or failure at one's employment and the criticism of superiors, and the constant attempts by one's inferiors to undermine one's position and authority, certainly can and does lead to unfortunate imbalances both in the mind and in the body.

The prescribed treatment for this, which I have found most successful, is to counsel the individuals so afflicted to alter their lifestyles to a more relaxed and less demanding vocation, to frequently attend musical performances, the Kabuki Theater and other relaxing pastimes; to work outside in their gardens, to acquire a hobby, or even a pet. Also to make frequent excursions in the country and to take walks in pleasing areas such as woods, the mountains or near the sea.

It is very clear to me that farmers and fishermen do not seem to suffer from the same afflictions and mental imbalances as merchants and bureaucrats or city dwellers in general.

And that perhaps their occupations and quiet modes of living seem to benefit the farmers and the peasant, the fisherman, the small tradesman. In fact, generally speaking my years as a physician have taught me that the general problems the lower classes seem to develop physically are mainly due to accident or physical overexertion. Whereupon the upper classes in the city suffer from numerous maladies which are totally unknown in the country. This, of course, does not include epidemics such as influenza and small pox, whose demonic powers afflict the entire population.

I have found that in a mental imbalance a garden is better than a shelf full of medication, or all the advice and treatment that I can give. I find that diet, moderate exercise, moderate sexual activity and moderate use of alcohol can bring about remarkable change in an individual. Of course, with all of these remedies the application of the Universal Life Force Energy of Reiki is indispensable. Whatever the cause in this present life of the illness, and whatever the cure we can devise, superseding all of this are the compassionate activities of Medicine King Buddha which are manifested through his practitioners.

In order to cut the root of the affliction, the sword of the compassionate activity of the Buddha must be employed. In our knowledge as healers we can prescribe remedies, administer massage, change lifestyles, and give kind advice and listen with a kind ear. We can try to correct attitudes, whether religious or cultural, which lead to imbalance. We can employ mediums and exorcists to remove negative influences, but most of all we can employ the Universal Life Force Energy of Reiki which issues forth from the compassionate heart essence of Medicine Buddha.

Before closing I would like to say one more thing: In the West in Europe and America, it has become the custom to confine sufferers of mental imbalance in asylums for the insane. I firmly believe that incarceration and confinement in such an institution could only produce aberration in even a normal individual such as myself, therefore I firmly believe that our Oriental custom of keeping such individuals at home tended by the family is far more beneficial to the individual and the family than institutionalization. No matter how compassionate the medical staff of such institutions are they cannot provide the love and support that devoted family members can provide. And I remind all of you that your ethical obligations to your family far supersede any inconvenience that such individuals might cause.

When these individuals were babies no one minded caring for them and, even though they are now adults, their affliction renders them as helpless as a newborn child. The fact that they are adults should not matter and they should be treated with the same amount of love and care as an infant who has similar needs.

This is our obligation as human beings and such obligation is the structure of our society and of course is found in the teachings of the Buddha and Confucius.

Now that I have spoken on this matter, on the following Sunday, on the 17th of August, I would invite all of you from 4 p.m. to 11 p.m. to attend a discussion on these subjects at my home. Dinner will be served at 6 p.m. and there will be an abundance of food and a certain amount of sake for your consumption.

Please, dress casually and not formally in our own national clothing as weather permitting we will adjourn to my garden for some discussion and perhaps some poetry reading, since it is the full moon. I imagine such an evening would be most enjoyable.

15

ON DEATH AND DYING

Translated from Dr. Usui's notes:

Today an 8-year old child died in my arms. It was struck down by one of those demonic conveyances known as the automobile. Its mother brought it to me and it died in my arms.

This led me to contemplate the matter of dying. As a physician I have seen the many faces of death and none of them cause me revulsion or terror, for it is the end of us all. A natural progression from birth through maturity.

In old times the Samurai Lords proclaimed, "Let us pass as the cherry blossom falling in springtime." Many wise philosophers have interpreted this to mean: Let us die in the blossom of youth before old age and sickness comes upon us. I do not believe that this is what it means.

We would become bored if the cherry blossoms remained on the tree forever. It would no longer inspire us, nor fill our hearts with beauty, and furthermore there would be no fruit. Rather, I believe that in the springtime first comes the bud, then the leaf, and then the blossom. The blossom then fulfills its function and is fertilized by the happy bees. Its function then fulfilled it passes, its petals fall to the ground and the fruit comes, containing within it the seed of new life.

This is the way that things have been and ought to be, for without renewal there is stagnation. Then why do so many fear death?

The first is that they do not understand its true nature. The second and more important, if they are Buddhist or Christian, or perhaps Muslim or Hindu, they may feel they have failed to live up to the moral precepts that their belief system demands of them. I will discuss this a little later.

The atheistic hedonist feels that he will be deprived of his enjoyment and simply go down into nothingness. I will deal with him first.

True, if one does go down into nothingness, one is deprived of one's pleasures. But one no longer suffers pain or heartbreak. I do not believe that nothingness is the end, but if I did, I would have no cause whatever to fear it.

I look back on my life to this point and see that the scant pleasures I have derived and experience, are far outweighed by the suffering, struggles, pain and heartbreak that I have endured. Every day that I arise I know that in some way I will experience pain. And I do not know if I will experience happiness or satisfaction.

Weeks go by without having the experience of something truly pleasurable. But not one day goes by without some sort of pain or distress. So why is life terribly important? And why, if I believe that all this would cease, should I have any fear of its cessation? Rather, it would seem that I would welcome it, so why should the atheistic hedonist fear death? The only reason I can think of is that the atheistic hedonist is not really an atheist and perhaps there is something waiting on the 'other side'!

Now, let us progress on to the Shinto believer. I have never really met a Shinto who had any fear of death at all. The Shinto believer believes he or she simply becomes an ancestor or a kami and no longer has to deal with the inconveniences of a body. One doesn't need a house, any tree or stone or even fence post will serve for the night. Some kamis who particularly like an area will choose to abide there, with none of the inconveniences a human would have.

A kami doesn't get wet when it rains, nor does it suffer from heat or cold, or toil for his food. His religious descendants graciously supply it. If they fail in this duty for some reason, the kami has ways and means of reminding them of their duty. Thus, the Shinto do not fear death.

As I was walking in the park near my home, a few days ago, I heard two elderly lady adherents of Shinto discussing their coming transition. They were really looking forward to it. They were considering all the juicy bits of gossip and talk they would be able to overhear in their non-corporeal form. Also one of the ladies felt that her grandson-in-law could probably do with a good scare supplied by a thorough haunting. I find this attitude delightful and healthy and needless to say most amusing.

Now let's go to the unfortunate Christians. Whether Japanese or Western, the Christians believe that they only have one chance to make good. To use one of their own expressions, if they do not walk the 'straight and narrow', then they will be damned forever.

From what I understand, the Islamic peoples hold approximately the same belief. What a terrible fate, because I am certain if this is really the case, the Christian Heaven is vacant of occupancy and its hell is like an overflowing sake cup, dripping its contents from rim to table. Why do I say this?

Christianity is so filled with so many 'Thou shalt nots' and 'Thou shalts' that nobody would be able to fulfill the giri entailed therein. So having stumbled on the 'straight and narrow' as any human being would, then they are destined for eternal judgment and hell.

Now as a Buddhist, I must believe that the Christian God exists, but I believe that he is much kinder and much more compassionate than his proponents are. I have read the New Testament and find that the image of Jesus portrayed therein is far from wrathful and vengeful. In fact he spoke of love rather than condemnation, a lesson that many of his followers could well take to heart. He seemed to me to be somewhat of a male form of our Kannon, our Lady of Mercy, whose compassionate eyes gaze on all beings.

So if one truly believes in this deity, Christ, then one should have no fear of death. Because it says that he will gather his elect to himself and to his father. Perhaps however, it is fear of one's own shortcomings and willful violation of the ordinances that they should be obeying, which lead to these fears.

I attended an Anglican Church service recently where the congregation fervently confessed that they had 'not done those things they ought to have done, and they had done those things they ought not to have done'. My question was why? If they know what they are supposed to do, then they are surely capable of doing it and Heaven knows their deity has made it abundantly clear what they are not supposed to do, yet apparently as exhibited by their confession, they seem to have heedlessly done them anyway.

This is very confusing to me. What is even more confusing is that at the end of their confession they solemnly promise not to do them again and to do those things they are supposed to do, then the very next Sunday they say the same confession again. And the Sunday after that, and so on.

Perhaps this is why Christian people have a fear of death. My advice to them is to believe what their deity tells them, that he is forgiving, but my other advice is to try their best to do those things that he has told them to do, and not to do those things that he has counseled them not to do.

After reading the New Testament, I think with some understanding, I feel that relying on the promises he has made and trying to do their best under the trying circumstances of this samsaric world, they should have no fear about the future disposition of their mind streams.

Now, to the Hindu, the Hindu like the Buddhist rationally believes that this life is only one in many. The Hindu is supplied with a list of "do's" and "don'ts" and sacrifices to make and rituals to perform. These are stated very clearly. If the Hindu is able to do this, then he has no fear of a good rebirth. From the Hindus I have met and communicated with, they don't particularly seem to fear death, because they strive to fulfill their religious duties very much as the Buddhist does.

Now, we come to the Buddhist. The Buddhas have taught rules of conduct, which are most reasonable; to refrain from killing, lying, thievery, sexual misconduct, and the indiscriminate use of intoxicants, is most reasonable. The so-called "sixth rule of conduct", is even more reasonable: to try to better one's spiritual state while in the body.

I could give thousands of examples but feel I don't need to, about the reasons that the first five should be obeyed. The sixth, any rational being can see the benefit and I don't think these are only for Buddhists. Virtually all of our Shinto believers have accepted and adopted them, admitting that the concept of moral conduct is truly important, as it is the basis for one's own progression along the spiritual path. Also, if the five are observed one doesn't cause disharmony in the community and bring suffering upon themselves or others. By simply observing these ordinances, the Buddhas tell us that one will gain a fortunate rebirth, so Buddhists have no true reason to fear death.

In summary, I believe that fear of death is fear of Self, and this should not be so. Truly, if one strives to live a proper life, as most people do, and give it their best effort, then death should hold no fear, but be looked upon as a natural progression and renewal. For the Buddhist it provides a chance to repair mistakes made in past lives, and to move forward to greater realization. Thus, it is to be accepted and embraced as the normal order of human existence.

For those who fear death, I have this advice: We are told that both the Christian God and Buddha Amida are filled with compassion. How then could they want even one being to suffer? Therefore, it seems only correct to me and I do believe in their compassion, that they would not let one being suffer needlessly, nor would they desire to punish that being in any way whatever.

We are all joined together by the chain that is Life on this planet, and to us Life should be precious and a unity. At the same time, we should realize that death is an illusion and that in so-called life we are a unity, so in death that unity is unaffected.

As a physician I have seen death, but I have also seen life and the multitude of stages between the two, and I do perceive it as a wheel whose hub is the grandeur of the universe.

When we were in the womb we did not fear birth because at that time we had no comprehension of its meaning. It is the same now. Unless we have memories from previous lives that few of us do, then we have no comprehension of the reality of death as a simple transformation. Since we did not fear birth, why should we fear death? It is just the doorway to rebirth. Doors have two sides and doorways lead from one room to another. Death is not more than a doorway and we should not fear to grasp its handle, slide it aside, and pass through.

There is a Buddhist story about the peasant who pleased his Lord and inherited a great castle. The peasant had lived before that in a one-room hut. The peasant moved into the castle, but when the other Lords in the area came to visit him, they found he, his family, and all his possessions living in the entry hall.

They asked him why and he answered that was what his family and he needed. To his amazement they explained that there were many rooms filled with treasures and objects of beauty. Simply because he had not experienced them, didn't mean that they did not exist, nor that they would hold terrors for him. They showed him the means to open the shoji screens and pass from one room to another. He was amazed and pleased and filled with joy at what he saw was his.

Of course, most of us are that man living in our single room, this life, and not knowing the wonders that await us in the other rooms of our castle. The kind Lords who visited him, of course, are the Buddhas, who explained to him that this castle had more than one room and in their kindness demonstrated to him the wealth of possessions that he possessed.

So let us look on death as nothing to fear, but an adventure, an exploration if you will, of a grand palace with many rooms. When the time for our transition approaches, let us not fear to grasp the door handle and slide it aside and pass through, experiencing the wonders of rebirth and spiritual evolution.

16

JOYOUS OBLIGATION OR GIRI

The following is my introduction to the Japanese concept of giri, to help the reader better understand the lecture I have included, which was given by Dr. Usui in the garden of his home to fifteen of his graduating students, and is one of the few dated documents.

The word 'giri' is a Japanese word somewhat difficult to translate into English. It has variously been translated 'debt', 'obligation', 'burden', 'responsibility', 'vow', 'contract', and it is all of these things and more. Before presenting Dr. Usui's lecture, I feel it is extremely important to explain this concept, which we have translated as 'obligation.'

The entire structure of Japanese society and the cement that has held it together since prehistoric times is based on giri. In order to understand Japanese culture, social structure, and mindset, it is totally necessary to understand the concept of giri. Everyone in Japan has a burden of giri that they owe to others, and at the same time giri is owed to them by others.

Let's take an example of a young lady whom we will call Yoriko. The first giri she acquired was that to her parents. At the moment of her conception she acquired the obligation to her parents for conceiving her. She acquired nine months of giri during her gestation, and giri toward her mother at birth, and to her entire ancestral line by the fact that she was born into it.

Also since she was born on the Japanese Islands, she acquired giri to the Emperor and to government authority. As she was born middle class, she acquired giri to the middle class. As her parents' servants served her, she acquired giri to each of the servants. She was taught by tutors and, thus, acquired giri there. When she married, she not only acquired all of her husband's giri, but giri to him and all of his immediate relatives. As she began to work in his business selling silk to customers in his shop, she acquired giri to his customers. As she did her shopping at the fishmonger, the vegetable vender, the rice merchant, and the noodle maker, she acquired giri to them.

This is not to say that only she acquired giri; at the same time at every interaction anyone she came in contact with acquired giri toward her.

Let us examine categorically the giri she acquired and the giri that was 'owed' her by others, giri toward parents, relatives and ancestors. Since Yoriko was born into her family, as soon as she breathed her first breath of air she owed the following general giri:

To be obedient to her parents and elders;
Never to dishonor her parents, relatives or clan;
To work for the benefit of her parents, relatives, and clan.

In turn her parents, relatives, and clan acquired the following giri toward her:

To feed and clothe her all of her life if necessary;
To protect her from harm in all circumstances;

To see that she was educated according to the standards of her social position;

To give her a job when she was old enough so she could support herself;

To find her a husband of suitable station and qualities;

The giri that she acquired toward the government:

To be totally obedient to its laws.

The government's giri to her:

To protect her and in modern times, to educate her. If it is the government who educates her, she acquires that giri and must repay it by performing her work well and paying her taxes, etc.

When she was attending school, she would naturally have acquired personal giri to each of her teachers, which would mean treating them with respect and kindness.

When married, she would owe allegiance to her husband's family in the same way she would to her own. They would owe her the same giri that they would owe their own daughter. As she was cared for by servants with her own family or her husband's, the servants would owe her the giri to serve her properly and honorably to the best of their ability. She would owe them financial support and the kindness and respect due their station in life. As she managed her husband's business of silk merchant, his employees would owe her the giri due their boss; that is, honest and diligent conduct in pursuit of their employment.

She in turn would have the obligation to treat them fairly and justly and with the respect due their position in life. To the customers she would have the giri of providing service in the manner that they desired and supplying the highest quality merchandise at a fair price. When shopping for her household needs her giri would generally be loyalty to trading at certain businesses and not insisting on an unjust price when purchasing their merchandise. They would owe her the obligation of providing fresh, quality merchandise without demanding an unfair price.

Although Yoriko did not sign an agreement nor contract to her parents, relatives, government, teachers, servants, husband's family and relatives, employees, customers, or the stores at which she shopped, and made no conscious commitment, nevertheless these bonds were formed; by simply living and existing and interacting with her society she acquired this giri. This is called 'daily giri' or 'ordinary giri'.

There is another kind of giri that is 'intentionally acquired giri'. For instance if Yoriko decided to learn the tea ceremony or flower arrangement from a Master, she would acquire a very special giri that would relate to her specific teacher.

If Yoriko found that she had no talent for the silk trade and needed to learn something else to support herself and found that she had a proclivity for pottery making, she would go to a Master Potter to learn her trade. She would then have acquired a lifelong giri to the Master, his family, and guild. What this means is, she would pay him in money and services during her apprenticeship. She would also hold him in due honor as her teacher, respecting members of his family; she would praise his abilities to everyone whom she had contact with if it was appropriate to do so. When on her own she would say, 'Master X was my teacher. All that I have learned came from his wisdom.'

The most important giri she would have, however, would be to make each pot to the best of her ability because its quality and beauty would be a direct reflection on her teacher. Her conduct in dealing with customers would be a direct reflection on the moral teaching he gave her as he taught her to make pots. He in turn would be required to teach her the trade to the best of his ability and teach her the morals of the pottery businesses.

Say that Yoriko is a modern girl and after being educated at a technical school, gets a job making computer chips at Toshiba. She is trained by a Master computer chipmaker; he has given her the gift of a profession, just as the potter would have done. She owes him the same giri; because Toshiba is employing her she owes them the giri of giving the best service possible. In turn, they owe her the giri of her wages and the responsibility to look after her health care, general well being, safety on the job, and provision for her retirement.

A number of years ago when economic problems developed in Japan and downsizing had to occur, many middle level executives and upper level executives committed suicide. The upper level executive because they had let down the company in general and the lower level executives because they were so ashamed that they were unable to fulfill their giri to their subordinates.

This is the seriousness with which Japanese view giri. A person who does not honor his or her obligations is looked upon as a person of no worth and becomes an outcast, a 'non-person'. A person who goes to great length to fulfill his obligation is looked upon with complete approval and greatly honored.

In the Japanese tong called the yakuza, which is extremely old-fashioned and filled with the concept of obligation and honor, a member high or low who has failed in honoring an obligation whatever the cause will apologize to his superior by severing the little finger of his right hand and presenting it to his boss.

Believe it or not in modern industry in the last twenty years this custom has become fashionable. When I was in Japan in 1977, my friend Dennis introduced me to a friend of his who was a high ranking ministerial executive in MITI. I noticed that he was missing both little fingers and asked Dennis if he was yakuza. Dennis said, "No, but he had a very conservative boss and had made two very serious mistakes."

Dennis then told me the story of a young man that had seduced his boss' daughter. He had actually offered the boss to sever his own 'member', to repair the mistake. The boss fortunately had a sense of humor and modern thinking. He laughed uproariously as the story goes and said, no, thank you, he had one of his own and suggested the whole matter could be solved, if he simply married the daughter; that obviously the boy loved the girl and the girl loved the boy, that he had noticed the boy was very hard working and devoted to his duty and that, since the boss was a modern man, he would overlook the difference in social status and welcome him as a son-in-law.

Dennis' father knew the man very well, and the man had been thoroughly against the marriage until the young man had made the offer and was so heroic in discharging his giri that the boss' opinion had immediately changed. The boy, whom he had viewed a ne'er-do-well and defiler of his daughter, had instantly become a man of virtue and honor. This is another example of the importance of discharging one's giri or obligation in Japanese culture.

And so goes giri. Interestingly, the way, the Japanese language has created a new phrase and word over the last thirty years: 'gaijin' is the usual term applied to a foreigner, particularly Westerners. However, the new phrase geigo gaijin has been created. It means 'special foreigner' and is applied to

Westerners who understand the concept of giri. (General Douglas MacArthur was the first Westerner this was applied to.)

Lecture to His Graduating Students,

Held in the garden of his home on June 11, 1916
Translated from Dr. Usui's notes

Today we have gathered here at my home. You are going to be graduating and going your own ways. Two of you will be returning to your monastery, and the rest of you will be dispersing to your employment or to further education.

Two of you are monks and the remainder are laymen, yet all of you are healers and I wish to speak to you about the giri (obligation) which that entails. You have completed your training with me in the system of Reiki and, of course, all of you have finished your education, yet in another way, you have not. You see, our very first giri is to continue to learn. Some of you, particularly those of you who are doctors, consider that you are filled with all the wisdom and knowledge that you need, and that there is no more.

This is not so. Science is progressing and what we know today will be obsolete tomorrow. It is in my lifetime that Koch and Semmelweiss have discovered bacterium and brought forth the theory of contagion. In the beginning, they were laughed at by their colleagues and even ridiculed, but today their theories are regarded as fact and the dread affliction of postnatal mother's childbed fever has been eradicated.

We have an obligation to pursue studies of both the physical and spiritual means for alleviating suffering and eradicating disease. So, it is very important that we accept our first obligation, which is to continue to acquire further methods to alleviate suffering.

As Japanese, and I will add Dr. Kim, Koreans, we are part of a very old society with customs established over millennia. We are looking to the West for the science and knowledge of medicine, physics, chemistry, and mechanics, but in doing so we must not lose sight of the constraints and obligations which our ancestral cultures place upon us.

I feel it is important today to speak to you about what it truly entails to be healers and to speak to you of the profound obligations that you have assumed. Because of the way that morals have degenerated over the past few years in this country, I feel impelled to speak to you, although I wish I did not have to. However, with modernization and Western influence, the sacred bond has been weakened and has lost its strength.

This is due to the fact that many of you are abandoning the practices and morals of the past and along with Western science are adopting the same kind of materialism as is practiced in the West. I am not saying that Western science is wrong in any way. Nor am I saying that it is inappropriate for us to look to the West for its scientific knowledge, but we do not have to adopt the same moral conduct in order to adopt the science.

For thousands of years our people have understood the concept of giri and it has become the very basis of our culture and behavior. Some think it is outmoded and out of fashion but they are deluded. Western culture, though strong in science, is very young and we are very old. It is necessary for us to apply discrimination in choosing what is right and in rejecting what is wrong.

For three hundred years, we had peace under the Tokugawa Shogunate, but recently we have engaged in war with Russia over Sakhalin Island. We have won of course, but what is the cost of that victory. The European powers and America are now engaged in a Great War in Europe and much suffering and death is the result. Fortunately we are not participating, but that is no guarantee we will not be doing so in the future.

Therefore, as I mentioned before, it is necessary for us to adopt and learn the scientific methodology that the West presents to us, but with that same knowledge we need not adopt the misconceptions and mistakes which are also inherent in Western culture. To do that would only bring much suffering upon us, and it would only bring disaster.

It is not the fault of the Westerner in any way that he does not understand or subscribe to our system of giri or moral conduct. This system of obligation and our precepts of morality have existed on these islands since they were created. It is an inherent part of the Japanese culture and it has always been so.

Our fathers have taught us, our grandfathers taught our fathers, our great grandfathers our grandfathers, and so on. It is one of our obligations to impart the concept of giri and the foundations of civilization to Westerners. If there is no one to instruct them in duty or obligation, how will they learn?

We all know that it is not appropriate for an adult to empty his bladder or void his bowels at any time or at any place. If we did this it would bring public censure upon us and create a problem for our servants or the host in whose house we are being entertained. Yet in the past we have all done this.

When we were children we voided our bladder and emptied our bowels fully clothed and in any place we happened to be, no matter how inappropriate. But can a child be blamed for this action? No it can not.

The child cannot be blamed as it simply means that it has not been taught. It is the responsibility of the parent to teach the child these things, as it is our obligation to teach foreigners about giri. If we do not, we have failed in our own giri, and since we understand the significance of obligation, we then find ourselves in a worse condition, particularly if we are too lazy to bother teaching them. This is a point that will need to be discussed later.

Fourteen of you are Japanese and one is a Korean who has been born here. Therefore you understand giri. You cannot be a healer, a nurse, a chemist, a pharmacist, a mechanic, or anything else properly, unless you hold to your obligations.

You must show to the world that you have honor and face by fulfilling those obligations your society and your family requires of you. If you do not, then whatever you do, you could be another Koch or Semmelweiss, or even Emperor or a Shogun, the bravest warrior in battle, and yet if you have not fulfilled your obligations, you would be nothing. A person even lower than the lowest caste person, an eta. In fact, an emperor who does not keep his obligation is lower than a carrier of human faeces who does fulfill his giri.

Let us look at the specific obligations of a healer:

In dealing with the general public, one must first realize the obligation to be grave, and not be given to frivolity. One must never, and I truly mean never, show oneself to one's patient after consuming even the tiniest amount of alcohol. If one smokes tobacco, one must not do so when counseling with a patient.

One must not be seen with questionable companions or seeking about for loose women. One should not be flamboyant in one's dress, so as to call unfortunate attention to oneself. One's home life should be above reproach, even when the servants are not present. One should not inappropriately comport oneself in the presence of the servants for you know it is said that a servant's tongue is like a dagger; it can stab in many directions.

One must treat one's subordinates with the utmost respect, never administering corporal punishment. If a servant has committed an act worthy of corporal punishment, then that act is also worthy of discharge. Discharge is far better, as it removes the problem from one's household and at the same time removes the cause that disturbs you.

It is of course important to treat all of one's subordinates with compassion and understanding. You know very well that some days you rise from your futon in a dark mood. Take into consideration that they do as well and those two dark moods might be concurrent. This could lead on both parts to serious misunderstanding and unfortunate consequences. Therefore, it is incumbent upon us to realize that persons other than ourselves tend to have days of unfortunate circumstances, and even though the person is a subordinate, to treat them in a manner that we would wish our superiors to treat us in similar circumstances.

It is said that in the days of Ieyasu Tokugawa, that there was a certain general who had a stomach complaint which afflicted him constantly. This unfortunate man would punish the mistakes of his subordinates with extreme severity. One day he made a small mistake and the Shogun immediately sentenced him to death. In amazement, he asked the Shogun why such a small mistake had caused his death. The Shogun replied, 'Sir, I am only following your example.' The general immediately repented and was forgiven his small error, by the Shogun. Therefore, take this into consideration and hold it in mind.

Another story also comes from about that same period regarding giri. A woman lived on the fief of a Daimyo and wove rice straw shoes for her living. Every year she would ask the Daimyo the price for some rice straw.

Every year he would say, 'Simply take it.' She would say 'No, I make a profit from it and it is your rice straw.' He would say, 'But I have no use for it.' She would reply, 'Nevertheless it belongs to you and it is not mine.' He then would chuckle, and demand a small price. When she had made the shoes and collected her profit she would then go to his steward and pay the amount.

She was taken sick one year and could not work. As she was a widow, supporting her grandchildren, the family was in serious trouble. She was very surprised when the Daimyo appeared with food, and a bag of coins, at her door.

She inquired why he had come and was told, 'Honored Aunt, over many years you have served me faithfully, insisting on giving me what is my right although I did not want to take it. You have more than fulfilled the obligation of a loyal subject to your Lord. Would that all Samurai be as scrupulous in discharging their obligations. Therefore, now you must let me as your Lord discharge my obligation to you, or I shall have no face.'

The woman understanding this gratefully accepted the food and coins. She recovered and served him faithfully many more years.

Dr. Usui does not give any indication in his lecture that she repaid the food and coins. She did not, and the Japanese would have understood this. The Daimyo did not grant her a loan but fulfilled his obligation to her. She understood this. If she had tried to repay the money and food, she would have terribly shamed him and taken away his face. It was not a gift to her out of charity even though I am sure he would have felt charitable toward her. She would not most likely have taken his charity, for the classic Japanese proverb states: 'A beggar is without honor.' However, she would have allowed him to fulfill his obligation to her. This is a perfect example that illustrates how giri works.

Dr. Usui continues:

A Christian would say, her Daimyo recognized that she had been faithful in a small thing to him, so he was faithful to her. Thus, we can take this to heart and hold in our mind that even the smallest obligation is important to fulfill. If we do not fulfill small obligations, how then can we be willing to fulfill greater and even more important obligations?

Unfortunately, many people today would think that the woman's act was senseless. If she could acquire free rice straw, she was stupid to have paid for it. She would have lost some profit.

Clearly, she was not stupid. She honestly fulfilled an obligation that she recognized. Whether the Daimyo considered it important or not, was not the question. She considered it important. Even though it was his straw, it was her obligation. It would have been most unlikely that he would even have taken notice of the straw. He obviously did not care about it and asked her to take it. But she knew, better than he did, her obligation, as the straw was his. He had paid his tenants to grow it for its rice. He had taken the rice, the straw remained, but it was also his. She had no right to it. She honored his rights to his straw. And although he would have burned the straw to clear the field, it was his straw to burn and not hers. She recognized his right and her obligation and like an ethical person, fulfilled that obligation.

Even if he was not kind, but greedy, he still would have fulfilled his obligation to the letter; if he had not, it would have become apparent to everyone that he had not, and he would have lost a great deal of face. Instead, they both gained face through her acts. She gained face by paying, he by fulfilling his obligation.

This is the way that society functions optimally. When every individual fulfills his obligation, there is little need for civil or criminal law. There is little need for police, for when people can recognize their obligations and are set on fulfilling them, there are no disputes. That is why from the year 1616 to the year 1867 peace reigned and prosperity abounded in Japan.

By the example of the Tokugawa Shoguns people fulfilled their obligations to one another, government, and Emperor.

Let us further explore the obligation of a healer. What we have essentially covered, is that before fulfilling one's obligation to one's patients, one has to fulfill one's primary obligations. If one does not, then it should be clearly evident that this person does not have the proper moral conduct or inclination to be a healer.

Dr. Usui is saying here that the moral conduct, to which he referred, was keeping one's obligations. The Japanese theory of moral conduct is intertwined so much with giri that the two are inseparable. When one performs any action, drunkenness, sexual misconduct, thievery, etc., one has failed to properly execute one's giri in relation to family and society.

It must be understood that true Japanese morality is based upon fulfillment of obligation and if one properly executes this, then one's life will be moral and in perfect order, i.e., one does not refrain from going to a prostitute because it is a religious sin, but because one's action would reflect upon one's social class and family and, therefore, would be a failure to maintain the obligation to one's family or class. A poor man might go to a lowly prostitute without censure. A middle class man would have to go to a prostitute of his own class to avoid censure and the visits could not be too frequent.

Japanese instinctively understand when the line would be crossed bringing censure and loss of face. Unfortunately, I do not have such complete understanding of Japanese culture as to know when that line would be crossed. For example, when I was visiting Japan my friend and I were hiking in the mountains. We came upon a small lake in which a number of the local farm hands were bathing. It was extremely hot and I was covered with perspiration. I immediately began to strip off my clothes with full intention of diving in and joining the lucky people. My friend immediately restrained me and explained that it would be most inappropriate for us to do so.

As we traveled on, both profusely perspiring, I asked him to explain what happened. He told me they were peasant farmers and it was totally appropriate for them to do so. But that he and I were not peasants and that for the son of an American General and an Executive, it was not appropriate. We later came to a stream in the mountains in a totally deserted area; then it was appropriate; there were no other people around. It was not inappropriate to bathe with such people, such as in a public bath. But even if the lake had been empty of people, but if someone could have seen us bathing in a primitive situation and disrobing in the open air in the presence of people of a lower class, was not a good example for them, even though they were participating in it. More was expected of people of our class.

Dr. Usui continues:

I have talked about moral conduct in general, but a particular moral conduct is incumbent upon the healer. This particular giri is even more important and binding than the general moral conduct our society prescribes.

The first is: One must never, and this is absolute, knowingly take any action that will cause harm to one's patient. This is why it is much better not to act according to allopathic discipline prescribing a treatment, unless one is absolutely certain of benefit to the patient. One has the certainty that if one uses Reiki on behalf of the patient, one can cause no harm. Whereas the incorrect allopathic or Chinese remedy could actually worsen the condition. One has the obligation to act if one knows how, and refrain from acting, an even stronger obligation, if one is not certain of the benefit of the treatment. I realize that this is a difficult challenge, because the patient will insist: 'Doctor, do something for this condition. Help me.'

Many doctors, when they do not know the cause and cure of an ailment will prescribe a laxative for a patient, for a laxative is obviously a drug that has an almost immediate and recognizable result and most doctors feel this does no harm. They are generally right in assuming so, but many of you as doctors know that if the person is suffering from gall stones, appendicitis, or a thinning of the intestinal wall, a laxative could cause death.

Other doctors feel that the prescription of a placebo might be beneficial. I do not feel this is true; first, this must necessitate a lie to the patient. The doctor by saying 'This is a pill that will help your problem' is first, lying by saying although I do not know what is wrong with you, or I do not believe anything is wrong with you, I refuse to tell you this; instead I will pretend to know what is wrong with you, or pretend that even though you have nothing wrong with you, there is something wrong with you. Then a second lie must be told, 'This pill will help you get over what I don't know is wrong with you, or this pill will help you get over the nothing that is wrong with you.'

So I have told two lies to the patient and a third lie to myself, for I have said to myself the patient is too stupid to understand if I explain it to him, that I did not know what his problem was, or that he has no problem. The real reason I have told him the first two lies is, first, he might not pay me; and second, he might leave, go find another doctor, and never come back to me.

So I have lied to myself twice more by denying that these are my true motivations, and therefore violated the ethics of my profession. I have deceived a person and I may have killed him because, say that he really has a dangerous condition, that I am either too stupid, or that my training is insufficient to recognize, and say that there is a known and easy cure for that condition. If I do not explain truthfully, he might never get treatment and then die. And his death would be upon my head, just as most certainly as if I had plunged a lancet into his heart.

I will give you an example of this. A man had been to many doctors, both Western and Chinese who could not understand why he had a rash under his arms and in his groin. He was a wealthy man. They prescribed purging, injections of metal salts, salves ranging from the palliative to the aggressive, bathing, washings, poulticing, and all to no avail. He had recently developed trouble in breathing and pains across his chest similar to a coronary disease. He came to me weak, wheezing, itching and in desperation. I had never seen anything quite like this before myself, but took the time, as was my obligation, to carefully question him. After about an hour I discovered that the condition only developed when he walked on the beach. I suggested an allergy. He did not think so.

I then questioned what he did on the beach. Sometimes he would watch the sunset, sometimes he would simply meditate, sometimes he would read, sometimes he would write poetry and sometimes he would bathe. I told him not to go walking on the beach or visiting it. He did so. There was no change in his condition. I then questioned him further and like Mr. Conan Doyle's Sherlock Holmes, found the clue that led to the answer.

My patient was very fond of crab. His wife and mother were not. At the place where the sand joined the village was a stand that served luscious crab grilled with sugar, spices, and soy sauce. On every trip to the beach the high point of his peregrination would be, before returning home to enjoy his favorite dish. When I forbade the visits to the beach, he agreed to forego it, but not his crab.

He sent his servant every day to the crab stand. I suggested at that moment, when the rising sun of realization dawned within my mind stream, that he would have to forgo his crab. He agreed, almost in tears. He came back to my office three days later, both sad and joyous. The rash and the breathing problem had totally disappeared, and he indicated to me he was feeling fine. But sad that for the rest of his life he would no longer be able to enjoy crabs.

I suggested to him that certain types of shrimp when prepared with soy, spices, and sugar, tasted about the same, he agreed to try them and a week later burst into my office while I was seeing another patient and presented me with a substantial bonus and a small antique silver statue of Kannon. He had discovered that he not only liked the shrimp better then the crab, but that it caused him no further distress. Also his wife and mother confessed that their principal aversion to crab was having to look at it while they boiled and cleaned it. They had no objection to shelling the small shrimp and preparing them. Thus, he could have them whenever he wanted. His wife and mother even prepared him a small lunch packet containing shrimp and the pickle he enjoyed, so he could take them to the beach with him. He therefore confessed that he was saving a substantial amount of money by eating at home.

We can see some amusement in this anecdote, but it is a serious example and a case in point. His allergy was progressing and becoming more severe, breathing problems were developing, and at some future time a severe seafood anaphylaxis could have occurred at any time after a meal of crab and resulted in his death. If I had followed the usual protocol of my colleagues, I would have prescribed a salve and a placebo. I would have acted without knowing the true cause of the illness and could have caused his death.

You'll probably enjoy this next story. A young Western widow came to me complaining that her menses had ceased. She had been to another doctor who had tried a number of remedies to bring on the menses without success. Her husband had been dead over a year. I began to question the girl thinking she was exhibiting all the symptoms of an early pregnancy. She said this could not possibly be, as her husband had been dead for over a year.

I sent her home, consulted all my books on gynecology and even borrowed some from a friend. I saw her two weeks later and her womb was clearly filling with fluid and was imitating a normal pregnancy. I decided to question her some more. Being careful to be exceedingly tactful, as she was a Western woman, we got to the point of sexual intercourse. Oh, yes, she had engaged eleven times over the past year but was suffering under the delusion that women could only become pregnant from their husbands because that was the way in which God had ordained it.

I explained carefully to her that this was not the case; she insisted that might be so for Japanese, but was not true for

Christian Westerners. I asked her to wait in my waiting room while I called a Western colleague and to his unrestrained amusement explained her peculiar belief. He agreed to see her and she and her mother returned to California and were never seen again in Japan. Since she was a healthy young woman, I assume the birth was normal and both she and her mother were proved wrong.

It is interesting for me to say here that I have never had a case quite like hers again, but I have treated a number of Western female patients who until I explained it to them, did not connect the act of sexual intercourse with their condition of pregnancy. I also examined a young Western man who frankly disclosed to me that he believed that kissing could result in pregnancy. I explained to him that whereas kissing might lead to the act, that kissing alone could not impregnate a girl.

I have also treated five young Western ladies who also believed that kissing was the primary cause of pregnancy. On questioning them I found that their mothers had all told them this in order to discourage the practice.

But to return to my patient and her original story. Had I prescribed laxative or attempted to bring on menses by other Western practices or Chinese herbs, I could well have caused a miscarriage, the subsequent death of the fetus and perhaps hemorrhage and death of the mother, but I refrained from treatment until I could research her problem, and then spent the time to judiciously question her and, thus, discovered the primary cause of her condition. I could either regale or bore you with many more anecdotes of this kind, but I won't bother, for it is time for us to go on.

Although we would like to think that our great knowledge of medical science enables us to cure any illness by the quick wave of a pen over the prescription pad, or a few flicks of our scalpel within the patient, this is not the case. As physicians and nurses, you know that patients die. Therefore, it is our giri to the patient to inform him or her of the truth so that they may prepare themselves for their inevitable passing. It is our obligation to hold out no false hopes for recovery or to not suggest useless and perhaps painful treatments so that we may charge for administering them.

It is our obligation to do all that we can by the prescription of opium and its derivatives to alleviate suffering. It is also an absolute obligation that we explain to him that although there is no physical cure for his affliction, that perhaps spiritual science can aid him. We, however, are obligated to make no promises, but regularly administer Reiki treatment, both to assist and in alleviating the pain. Whatever is best for the patient and will relieve suffering, is ultimately what we must choose. It is our giri to do so.

Another form of giri is the obligation we have to those in the spiritual lineage of Reiki to pass on their teaching. But it is not only they and our positions that are a part of this lineage. My chemistry professor was a Christian Korean. He was Christian because the Christians bestowed benefit on him and his family. He confessed to me that he did not really believe in anything except science. In fact, he denied any religious conviction and ascribed all his knowledge of such things to a German Western philosopher, Karl Marx, who I understand is now in vogue in certain circles in the West, and whose philosophy is presently disrupting our old enemy, Russia.

Yet, he taught me chemistry and I have used that knowledge of chemical compounds to compound both external and internal medications that I have applied to relieve human suffering. We must, therefore, assume as Buddhists that some action in his previous life has separated this unfortunate Korean who says he is a Christian Marxist from the understanding of spirituality and his own nature.

Yet, through me and many of his students, he has greatly benefited many suffering beings by his teaching. So we must assume that whatever karmic action he committed, though it has separated understanding from his mind, has not separated him from the great river of knowledge which alleviates suffering, and which flows forth from the great compassion of Medicine King Buddha.

In this life, it is not his karma to understand this, but I am sure that the compassion of Medicine King Buddha will allow him to understand it in a future life.

After my graduation and before his passing, he and I had many talks about this Dr. Marx, though Dr. Marx is not a medical or scientific doctor, but a philosopher. It amused me to discover that his doctrine is much like Buddhism, although Buddha has been removed. Through his teaching he wishes to alleviate the suffering of the poor and ignorant peasant and worker, whom he believes to be exploited by others, to a higher level of understanding, freedom, and prosperity.

I do not think his goals are evil but fear if they are widely disseminated, they could be misunderstood and lead to violence. I have no real fear that they could establish themselves here because we are such socially conservative and responsible people, but I do fear that they could lead to much trouble and suffering elsewhere and could add to the social unrest in Russia, the Western democracies, and possibly China.

But we must go on.

I once had a physics professor who taught me a great deal about weights and counterbalances. He was a Western man and very scientific. He was not devout in any sense of the word and had only a passing interest in Buddhist teaching. He told me it was a little exotic for his taste. It is interesting, however, that near the end of his life he began to practice Zen, but that is not the point. He taught me about the application of force and leverage and an understanding of that science.

I later used this to design the traction splint that we are all now using. By the judicious use of pulleys and changing weights, I can adjust the traction pressure to the type of fracture and the weight and size of the person and the length of his or her leg, thus, aiding the healing of the fracture, as a simple weight and suspension would not be so effective because the pull would not be adjustable to the same degree of fineness as is my little invention.

So he therefore greatly benefited patients whom you and I have treated, and also many of my colleagues who are using my double pulley design.

I had a Western English teacher who taught me the language very well. You may say that this is not a science and in general terms I must agree. As you know, I have also learned some French and technical German from European associates and books that I have studied privately. Now each of those people also must be, according to my reasoning, in the lineage of Medicine Buddha.

Why would I say this? Because through my knowledge and ability to speak English, German, French, and also some Manchu and Korean, I can treat patients who know only those languages and minister to them with both medicine and Reiki. So my teachers, both formal and informal, since they have aided me in aiding others and giving proper treatment must be considered in that lineage.

It would behove you to sit down and consider just how many people consciously and unconsciously, directly or indirectly, are in the lineage of the teaching which relieves suffering, which comes from the compassionate mind and intention of Medicine Buddha. It is not just the Kobo Daishi and the great teachers of India and China, but anyone who has taught you even a scrap of knowledge that has allowed you to alleviate suffering and bring healing to sentient beings.

To each of them we owe giri. First, the giri to respect their knowledge and the gratitude that they have imparted it. But just as we owe the obligation to Medicine Buddha to become like him, we owe them the obligation to become like them and impart our store of knowledge to others. The only true way a teacher may be repaid the obligation which we owe him, is to utilize the knowledge that he gained and imparted to us, adding to it according to our capabilities, and by passing it on to others, so that the benefit of that knowledge and wisdom not be lost, but continue down to our posterity. This brings to mind another small obligation, that if we find that a bit of knowledge is incorrect or defective in some way or incomplete, we should not blame our teacher, because the progress of knowledge is a continuous process and increases from generation to generation.

When we have discovered this we have an obligation to correct it and add to it, before we pass it on. Some might think they have an obligation to correct their teacher and this is true, but only if the teacher's disposition is one that would lend to correction from a student. There are many like this; there are some however, fortunately in a minority, who would be disturbed by such a correction and not take it well. In such a case our giri to that teacher for all the correct information he had imparted to us would urge us not to disturb him, and particularly not to argue with him over that small point. So this you must also keep in mind. Remember the teaching of Musashi who says, 'Evaluate the individual, examine the situation before acting, and then act according to what is appropriate.'

Now the second great obligation we have, whether Buddhist or not, is to aid all sentient beings. I notice my Shinto student smiling and saying to me, 'But Shintoists believe the same', and I know this to be true. We cannot fulfill our first obligations to Medicine King Buddha if we do not fulfill our second obligation. Yet by fulfilling our second obligation we automatically and simultaneously fulfill our first obligation.

By setting forth according to our capabilities and bringing healing, comfort and solace to beings, without regard for their social position or financial stability, we alleviate suffering and, thus, in this very life become like Medicine King Buddha. Whether we do it by allopathy, naturopathy, homeopathy, chiropractic, pharmaceutically, or spiritually, we have become like him and, like him are performing Buddha activity. When we teach another our discipline we are becoming even more like him by passing on the knowledge and training that will enable others to relieve suffering. So not only is it our obligation to heal, but it is our obligation also, sometimes I think an even more important one, to teach others to heal. I can see 30 patients a day at the very most, but if I train 30 healers, they can see 360 patients. And if they in their lifetime train 30 each, then there will be 10,800 patients, and if they train 30 each... just in one lifetime you can then see how much suffering can be alleviated.

But it is our sacred duty and obligation to train them properly, not only in the physical part of the discipline, but in the moral, ethical and spiritual as well. We will know that we have succeeded if we do this, and that no matter what, whether we gain fame and fortune, or remain a little known physician living in a building on the side of a mountain treating the sore feet of peasants, if we have only taught but a few, or just one properly, with certainty, we have accomplished something in this life-span.

Many of my colleagues ask why I take time from making money to teach young dullards like you. It is simple. I cannot take even a hair's breadth of my fortunes and possessions into my next life. Some day I will appear before Emma-O, Lord of the Dead, for judgment and then my next life will be determined. Since I can't take any of my possessions with me, and since he is known to be incorruptible anyway, I cannot pay him a bribe, but I can show him my honor and my students. You are my true wealth. This is true. But of course this is not the only reason I am teaching you.

I feel the truth of what I am saying, and that knowledge alone determines my action. After today, you will go to different places and do different things. I may see some of you again, others I may never see. Dr. Kim will be returning to Korea. You two brothers will be returning to your monastery. Others of you will go into city or country practice. Kinjero I know I will see again, as he will be acting as surgical nurse and anesthesiologist to the French doctors in Tokyo.

But as each of you go your way and begin your healing practice, I am asking you now to remember your giri to me to act morally, to always speak the truth, to not say things you do not mean, to say things that you mean, keep your obligation to country, to your parents, to your clan, to your patients, to your friends, to your colleagues, but more importantly than all of us, to Medicine King Buddha, for by doing so, you fulfill all of your giri to me, and by doing so you will fulfill your giri to all beings. And to all of us, your teachers from Medicine King Buddha to this woolly headed old doctor, teach! For then you will have truly fulfilled your obligation.

Now my servant has prepared a delightful supper for us. When I was writing this lecture and it brought to mind my dear patient and his allergy to crab, I remembered that he introduced me to this wonderful dish, so among the other poor offerings which have been set out for you, there is a large bowl of succulent crab. So let us now go and have a taste of what that poor and unfortunate man is missing.

17

PERSONAL LIFE

It may seem to Western readers that Dr. Usui is intruding far too much in the life of his students, but by Japanese standards, this is not true. A teacher in Japan, then as now, was expected not only to teach the subject of his expertise, but also to prepare his student for life. In the old days this was also true in Europe, but in our modern society this admirable practice seems to have almost completely disappeared. So understanding the times and the compassionate spirit in that it was written, let us examine Dr. Usui's advice on the proper and ethical way to conduct one's personal life.

The Perfect Way to Live in Harmony
Translated from Dr. Usui's notes

I have considered talking on a variety of subjects, but now that we have come together here today I think it would be good if we discussed the general manner in which a healer should conduct his life. The first thing I want to mention is that I am not taking a prudish stance, only a practical one.

Many of you are Buddhists, as I am, and many of you follow the "Path of the Gods", others of you follow no specific religious path, so it is reason, rather than religion that I choose to speak of.

It is imperative that we first examine what the aim of our life will be. We all know that we owe a debt to our family, our country, and the human race itself. For we are not separate but part of this dynamic whole. We are a part of the life that exists in this world system.

Therefore, it is natural that we realize this debt and repay it by service. I am sure that every one of you wishes that something remains when your footsteps have vanished from this walk of life; and that something ideally be of benefit to others. Therefore, the first thing we will consider, is the contribution we can make to human knowledge and welfare.

This is a very personal matter, and you decide on your profession according to your own inclinations. All of us here today have chosen to be healers, physicians, nurses, and lay healers. By doing so each of us has chosen to make a contribution. In doing this you have assured your happiness and satisfaction. No greater satisfaction can be experienced than the happiness and satisfaction that one gives rise to by aiding a fellow being.

But of course, this is not our only consideration in life. You must also earn your own living and fulfill your obligation to family and community. You need to secure a place to live, bring food to your table for yourself and your family, and so I have decided to share some advice that I hope all of you will follow, for it has led me and many others to happiness. It is based on my own experience as well as theirs.

Choosing a Home

One must be most circumspect when choosing a dwelling place. First, it is wise to hire a geomancer and make certain the Feng Shui of the area is proper. Then one should build within one's means. Our forebears found that simple, unadorned homes brought happiness and peace. One should not go deeply in debt to provide a large or ostentatious dwelling, for repayment of the debt and fears and anxieties concerning it, will distress one's internal harmony. If one has not the means to construct a large home without difficulties, then one should construct a smaller, more modest dwelling. One should always leave a place for a garden, however modest.

You need not do this, of course, if you are living in the country rather than the city, for the beautiful vistas and pleasant surroundings will serve the garden's purpose. For what is a garden, but a bit of country brought into the city for those of us who must suffer the burden of metropolitan life? A home without a garden is like a body without a mind stream, or a mind without spirituality.

Thus, one should plan for one's garden in planning for one's home. Even if the size and opulence of your dwelling must suffer by providing space and expense for a garden, it is necessary to make that sacrifice. The most important thing for a person to do is to maintain inner harmony and one cannot do this in an urban area without a garden.

Now as to one's dwelling. Even though small, it should be airy and it should be arranged so as to suggest space. It should not be terribly cluttered with too many possessions, nor overly decorated with screens, wall paintings, and other adornments. These only serve to distract the eye and mind; rather, it should be a place for calm retreat and reflection.

Choosing One's Wife

If one has chosen the life of a householder, then of course, a wife is required. Your parents and relatives will naturally provide the needed girl but, this may seem out of character for me saying this and this is not due to modernism on my part, but before agreeing to the marriage, one should get to know the girl and if perhaps the parents and relatives have made a mistake, which they probably have not; but should this unfortunate case arise, then one should consider suggesting, then insisting, on an alternative choice.

A proper wife must be modest in demeanor and behavior and should be of the same or near social class. A wife of lower class would not be well trained to one's expectations. A wife of a higher social class has the tendency, because of her position and wealth, to attempt to dominate her husband. Neither situation is to be desired. Therefore it is always better to marry an equal rather than a superior or an inferior person.

She should be well trained in household duties, not given to a great deal of gossip nor gadding about. She should be both modest in appearance and interior qualities. Her spiritual radiation should be the same as her husband's, because I can tell you from the experience of some of my friends that unless this is so, harmony can vanish overnight and dissension move in with her baggage.

Sometimes it is necessary for relatives of your wife to share your dwelling and, of course, it is the custom that you care for your mother or perhaps other female relatives who are without protection. It is extremely important before marrying that you assure yourself that her relatives are compatible with your mode of life, and that she is compatible with the relatives you have taken under your protection. If these important points are not examined and dealt with, the harmony of your household will be that of the realm of the warring gods.

Once these matters have been considered and dealt with, one should have long talks with the prospective candidate. You should fully open your heart to her, telling her of your aspirations and intentions and encouraging her to tell you of her wishes and desires. When this is accomplished and you find that your ambitions are acceptable to her and that hers are acceptable to you, and you are in harmony with one another, then and only then should you consent for the marriage to be arranged.

You both must consider that your entire lives will be spent together and then if harmony and affection do not exist between the two of you, then only sadness and misery for you both can be the result. Therefore you should take all steps necessary to assure that you will be able to live in harmony and affection. If you do not, then a marriage can lead only to disaster and suffering.

Servants

One should be even more careful in the choice of one's servants than of one's wife. It is better to depend on servant families that have served your family over a period of time. Their loyalties are usually assured. Remember that servants are privy to your every action and are trusted with your innermost doings. Servants should not be given to the use of intoxicants and be most moral in their conduct and activities.

In choosing female cooks and maids one should not choose the beautiful and elegant, but the simple and plain. This will lead to domestic harmony, peace, and satisfaction in your household. In all dealings with servants, one should be fair and honest, but at the same time maintain authority as the employer. Familiarity with servants is a necessary and good thing and one always should be friendly and willing to give help and assistance and always lend a willing ear to their troubles and problems which, even though they seem trivial to you, are of great importance to the individual concerned, and worthy of your attention and consideration. One should listen to their advice and heed their warnings and complaints.

At one time there was a very wealthy Daimyo and a powerful man in the Bafuku. He was a just and honest man and treated his servants well, considering their needs sometimes even above that of his family. His household was always most harmonious, his sake and tea always served hot and his sashimi cold and fresh. His rooms were always ordered and his pen, ink, and paper, always at hand when he needed it.

Not so with his neighbor. His neighbor was known for his excesses and treated his servants like animals always willing to administer corporal punishment at the slightest distraction.

One day that neighbor and other ambitious men planned a coup against the Shogun. This would have resulted in the death of the just neighbor and his family. The mean-spirited Lord's servants overheard his insidious plotting and, because of their mistreatment at his hands, had no great loyalty to him. They were indiscreet when speaking to the just Lord's servants in the market. The just Lord's servants being loyal and discreet reported this to him. He immediately sent messengers to the proper authorities. The plot was uncovered and the pernicious plotter and his associates lost their lives and land that were added to the fief of his righteous neighbor.

This is a true story that comes to us out of history. Because one man treated his servants well, he gained advancement and notoriety of a positive sort. Because the other man had mistreated his servants, he lost all and for many years thereafter, he and his associates were spoken of as accursed.

Thus, one can see the importance of treating one's servants properly and justly. If one is to treat their servants in this manner, one should treat one's wife and family in the same manner. Remember that it was the betrayal of Goshiwara's mistreated wife that led to her betrayal and the destruction of the Fujiwara's power and the death of young Emperor Antaku.

Also remember that if one treats one's sons and daughters justly their loyalty to you will be assured and secured for your posterity, which now brings us to the all-important subject of children.

Children

An ancient proverb says that a man lives on in his children, and this is true. One's reputation in the community is dependent upon the conduct of one's children. They are all small mirrors that reflect the parents' honor and ethics; therefore, one should take great care in their raising. For if you do not, then I can tell you from many examples that only sorrow and unhappiness will be the result in your old age. Much time and care should be spent in their education, both in learning in the arts and sciences and in their ethical and spiritual training.

One should never be unjust in your treatment, but maintain discipline and authority. If possible one should meet with them every day and speak to them of necessary things. One should not be too severe, but also never lax. Corporal punishment should be a last resort and proper comportment and demeanor should always be enforced even if corporal punishment is necessary. Both sons and daughters should be taught modesty and the importance of the household's harmony emphasized. Should all of these fail then, hard as it might be, the child if necessary should be turned out for the benefit of the harmony of the household.

When the child has reached early adulthood and is able to function on his/her own, their patrimony should be given them and then they should be expelled from the household. However, if one has diligently fulfilled one's duty in ethical, moral, and spiritual training, this should not prove necessary.

The Household

One should always strive to maintain neatness, cleanliness, and order in the household. The reasons for this should be apparent.

If there is filth and disorder, disease and vermin can abound. If there is disorder and untidiness the mind will continually be distracted. One should maintain at least two or three cats as they serve the primary purpose of eradicating and discouraging rodent infestations. Their independence, self-containment, and demeanor are always conducive to harmony and peace. The way in which a mother cat cares for her kittens is a fine example to us all. They should be given free run of the house.

Sometimes it is necessary to maintain dogs for their ability at guardianship. If so they should be maintained in kennels away from the house and never permitted in living quarters. Birds are fine pets and no house is complete without a few. Their songs and beauty are a true adornment to one's life.

A few lizards can be easily purchased to inhabit one's home. They are excellent in that they eradicate some of the more noisome insects that might gain entry.

No garden is complete without a number of frogs. Their songs at twilight are some of the most soothing sounds that the human ear may experience. Crickets are also pleasant to have about but care should be taken that they remain caged. I have known of libraries and precious scrolls that crickets have completely destroyed. If one gravid female cricket is allowed to escape then I am afraid that true disaster has come to your house.

Naturalists tell us that crickets are most prolific and that one female can be responsible for bringing 10,000 young into the world. If one maintains one's house in cleanliness and order, it is a reflection of one's inner life and can only bring harmony and peace.

On Appearance, Hygiene and Attitude

It is extremely important for we who are engaged in the healing profession to always be clean and neat in person. It is also a reflection of our motivation and an example to our patients. One's hair always should be well groomed, one's garments modest and clean, one should bathe daily and give special attention to one's nails. One should thoroughly wash one's hands with soap after any contact with a patient, and most certainly after attending to one's bodily functions. This is not only common politeness, but also prevents the spread of disease from patient to patient.

We very well know from the great discovery and teachings of Semmelweiss that before his discoveries, the filthy hands of the physicians and midwives transported the dreaded childbed fever from one patient to another, and this contagion of course, resulted in the death of uncountable women. As we are daily in contact with the sick and diseased, it is truly necessary to maintain this superior degree of cleanliness.

We should be temperate in our habits, neither eating nor drinking too much, and never appearing in public intoxicated and disheveled. It is said that sake can not only befuddle the mind but destroy one's reputation and standing in the community. This is absolutely true. Dr. Ito is physician to the Emperor Meiji. He has replaced the prior physician, as his predecessor had once been seen publicly intoxicated. For an ordinary layperson their neighbors and relatives act as a judge. For the healer, his patients are added to this list.

I am not saying it is wrong to consume sake. I do so frequently and with enjoyment, but drunkenness is never necessary and is totally an example of one's lack of personal discipline and shows a marked defect in one's character.

Now about visits to women: At some time in their life most single and married men find it necessary to visit women. One should be certain that if one takes a mistress she should be of one's own social class. One should be discreet in this behavior and one's relationships should never be a public performance. I find it best and far less distracting to maintain a celibate existence. All of you could profit from this example.

As to politics, I simply find it distracting. The government is going to do what it wishes to do and as a loyal subject, it is my obligation to support the government, and this discussion of how things should be, or ought to be, or should not be, or ought not to be, is a fruitless waste of time and breath. Our discussions cannot change anything and, if treasonous, can bring on trouble, legal involvement and sometimes even death. It is even better to totally absent oneself from these discussions and endeavors, so as to maintain one's peace and harmony.

Simply by following this advice which I have given you today, I am sure that you, should you follow it, will live long happy and peaceful lives, fulfilling your obligations to your nation, your community, your family and ancestors, and all beings.

This is all that I have to say for today. Thank you.

18

CHARACTER OF THE PRACTITIONER OF THE HIGHER LEVELS

Ethics and individual character are extremely important in Japanese culture, and I do believe in our culture as well. For honor, ethical behavior, honesty and forthrightness are the basis upon which a civilization is constructed. Dr. Usui makes it pristinely clear in the following lecture that these virtues are indispensable to a practitioner of the healing arts.

The Character of the Practitioner of the Teachings Of "The Tantra of the Lightning Flash"

Translated from Dr. Usui's Notes

The character of the person who is practicing the higher levels of the "Tantra of the Lightning Flash", should be one who is dedicated to healing, not to self-aggrandizement, ego-satisfaction, or material profit. What is so amazing about this system is that all of these things will come to us: fame, fortune, and recognition, if it is practiced with a pure mind and dedication to healing.

The individual who is initiated must be of good character, but most of all they should have the mental capacity to absorb the wisdom that is contained within each level (Degree) of the Reiki system. They should be stable individuals, not flitting from this healing system to that healing system like a careless butterfly feeding on each of the blossoms of a peony. They should be willing to devote themselves to the perfection of one system, before continuing on and seeking other systems.

The knowledge of healing that is contained within the "Tantra of the Lightning Flash" is vast and as profound as the sky. It is as wide and deep as the ocean and it is inexhaustible. It is fine to use other adjuncts such as massage, shiatsu, and so on to aid the individual. It is even proper to incorporate things such as Tai Chi, body movement, and exercise, which when the Tantra was written were unimportant, because people had more physical activity in that day.

The lack of physical activity does cause blockage in modern individuals, particularly the bureaucrat who has to sit in his chair for ten hours per day, or the executive with a zaibatsu who has to do exactly the same thing, using his mind and not his body. So, these things are beneficial and can be incorporated, but other systems which indicate they channel spiritual energy from this or that source for healing are unnecessary and a waste of valuable time and endeavor, because within the system of the "Lightning Flash", all of this is contained.

If one owns a warehouse that is filled with all manner of delightful possessions, fine foods, beautiful furniture and clothing and jewels, it is not necessary to go down to the fish market and acquire a new dead fish that is not as delectable or as fresh or as consumable as what one already has in one's warehouse. In fact, it would be foolish, particularly since that fish might be old and tainted, or perhaps someone has intentionally put poison into that fish.

In your storehouse you know the origin of every item, whether it is a food item, whether it is clothing, a cooking utensil, a map, a piece of furniture, or whether it is a garment. You know that these items have come from the best manufacturer with the highest reputation, and are of the finest quality possible. Therefore, it is not necessary to seek from someone else's storehouse when you do not know the pedigree of the item that you wish to acquire.

This is not to say that you are to disparage the other merchant's merchandise. It is the simple truth that you have no need of another merchant's merchandise because you yourself possess a higher quality, finer manufactured merchandise, so there is no reason to seek abroad for something which you possess already, which is of better quality than you can find elsewhere.

Also if you are preparing a dish to serve to your friends at a party you are giving, you find the ingredients for the recipe. You use your own trusted source for the squid, the octopus, and the fish, for the rice, the spices, the soy, and the miso. The good housewife, when she is shopping, knows the merchants that she is buying from; she has traded there in the past and knows the quality of the commodity they are purveying. Let us say that the housewife has all the ingredients for her recipe to make a very fine dish for her friends and her husband's friends that are coming to dinner. Everything is there and sufficient to be cooked and to go on the hibachi.

There is a knock on her door. She opens the door and there is a peddler there. He says he has this wonderful ingredient that will improve anything she mixes it with. She does not know this peddler; he may be good and what he says may be true, or he may be lying and what he says may not be true.

The prudent housewife is not going to buy his ingredient and combine it in her dish. Perhaps it could improve the dish; perhaps it could spoil the dish. Perhaps it could even poison those who partake of the dish.

She is going to say, 'No, I am sorry. I already have my ingredients. I know where they came from. I don't know you. I am not familiar with what you are bringing me. And besides all of that, my dish does not call for your ingredient. I have all the needed ingredients. I am sorry, but you must go somewhere else.'

You are that housewife. The dish you are preparing is the dish that heals the suffering of all sentient beings that are the guests that you are entertaining and presenting this dish to. Thus, when you are preparing this dish you must follow the recipe. You must be certain that your ingredients are known to you and that the purveyor of those ingredients, all of the Buddhas and Bodhisattvas, are of impeccable reputation. The things they purvey are of benefit and impeccable source. Therefore, when you prepare this dish that you will share with all sentient beings who are your guests, you know with certainty that this dish will be tasty, nutritious, and will cause no harm, and only bring benefit.

The peddler who was at your door might be a good and beneficial person, and the ingredient he is purveying may be a good and beneficial ingredient. But you have not had the time to get to know him. You do not know from where he came, and you do not know his intentions in selling you the ingredient. Most of all, your recipe does not even call for this particular ingredient. So it would be stupid of you to buy that ingredient on his say-so, and put it into the dish. No housewife in all the islands would do something like that in preparing an ordinary mundane meal for her family, husband or friends, so how much more important is it to not be stupid and incorporate some strange ingredient into your teaching when you already have all the ingredients and your recipe does not even call for this ingredient.

This should make my point.

The other thing I wanted to mention about the people who will be practicing this path: They cannot be stupid and have low intelligence and understanding. They have to have an understanding that, contained within the system of the "Lightning Flash" is all that is necessary for the performance of each function.

No strange new ingredients, perhaps brought by a kami in a dream, perhaps brought by a self-important practitioner of some self-sprung local belief, or anything like that should be incorporated into this system.

What should be incorporated into this system, if you feel a need to incorporate something, are those systems which have a lineage: Tai Chi, other physical exercises, means of beneficial massage, external allopathic medication such as sulfa, which a practitioner of that form of medicine, in other words a physician who is practicing that system, would know how to administer in moderation for the particular problem the patient is suffering.

We must remember clearly and distinctly that all true healing medical knowledge springs from the heart of Vaidurya Probassa Buddha, the Medicine King Buddha, and that it is not to be disparaged. But we must be sure before any curative is applied that it is derived from a proven healing system, and not something which one has created out of the fog and mist and floating gossamer of their own imagination. Allopathic medicine is a true system, Tai Chi is that, Shiatsu is that, and massage is that. They are all legitimate methodologies of healing; chiropractic medicine is that, but there are many things that have been created out of mist and floating gossamer and falling feathers that are not that. So you must be careful to discern which is that and which is not that.

The other subject I want to mention is that the individuals practicing must be stable individuals, and what I mean to say very clearly without dissimulation: is they cannot have their home constantly aroused, husband and wife fighting, or children fighting, or bills not being paid, and disruption in the household that unsettles the mind of the practitioner.

When one's mind is unsettled and worrying over other things, dwelling on interpersonal relationships, dwelling on the bill collector bringing the legal officials to the door, dwelling on the landlord throwing one out the door of one's dwelling, worrying about one's possessions being taken by creditors, worrying about one's wife having sex with someone else, worrying about one's husband having sex with someone else, worrying about having sex with someone else; all of these are distractions.

If one has these distractions, one is not able to practice the "Tantra" with the proper clarity of mind and with full efficiency.

So before practicing healing others, it is necessary to heal your own life, to bring stability into your own life, so this must be kept in mind. If you see a student, no matter how sincere, who is having all of these problems, it is proper to give refuge, but it is not proper to give initiation beyond the lay practice.

So the person's life must be stable; and I am not saying that they must have money and a nice house and so on. They could be a mendicant, traveling the world for the benefit of beings, but they must be doing that because they choose to, not because the landlord has put them out of the door or because the prefecture police are looking for them.

They could be poor, they could be rich, they could be in the middle; they could be very smart, they could be only a little smart. That, we are saying, is not important, just so long as they are intelligent enough to comprehend the basic steps and the methodology of the teaching. But whatever lifestyle they lead, they must have stability.

Rich people sometimes have less stability than poor people do because they worry about someone getting their money and making more; so, their minds are often scattered, and dwelling incessantly on money, whereas some poor people are not. Yet, some poor people are constantly wondering about where the next bowl of rice will come from. This does not make a good practitioner, either. So, the rich practitioner may not necessarily be a good practitioner, and the poor practitioner must know where his next bowl of rice is coming from and not expect Reiki to provide it. The rich person must organize and put his business worries aside, because all of these are distractions.

So this is all I have to say today. Sayonara. And this time I mean it!

19

DR. USUI ON SECTARIANISM

In this chapter, Dr. Usui clearly and forcefully expresses his views on sectarianism; incidentally from Dr. Usui's comment below, the following notes were written some time in 1919.

The Traps of Sectarianism

Translated from Dr. Usui's Notes

I was asked today by a friend, Ushima, why I didn't build a temple, and why I did not begin conducting healing ceremonies. The answer is most simple, I am not a priest. I am a physician.

I believe the two can be combined in one person, but my karma has not dictated that they combine in this humble person. I am 57 years old and even if I had the time, I do not think I could absorb the amount of learning at my advanced age that it requires becoming a Bonze.

My friend Watanabe Bonze fulfills that function admirably since he studied these things from the age of 11. When he was a young man, he even made the walking pilgrimage through the country as a homeless brother.

Ushima also brought up another important question that I had not even considered. And indeed, it is an important one. Ushima is Shinran. His primary devotion is to Amida Buddha, but for years he has also practiced our Medicine King Buddha. We discussed whether it was necessary for him to give up his Shinran practice and begin the practice of the Shingon form. Many of our people are Tendai still and their Bonze and families object to their taking up Shingon practice when their family religion is Tendai.

I have given this much thought, and because at the preliminary level of ordinary practice it does not matter, Watanabe, Ushima, and I feel we should discuss this. Watanabe is of the opinion that since Mahavairochana is not directly involved, that it does not matter from which school the practices are taken. Ushima on the other hand, being an accountant by profession, feels that standardization is of some importance. Neither Watanabe nor I feel this.

For instance, one of our best practitioners, who is from Panmunjom in Korea, Mr. Kim Yang Su, does not belong to any Japanese school, but is a Korean Amida follower of the Tantric sort, the practice of his school being the one that has caused a certain amount of scandal lately in Tokyo and certainly has elicited disapproving glances from both religious and civil authorities.

But I believe, and he has assured me, that their practices in actuality are in no way scandalous, nor are their doctrinal beliefs, but they are just misunderstood by the uninitiated and generally somewhat stupid populace, and even more stupid and rumor-mongering civilian authorities who for other reasons wish an excuse to dislike the Korean people.

His abilities at healing are exemplary; his traditional Korean herbal medicine and Kundhyo massage techniques have produced results of a most extraordinary nature. Now that we are friends and a bond of mutual trust and respect has been established and is further developing between us, he has confided in me that ever since he was a young man, he has used the energies of Medicine King Buddha even though without formal direction in his treatment agenda.

This has most heartened me and I believe that if this same energy of healing is exuded through him, having an origin in the training of the disciplines of his school, then perhaps most likely the origin of the Buddhist training and the methodology of manifestation and invocation is unimportant.

My friend Mariko Sasaki made a pertinent point when another matter of little importance was being discussed by her and her husband at their full moon poetry reading. The point was, that there is only one Buddha Shakyamuni: no Zen Shakyamuni, no Tendai Shakyamuni, no Shinran Shakyamuni, and so on.

Considering this point, I must conclude that, even though for most Japanese, it is unthinkable that there is not necessarily a Shakyamuni for the Japanese, a Shakyamuni for the Koreans, a Shakyamuni for the Chinese, and even for the Europeans or Americans. After all, the Sutras do not tell us that he was born in Kyoto, but rather in some wild place on the Indian sub-continent. But of course, he must have been Japanese in a previous incarnation.

Following this line of thought, we must remember that Kobo Daishi did not receive his teaching on Haihe Mountain but in the barbarous realm of the pig and garlic eaters. But surprise! His teachers did not receive it in the Northern or Southern capital, but from adventurous, dedicated, devoted, kind travelers who, in order to work for the benefit of the

Dr. Usui on Sectarianism 201

ignorant Han, had trekked long distances in adverse conditions from that barbarous place of mosquitoes, elephants, and tigers, known as India.

I am sure many of our religious authorities, if not publicly, have probably privately within the tightly closed closet of their own minds, questioned the wisdom of Shakyamuni to have been born in such a disagreeable and barbarous place as India, when he could have just as easily been born in the only civilized domain in this world system: our beautiful civilized, sacred islands, inhabited by the polite, unassuming, gentle, peace-loving, humble descendants of the Sun Goddess.

After deeply contemplating these matters, I can only conclude that since there is only one Shakyamuni, there most probably is only one Amida, only one Fudo, and unfortunately only one Medicine King. Looking at the matter in this way, and being well aware of the truth contained in the Sutras where the Sage states that 'the wheel is turned for every being according to their desires and mental structure' [Note by Lama Yeshe: Probably 'needs and inclinations'] and that the validity of the Vehicle of the Elders is in no way compromised or superseded by the Great Vehicle. Nor is the Lotus Sutra, the foundation upon which Tendai is built, superseded by the Mahavairochana Tantra, nor as some of our Zen brothers would have us believe, superseded by the Heart Sutra; not as our Honin brothers would have us believe, by the works of Honin — nor our Nicherin Brothers by the repetition of the thought of a single mantra which I myself and many scholars have nowhere found in any of the Sutras or other teachings of Buddha, but which was apparently only known to Nicherin.

Let us try then to look at the teachings with a broader view, using the simile that has always been used by practitioners of the Bodhidharma, that the Buddha, his teaching, and the Assembly are Three Precious Jewels and each of these jewels has many facets. The facets of the Buddha, for instance, are Shakyamuni, Amida, Medicine King, Kannon, Fudo, Mahavairochana and Manjushri and so on. Each facet a Buddha radiating the brilliant light of his particular wisdom to benefit beings, and each facet of the Dharma jewel a different school, whether here in Japan, China, Korea, Siam, French Indo China, Ceylon, Tibet or India. And that the Sangha jewel is faceted. Each one of us is one of those facets, shining with its own light, working for the benefit of others and our own enlightenment.

Yet each of these jewels are not sundered or broken into pieces but remain non-dual, and that each and every facet is totally inseparable from all the other facets, for in order for their existence to remain, they must be one.

In the light of this information, gained by my meditation, I can only conclude that wherever the source or practice of Medicine King, Amida, or any other Buddha or Bodhisattva, it is valid and that the Buddha or Bodhisattva disperses and makes available his energies through the individual practicing that system, regardless of the country in which the system is promulgated and regardless of the school which is promulgating it. So we may conclude that even Chinese and Koreans, the Indo-Chinese, and even those who follow the Way of the Elders can manifest healing energy from the Buddhas.

So let us set aside our outdated sectarian views as we would discard a pair of old filthy and worn tabis and look to the essence of what we are practicing, in place of the outward forms which our minds are so attached to, which we jealously guard as we would our family's history, and upon which we place so much misguided importance.

20

THE GARDEN OF WILLOW TREES

It was through the insistence of people like Dr. Usui that in 1921, funds were made available both from the secular government and the Imperial Privy Purse for the establishment of training programs in medicine and nursing for intelligent young people of all social levels. In the 1920s the Imperial Army and Navy established numerous military training programs to train young officers both at home and abroad for the medical professions. It was military money that purchased Japan's first X-ray machine and hired a German specialist to train local medical students in its use.

I do not know where the following speech was given or to what group or when, other than it was shortly after the influenza epidemic, and therefore was somewhere between 1918 and 1920, and that we know the Minister of Health was present as well as two Imperial physicians.

It is interesting to ponder how much influence Dr. Usui's speech may have had in prompting the changes that took place during the 1920s in Japan. I would like to think he was partly responsible and that his efforts led to the evolution of the fine health care system in Japan today.

Speech Held to an Assembly of Physicians in the Presence of the Minister of Health
Translated from Dr. Usui's Notes

I am most graciously pleased to have been invited to speak today before this august assembly of my worthy colleagues.

I first must apologize profoundly, however: I had intended to speak today on the progress made in my colleagues' and my experimentation on the artificial culture of mycobacterium tuberculosis. However, unfortunately, I seem to have left my notes at home, or on the train, or in the hired carriage which brought me here.

Instead, I have therefore chosen to speak today about a garden that I know of, a "Garden of Willows", as it were.

Once a kind Lord purchased a portion of land and planted a willow garden there. He carefully bought the finest stock of trees, had the ground prepared by his gardeners, and planted the trees. The young trees flourished beautifully, but then the kind Lord passed on to his next life.

His sons and daughters had other interests and soon the willows became neglected. Some actually died, some withered, and some became diseased. This was not the fault of the willows, but of the lack of care they received.

The Emperor Meiji was the kind Lord who planted the garden by establishing health care for all and encouraging the cultivation of our peoples' health by encouraging the training of physicians and nurses. The careless children are our present administration who has neglected the garden.

Few physicians are being supported by our government and given training here on the home islands. Only those who travel abroad to Europe or America receive a proper education and such travel is limited to those with copious financial assets.

The recent influenza epidemic has shown that the number of doctors on the home island is woefully inadequate for the health crisis that we faced, and who is to say that some other disease other than influenza is not waiting in the wings to come on stage and cause greater death and suffering.

Some may say that I am remiss in my filial obligation to Emperor and Government by mentioning and making public this embarrassment, but as a physician I would be despicably remiss in my giri to the overall population of the home islands should I choose to keep silent. Under the Lord Emperor Meiji, our Government spent modest sums of cash for the training of physicians and nurses and reaped a rich harvest, but now those physicians who are the result of the Emperor's wise programs are now aging and soon will pass, as did the Emperor.

Enormous sums of money are now being spent on industrialization and military armaments, while little is being spent for the public welfare.

All of you gathered here at this conference including our most honorable and esteemed Minister of Health are men of influence within private business, Government, and the Imperial Court. I notice two of you are the Emperor's personal physicians and that one of you is physician to the Prime Minister whom I note is conspicuously absent from this gathering.

I also note that a number of you Japanese, Europeans, and Americans serve both the foreign and Japanese business community. I must remind you that during the recent influenza epidemic and then during the even more recent malaria epidemic that followed, that the infection spread from the poor and Yakusaka area to the more affluent areas and even into the Imperial Compound itself.

Proper isolation, quarantine and medical care could have prevented much of this spread. It is not only the poor that suffer from lack of trained physicians, but the affluent and the nobility as well. It has been shown throughout the last 300-year period that in Europe and China, epidemics began in the crowded slum areas, then spread outward to encompass the rural peasantry and the affluent nobility.

Modern science tells us that this can be prevented. Foundational work done by the great American military physician Dr. Walter Reed in America and by the German von Arnst in Heidelberg, give confirmation to this theory.

In America, both tubercular and leprous patients are being confined in sanitariums and leprosariums where they are given the best treatment available and many are cured, or at least their disease arrested and life extended.

If the sanatoriums only served the purpose of intensive care, that alone would be enough to urge us to continue the practice, but that is not the only advantage. I have many times seen the disease of tuberculosis of which I was going to speak today, because of its contagion, spread from one family member to another and then from that household in the village to numerous other households, where there was not one household totally free from the contagion.

If a serious epidemic similar to the influenza were to come to the home islands, we would not have sufficient physicians or nurses to deal with the crisis, nor would we have sufficient defenses to safeguard the health of the remaining population.

Therefore, I would urge that gardeners immediately be sent into the Willow Park, remove the choking weeds, cut new water ways, and again cultivate the ground, fertilizing and watering this beautiful Garden of Willows, so that the blight and death of the trees may be reversed, and that all can take pride in its restoration.

If we let this garden perish, it will bring dishonor both to the Lord that planted it and his descendants who failed to maintain it.

You did not expect to hear this from me today, I know. But sometimes the truth must be spoken plainly and without dissimulation for good to be accomplished. I look forward to hearing the remainder of your learned dissertations, but I remind you that if action for the training of physicians and nurses is not taken, there will be few left to deliver dissertations or hear them.

Physicians trained abroad cannot possibly meet the burden placed upon them by the population of the home islands. I would remind you that during our conflict with the Russians, because of the Emperor Meiji's wise provenance, there were sufficient physicians to serve with our Navy and Army, during the conflict, to bring solace to the injured and wounded.

I would also remind you that in the European conflict just past, even the industrialized European countries and America had a shortage of both physicians and nurses to serve their military needs.

If your compassion and humanism will not extend to your fellow man, then speaking to those of the Government, I say, let your own self interest motivate you in providing for the training of physicians and nurses for I, as many others, feel that even though we escaped the European conflict, there may soon be war in our sphere of influence and we will be most thankful and grateful that there are trained physicians and nurses to treat our injured and wounded.

Thank you, That is all that I, Usui, have to say.

21

SCIENTIFIC METHODOLOGY
VERSUS ORIENTAL SPIRITUALITY

In two excerpts from Dr. Usui's writings, the first, 'Use of
Reiki with Allopathic Medicine', Dr. Usui clearly states his belief in the beneficial union of the two. In the second excerpt,
'The Plum Orchard and a Dissertation on Inclination', he speaks
of what happens when science is divorced from spirituality.

Use of Reiki with Allopathic Medicine
Translated from Dr. Usui's notes

I have discovered that Reiki is an adjunct to healing by
ordinary physicians. At no time should the patient be treated
only with Reiki. The allopathic physician has tools that have
been given into his hands by the kind medical knowledge
revealed from the pristine mind of Medicine King Buddha.
All medicine, allopathic, surgical, naturopathic, and
herbological, springs from the pristine well-spring of healing that is the mind of Medicine King Buddha.

Therefore, the allopathic physician certainly should not be despised, nor the herbologist, nor the naturopathic physician. All of this knowledge is a complete whole revealed from the pristine well-spring of knowledge of healing, set forth so that all beings may receive healing according to their needs and according to their inclinations and mind set and the condition of their mind stream at the time the healing is given. The Reiki system, that of the "Lightning Flash", is direct application of the healing energy which flows from the mind of the Medicine Buddha. However, because of the condition of mankind, of its ignorance and obscurations brought about by the present dark ages, it is necessary also that other means may be applied and prove efficacious to the patient.

Reiki, sometimes when all other things have failed, will bring about a somewhat miraculous recovery. At other times it will augment and potentiate the treatment that the patient is receiving. At other times, due to the unfortunate karma of the patient, accumulated through many lifetimes and in this present lifetime, such as killing, cruelty, and hatred, the life span of a person will be shortened. Reiki at that time will be of no use or service, due to the past accumulations of karma. Nevertheless, it will alleviate the suffering and symptoms and assure that the being has a fortunate rebirth in his next incarnation.

It is through our own stupidity and the karma that we have created, that our illnesses and obscurations arise. Yet there is a remedy for these illnesses and obscurations brought on by our own ignorance, and that remedy is the teachings of the Buddhas and the Bodhisattvas, whose compassion flows forth like a mighty river, cleansing the three thousand fold universe of pain, suffering, hatred, malice, jealousy, and implanting within its place true knowledge and wisdom, which can serve as a beacon to those beings who are tossed about by the waves of sickness, old age, birth and death. It can lead them to the only true healing which comes from the pristine mind of enlightenment, which this "Tantra", the "Lightning Flash", sets forth.

I truly and firmly believe that, besides a system of healing, one can gain full and total enlightenment by its practice and application. The merits of beings who use this system and apply it with right mind can be accumulated, piled high as heaps the size of Mt. Meru. It can bring much benefit, healing, and supramundane knowledge to all mankind.

It is the storehouse of vital information. It is a map to enlightenment and it is a source of healing for all sentient beings. Therefore, it should be approached with reverence and awe, yet it should be applied in all the ten directions that suffering may be alleviated, and that enlightenment may be gained. Therefore, I will now repeat the prayer that I have directly taken from the "Tantra":

'We bow down, offer incense and pray to the Medicine King Buddha, Lord of Healing, Lord of the Lapis Lazuli Light. Throughout the ten directions and Three Times, may sickness be a name; a word heard no more. May suffering be only a dark memory; may diseases be banished from the hearts and minds of all sentient beings. May all people gain health, well-being, peace and prosperity. Thus, may the great Blessing Storehouse of the Buddhas pour forth a rain of auspiciousness to those who hear and read these words.'

The Plum Orchard, a Dissertation on Inclination
Translated from Dr. Usui's notes

Once, in a Northern Province, there was a farmer who owned a magnificent plum orchard. Throughout the province and even the entire country, his plums were viewed

 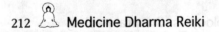

by any who had tasted them as absolutely superior and beyond compare. They were sought out and even appeared on the Imperial table and at important banquets.

Now, this man truly loved each and every tree in his orchard. He had even given them names of endearment. Each day he would venture into his orchard and talk to the trees.

The man had three sons. Finally he passed on and his eldest son inherited the orchard. Now the eldest son was somewhat scientifically inclined, as he had studied engineering. He immediately began to study plums and their cultivation. He wished to improve upon what his father had accomplished and carry on the tradition of plum culture and maybe even improve upon it.

This of course was an admirable aspiration and according to the best of Japanese tradition. However, it seemed that his attempts were always doomed to failure. No matter what techniques he used, the trees began to produce inferior fruit. His scientific method apparently was a doomed enterprise. No matter how much money, and he spent a considerable amount of it, was invested both in books and equipment, the quality of the plums continued to decline and even some of his trees died. In disgust he gave the orchard to his middle brother.

Now this middle brother was not scientifically inclined, but was a businessman. He was very cunning and successful in his business endeavors. Because of his vanity and his wish also to continue his family tradition, he wished to produce the superior plums of his father's time.

Since his orchard existed in an area devoted to the cultivation of plums he hired some of the locals to work the orchard, and after a few years the quality of the plums increased and they were again saleable but their quality never reached the superior heights of the plums which his father had grown. He concluded that the modern techniques had somehow damaged the trees or the soil and that although the plums were sellable, it was just another plum orchard and did not add a whit to his or his family's reputation.

The younger brother had been considered by his other two brothers as the ne'er do well of the family. He had been apprenticed to a Western technician who was versed in electrical science. He had failed miserably in grasping even the rudiments of this science and had been dismissed in shame by his mentor. He then chose to become a Zen monk, which lasted about a year and shamefully ended when his abbot discovered him with a young lady from the nearby village, engaging in un-Buddhist monk-like activities.

He had then gone to Tokyo and secured a job because of his English as an interpreter for a business house. He however had made a number of mistakes in the translation of important documents. These led to a serious misunderstanding and subsequent consequences, and again he was dismissed in shame. After that, the only job the young man could get was serving at an alehouse for foreign sailors.

The older brothers wishing to rescue their family name decided to present him with the family plum orchard. He chose to accept it and was overjoyed.

When he was a child and his father's favorite, he would accompany his father into the orchard and spend hours listening to his father's stories while his father tended his trees.

The young man on receipt of this wondrous gift of the orchard resolved to make something of himself. Now, along with the orchard he received the small but comfortable family home where his own mother lived with three family servants. Along with the orchard he inherited the responsibility to care for his mother and look out after her welfare. He readily agreed to this as he had great affection for his mother.

Now, left in the house were all of the senior brothers' scientific books, and in a shed on the orchard property many chemicals and fertilizers, all having been brought at great expense by his brother from Europe and America. In the long days and evenings of that summer he studied those books, so when next spring came he was ready. Following scientific methods, he began to tend his orchard, but within him an interesting shift happened.

He began to recall the happy days he had spent with his father in the orchard. His love for the land and the trees were rekindled. Sometimes he would even feel his father's presence and even hear his voice. He remembered the names of many of the trees and querying his mother and the servants, was able to ascertain the names of those whom he had forgotten.

He still, however, was diligently applying the modern agricultural techniques he had gleaned from his brothers' books and notes. That fall was a monumental surprise to everyone. The orchard bore a huge crop of plums that were even superior to those produced in his father's time. They were larger, sweeter, and juicier and had a magnificent color and fragrance.

That was five years ago. As I, Usui, write this, I am sitting at my writing desk eating one of this year's crops of those same magnificent plums, some of which were sent to me by the young man. You thought perhaps, this was simply a parable. It was not. It is a true story. I am currently treating the same young man's wife for an injury to her hip that she sustained while attempting the Western dance, known as the 'fox trot'. The young man told me his story and immediately it brought to mind my endeavor.

The older brother had no soul and no love for the land or trees. He felt that only the scientific method would triumph and that scientists had the answer for everything. The middle brother perhaps had love for the trees and the land, but he had more love for his own aggrandizement and no real time to devote to the orchard. He hired others who loved the land and the trees but did not have the gift of love that his father had. And so the orchard produced a somewhat mediocre fruit.

Now the younger son, my friend, had apparently not the wit or intelligence or fortunately the vanity of his brothers, but he had the soul. I have no doubt that his father walked with him in the orchard and that the trees and the Kamis of the area responded to his dreaminess and apparent lack of ambition.

I have come to know this man very well and found that he has a sharp intelligence, as well as the soul of a poet. This combination has led to his great success and the fame of his produce. His brothers in particular and his society in general were channeling his talents in a direction they approved of, but which was very wrong for him.

When he was allowed to follow his real inclinations, a magnificent success was the result. He was able to integrate the scientific knowledge of his older brother with the age-old knowledge and farming techniques of his father. The result was an unqualified success.

Now let us look at the broader implications of what we have learned from Mitsu's life. Unfortunately, in our society, and in other societies, we tend to force individuals into

a prescribed mold and fashion them into featureless duplicates of others.

I strongly believe this is wrong. I believe that within reason, every man should follow his own inclination as to
whatever means he chooses, to gain his livelihood. If this is
followed then one's creativity is not stifled and one's happiness and contentment and peace of mind are not destroyed. In fact, it is preserved and nurtured and leads to
great achievement, which could not have been achieved
otherwise. For a man who is not happy accomplishes little
in his endeavors. And a man who is not content, contrib-
utes little to the well-being of society.

I knew a young man once when I was very young, who
was from a family of teachers and poets. He had no inclination in those directions and to his family's horror rebelled
against their wishes and became a soldier. He fought val-
iantly in our conflict with Russia, made a name for himself,
and now serves the General Staff waiting for his promotion
to General himself. He is most respected and has been
decorated by the Emperor Meiji himself.

I do not encourage rebellion, but at the same time, I do not
encourage the stifling of children by their families either. I
believe that families should take careful notice and examine the inclinations of their children and allow them to
develop the talents with which they are born.

Now most of us are Buddhist or Shinto and we believe, or
at least protest our belief, in the continuity of the Mind
Stream. This very knowledge should clearly teach us that in
a family of three children each child is an individual with a
long history of previous incarnations, and therefore many
karmic inclinations, perhaps even differing, I should say
most likely differing, from those of his parents and siblings,

or even of his clan and station in life. It is not inconceivable that a pious person of low caste, who fulfilled his duties and obligations and loved and served the Buddha or Kami, might be born into a wealthy and noble household.

Therefore, we must not expect too much of our children, nor should we expect them to have the same goals and aspirations as we do. Rather we should evaluate their abilities and inclinations realistically and help them to accomplish their aspirations, even if they greatly differ from our own aspirations and inclinations. In this way we will escape sorrow, assist them also in escaping sorrow, and bring them and ourselves happiness and thereby benefit society.

We should respect that every individual has a long history of incarnations and therefore will have strong inclinations in a specific direction. I am not saying that if our child was a noteworthy thief in past incarnations that we should encourage his thievery in this present life. Perhaps it is our child's karma, should he have been a thief, to be reborn in a good and honest family so that this wrong inclination might be corrected, and his energies directed in a more socially acceptable direction, such as a government tax collector. Therefore, he would not wind up in prison and serve a necessary though opprobrious function for the civil government.

Sometimes, parents or a family do not seem to recognize the talents their children have. This would certainly be the case, if a fisherman in his previous life were to incarnate in the family of a poet or a poet and master of the tea ceremony in a family of fishermen.

Therefore, it should be a very great priority for parents to seek out the inclination and talents of their children and, thus, be able to direct the child into a happy, fruitful and productive profession.

On this matter, this is what I, Usui, have to say, but I wish to add something else that has come to mind. Originally, I began narrating this story of Mitsui to speak about inclination and children, but as I have been narrating it, other things have come to mind.

In the practitioner of medicine and Reiki it is important to combine both soul and scientific method and to do so diligently and with very direct involvement. Look at what happened to the plums under the first brother's cold and scientific approach to the problem. Observe what happened to the plums during the second brother's disinterested or self-centered approach. Most of all notice the marvelous results that the younger brother was able to bring about.

Therefore, I most ardently counsel you, that in your practice of medicine and Reiki you follow and cultivate the methodology of Mitsui, learning and applying all that scientific methodology affords you, but at the same time not casting aside or ignoring the tradition and soul of the healing arts. Not seeking to pursue your chosen profession in an indifferent way, seeking self-centered aggrandizement or notoriety, using the system for self-promotion, monetary gain or fame as a healer, but using the system as it was meant to be used as a way to bring comfort, happiness, and most importantly, healing to those beings who are suffering under a burden of pain and illness.

This is the very essence of what we are doing and this is the manner in which to approach it.

22

REFUGE AND DHARMA PRACTICE:
The Source of Healing Power

Where does the power of Reiki originate? What is its source and how may one acquire it? Dr. Usui explains here both the source and methodology of acquisition. His remarks are one of the cornerstones for the manner in which Medicine Dharma Reiki is taught. However, they are equally enlightning to the lay practitioner of simple hands-on Reiki as they reveal important background information.

They clearly establish that Reiki is an age-old spiritual discipline. They also inform about the requirements that need to be fulfilled before practice in the esoteric tradition of Reiki can be started.

On the Importance of Refuge And Empowerment
Translated from Dr. Usui's notes

People in the West are inherently thirsting for a spiritual path. Christianity, except in a very few cases, has proven to be a dry spring from which they can only drink dust and debris. The introduction of the inner system of Reiki with its deep and profound Buddhist connection, may very well be that spring which many of them are seeking. The refuge formulation itself, which I insist be promulgated before the student receives any of the inner initiations, covers the ground of a dedicated, pure, and spiritual path, which requires of one personal commitment, for the benefit of all sentient beings in the six realms of existence.

In order to successfully be a healer and by implication practice the inner system of Reiki, it is necessary that a being have this commitment. They must without question sincerely take Mahayana refuge.

The system of healing of the "Tantra of the Lightning Flash" requires that the practitioner be able to partake of the accumulated energy that is stored within the Merit Storehouse of all the Buddhas and Bodhisattvas. In order for the practitioner to partake of this energy which is within the Merit Storehouse of the Buddhas and Bodhisattvas, he or she must have taken with a clear and understanding mind, refuge in the Three Precious Ones. Furthermore, they must have awakened within themselves the enlightened intention to work for the benefit of all beings.

If this is not done, then there will be a blockage of the flow of energy from the Buddhas and Bodhisattvas, whether or not the person has received the initiation. Medicine Buddha himself, in the lay practice of Reiki, freely gives of His energy for the practitioner to accomplish the basic activity. Yet, when we are reaching for the higher activities, seeking the energy necessary not just simply to soothe and quiet an individual and work for their benefit in that way, but actually to perform a healing and bestow the more potent psycho-magical energy of the Merit Storehouse and make use of it, then we must have established a conduit.

An example would be that in the lay practice, it is like a kind water carrier who feels he can benefit a neighborhood by taking water from a pure, crystal spring and bring it to each home in a bucket. The spring is owned by a kind Daimyo who allows the individual to fill the bucket and then carry it to the people in the neighborhood. That pretty well in simile describes how the lay practice of Reiki functions. It is I who am the water carrier and it is you who are practicing the lay practice of Reiki that are the recipients of this water.

However, once you have engaged in the First Level of the inner system (Men Chhos or Medicine Dharma Reiki Level 1), it is the owner of the spring himself who has constructed a small canal from the source of the spring to your door. You can see the difference. This difference is very meaningful and profound. The owner of the spring of the Healing Water is Medicine King Buddha.

There is the Spring of Water that exercises the demons and the afflictions; the co-owners of that spring are the Bodhisattvas Wei-To (Vajrapani) and Fudo (Hayagriva).

There is the spring of the Water that repels the enemies; the owner of that is Hachiman Sama Bodhisattva (the Japanese God of War), the great Suma Kami.

In order to utilize the waters from these springs in a meaningful, effective way one must commit to the Buddhist path so that one may partake of the Merit Storehouse. One cannot simply become a Hinayana Buddhist, because there is no Merit Storehouse; the Hinayana path can be the stairway to selfishness. So, one needs to first take refuge with knowledge and intent in a one-pointed manner, and then confirm that refuge. The way to confirm refuge is to take the Vow of a Bodhisattva. To do so is to become a Mahayana Buddhist; then one may partake of the Merit Storehouse.

This does not automatically give you the Merit Storehouse. However, it gives you the ability to partake of the Merit Storehouse.

Thus, by the bestowal of initiation into the Deities pertinent to Medicine Dharma Reiki, you gain access to the Merit Storehouse. Otherwise, without these initiations, you are not able to draw from the Merit Storehouse. And if you are not able to draw from the Merit Storehouse, in that case, the words that you recite when you invoke the deities are meaningless nonsense. Well, not actually — they give honor to the particular Buddha when you praise Him, but that connection, if you have not taken refuge, is like a peasant sitting at home saying, 'The Emperor is good'. He is a great distance from the Emperor, so the Emperor may never hear these words.

After refuge when these words are said, it is as if a messenger carries these words to the Emperor, saying, 'The Emperor is good'. Initiations, however, bring you in the actual presence of the Emperor and you say those words to him directly. He is then pleased by your homage and he, therefore, bestows blessings.

But in order to pass the gate of the Imperial Compound, as in the old days, you have to have written permission by an official of the Court. That permission is the Refuge and Bodhichitta Vow. Then comes the official, your spiritual friend or teacher. You got past the gate, but there are all of these vicious Samurai there who are guarding the person of the Emperor. You are by the Gate, but they say, 'Do you have an appointment? Do you have an audience? And you don't know. You say 'I love the Emperor, and I came here', and they will say, 'That's nice. But that is not enough. Where is your invitation?'

Then your spiritual friend comes and says, 'The invitation is here to see the Emperor', and that is the initiation. You are then conducted into the Imperial Presence, you praise him, say your panegyrics, and the Emperor is pleased and bestows his blessing on you.

It is the same with the Buddhas: Refuge makes it possible for you to approach the Emperor, but does not give you permission to do so. It simply creates the possibility. The initiation is what gives the permission to 'approach the Emperor'. But if you don't have permission to approach. If you made it to the gate and, even though inside, waiting, was an Imperial Official to conduct you into the presence of the Emperor, and yet you had no pass to get in the gate, you still would not go before the Emperor. The gatekeeper would say, 'So sorry. I apologize, but you do not have the pass written out. I cannot let you in the gate to see your friend, even though the friend is waiting on the other side.'

So, this is an example of how the Refuge, the Bodhisattva Vow, and the Empowerment work in regard to each other. It is clear that for the people who are unwilling to make the commitment to take refuge, practice is not going to be successful even if they receive the initiations.

There are many people who are thirsting for a spiritual path. The practice of Mahayana Buddhism with its elevated concepts and universal compassion is the direction they are seeking, although they may not know it yet. It is the path that will shelter, preserve, instruct them, and that at last, brings them to enlightenment after empowering them to aid and benefit all sentient beings.

This teaching I am sharing now can be revised as if it did not come from myself, but is just a teaching. You are encouraged to use it when students inquire about the importance of refuge, but this teaching is particularly to understand the importance, the significance and the function of refuge in regard to the practice of the Medicine Dharma Kei system. It is very essential; so keep it in mind and adhere to the same concepts I have given you, if you want this "Tantra" to be carried successfully to the world.

23

THE ILL-FATED TRIP TO HOKKAIDO AND OTHER SUCH ADVENTURES

I am sure that many of us have had the experience of the holiday trip that was looked forward to with expectation and joy, but which then turned into a total and absolute nightmare. Dr. Usui has clearly had this experience, and not only once. Let us now journey with him to Hokkaido, an alpine Temple, and the Great Festival at Kamakura.

The translations in this chapter were included as they shed some light on Usui's personality.

The Trip to Hokkaido
Translated from Dr. Usui's notes

Today I returned from my trip to Hokkaido and am suffer- ing from complete exhaustion in body, mind, and spirit. It began with a train ride to our port of embarkation that I truly enjoyed. We then spent the night in Tokyo itself at a small hotel.

The reason for this trip was only to please Watanabe Bonze; his mother's brother owns a small hunting lodge on our Northernmost Island. Hunting has never been a really Japanese pastime as far as I am concerned, and most certainly has not been an avocation of mine, but to please my friend and his son, I chose to give in to their entreaties and spend one week in their and their relatives' company.

Personally, I consider it a most brutal thing to hunt and murder wild creatures in their natural environment. I feel it is much better to simply observe them, as they occupy their niche in the magnificent panorama of nature. To end their lives in such a brutal manner in such a peaceful and lovely setting is murder to my sensibilities. But to continue: we finally reached our port of embarkation that was terribly dismal. An early fall fog had engulfed the entire Northern portion of Honshu, so we set sail, or perhaps I should say set steam, into what seemed endless gray mist. The crossing, however, was smooth and we arrived on Hokkaido in the early evening.

Our host, who had not appreciated our large amount of baggage, had provided two open carriages. This necessitated the hiring of a small wagon from one of the local draymen. After considerable confusion and a certain amount of impatience, though politely masked, on the part of our hosts, we were away to the country lodge.

Unfortunately our host had not anticipated the inclement weather and for an hour and a half we suffered drizzle. One of the open carriages did have an extendible cover; as the drizzle increased to our host's insistence that it would not, an attempt was made to raise the cover.

This resulted in all of us being showered with dust, twigs, and a number of years' collection of leaves. As success seemed immanent, a large tearing sound was heard and the top split; however, it did afford a modicum of protection. If one leaned far enough back, or for the passenger far enough forward, one escaped the worst of the rain, to which the drizzle had turned while we were delaying to try and raise the cover.

As we neared our destination a constable on his horse met us. He had been sent by our host's wife and mother to ascertain if some mishap had occurred on our journey, as we were now two hours late. We assured him that other than being soaked to the skin and chilled, we were fine.

On arrival at our host's home, we discovered his wife, mother, maids and daughter, though exceedingly polite were more than displeased at our late arrival. An elaborate meal of local delicacies had been prepared, and had been awaiting us. Since much or it consisted of fresh sashimi, much of it had been spoiled. We satisfied ourselves with the dry somewhat inedible remains and I was most happy to acquaint myself with my futon.

The next morning dawned ominously gray. Horses were brought after a hasty breakfast of cold rice. We mounted and rode into a gloomy forest, seeking to find some innocent creatures to murder. After four hours of riding and walking in rain, drizzle or fog, it seemed that the wild creatures were much more intelligent than we, for in all of that time, we had seen three birds who looked as bedraggled and dejected as we. It was then discovered to our host's horror, that the hibachi, the charcoal, and tea ingredients had been somehow left behind, but we had cups and plates and bowls.

We then trudged another three hours home without refreshment. When we arrived at our host's, we found that we had not been expected for another three hours, so no food had been prepared. Our hostess, though smiling, was furious. We could all sense this, particularly her husband who walked and spoke very softly. A quick dish of noodles made of miso and tofu was prepared with promises of better things to come. I quickly, after eating, repaired to my room and prepared myself a salt-water mild carbolic gargle, as my throat was getting sore and not surprisingly, I was beginning to develop a cough.

A storm of terrifying proportions then commenced at about 8 o'clock that night. I had dozed fitfully off with a slight fever when my window blew open and I woke to discover that an icy trickle of water had been falling on my hips and legs from a leak in the ceiling. Fortunately two comforters had been provided and I had not made use of one. I carefully moved my futon to the other side of the room, drying myself and making use of the second comforter which, having remained unused in its cupboard, was as dry as could be expected in such a miserable climate.

About an hour later, I was roused by my host and told that a dinner had been prepared. The storm was raging outside. I felt I did not want to leave my futon, but politeness forced me to rise and dress, refresh myself and then enter the main room for dinner.

Knowing that I had been entertained by Westerners, my hostess had attempted, and I do say attempted with dismal failure, to prepare a surprise Western meal. This consisted of potatoes which I never really had become fond of, boiled to an unrecognizable mush, beet root pickled in sweetened rice vinegar, and a piece of venison fried in one solid piece and the consistency of a piece of old untanned dried leather.

Of course, I had to eat this, for courtesy forbade me to leave the table in disgust. Sake was served and although I usually only partake of one small cup, I decided for the sake of my health and hoping that perhaps my fever would be forestalled, I partook of a number of servings, and I will say that my mood considerably improved.

We spoke of the war raging between Russia and Japan, and how foolish the Russians were to think they could possess any of the territory of the Sacred Islands.

At about one in the morning, I repaired to my room looking forward to a good night's sleep when I discovered that the small leak had developed in my absence to a veritable torrent, thoroughly soaking the floor and the futon, having overflowed the chamber pot I had placed under it. Furthermore, three more leaks had developed, making the room uninhabitable.

I returned to the main room of the house and informed my host of the problem. As nothing could be done during the raging storm, my hostess's youngest maid was evicted from her room to sleep with my host's youngest daughter and I was given her room, which was snug and warm, but due to her devotion to one of the local Kamis smelled so strongly of the cheapest incense to which I am terribly allergic, that numerous times during the remainder of the night I feared suffocation.

My host's servant, who informed me that the storm was over and a delightful trip to the nearby village had been planned, awakened me quite early. I might add here that during the night, the combination of the overly-sweet odor of the incense, the sake, and beet root, not to mention the leather-like deer flesh, had begun to wage war in my stomach and I had to rush outside during the worst part of the storm to expel at least one of the combatants from my body.

I returned and was able to finally warm myself and return to sleep for what seemed a moment or two, before the cheerful man servant wakened me and informed me of the further torture my host had planned for me.

After a breakfast of sweetened gruel, which did my stomach a considerable amount of good, we boarded the open carriages again in a light mist and rolled through the mud to the country village. There, some of the local handicraft of some of the aboriginal peoples could be purchased, and to my delight I found a lovely tea pot with cups made by a local potter and purchased it as a gift for my mother. To my complete joy I was able to purchase a woolen kimono, padded with further layers of wool and lined in silk. I considered the purchase of this item the pinnacle of my holiday.

After a substantial lunch at the local inn, which I thoroughly enjoyed, I began to believe that I might derive some pleasure from my visit to Hokkaido. How terribly mistaken I was.

Half-way from the village to my host's home, was a small Shinto shrine to the same local goddess that the maid so fervently worshipped. Nothing would do unless we stopped. I should mention at this point that the sky was beginning to take on an ominous hue, which to me presaged more unfortunate weather.

My host, claiming constant habitation on the island since birth, assured me that we had plenty of time for a visit. We arrived, made obeisance and gave a small donation, whereupon the priest in charge of the shrine produced his blind and deformed daughter, who he claimed was a famous medium in these parts for the Kami who inhabited the shrine, and who had a message for all of us from 'the other side.'

For a moment I will digress here to say that I believe that there are those who have been blessed both by the Buddhas and the Kamis with the ability to communicate with the spirit world. Of this, I have no doubts whatsoever. However, there are those, and one finds them generally in poor rural shrines, who boast that they have the ability and do not. One only feels pity and sadness for them, considering the karma they may generate by giving false messages from one's ancestors or purported local Kami.

But to return to my sad and tragic narrative. The father then began to chant before we could make our exit and the daughter began to mumble and twitch. The assistant priest than appeared with paper, ink, and brush and began to interpret the message.

I was told to my horror that I would travel extensively to America, Europe, and China. This truly filled my heart with terror considering that this excursion, only a short one, was fraught with so much suffering and inconvenience. I resolved at that time that should Lord Mahavairochana grant me a safe return home, I would never travel any distance again.

Fortunately, I did reach home safely and upon arriving had a Saito Goma performed in thanksgiving for my safe return, and then strengthened my resolve into a vow that I would never travel extensively again.

But to return to my narrative: For approximately three hours the poor child twitched and mumbled, as my host's wife's mother had a great deal to communicate from 'the other side'. And my host's great grandfather had a similarly lengthy communique for my host. Finally the poor child fell into a swoon and was carried away by her mother and sister. We made a further donation and returned to the carriages.

We had not traveled half a mile before the sky veritably opened, drenching us with the heaviest rain yet. Within approximately half a mile of our host's home, one of the axles of the carriage in which I was riding fractured, the wheel came loose, and I was dumped from my seat face down in the mud. My host and his servants were able to un-stick me, clean me a small bit, and place me in the other carriage, promising me a hot bath as soon as we returned home.

Upon our arrival I was sadly informed that the wood used for the bath had become so soaked in the rain that it would not ignite. Some water was heated on the brazier and I washed as best I could, looking forward to wrapping in my new quilted kimono, only to discover that it had been left in the disabled carriage. A servant was sent for it and it arrived anon somewhat damp. It was then dried over a brazier for me and I wrapped in it feeling slightly revived by the dinner my hostess and her servants had hastily prepared.

I then discovered that during the small break in the weather, the roof of my room had been repaired and fresh futons and quilts had been provided. I, then pleading fatigue, returned to my room and slept very well.

The next morning I woke quite ill. The repeated soakings with cold rain had their expected effect. I rubbed my body thoroughly with camphor ointment, and taking from my pack the proper herbs with which I had providentially provided myself, gave the servant instructions on preparing me a tea.

I also dosed myself with syrup of ammonium chloride and ingested a small quantity of methyl morphine for my cough. I remained in bed for two days and having somewhat recovered was informed that we would hunt in the afternoon. A very wan sun looking as insipid as I felt had broken through the clouds and did provide some warmth.

After a small lunch we set out at about 1 p.m. and within 15 minutes had taken three pheasants. It sickened my heart to see such beautiful birds shot from the air to land in a broken heap on the moldy ground. But this was not the only horror in store for me.

In about an hour we came upon a grazing doe that was immediately dispatched by my host. It was only then that we noticed the two fawns that had been born the previous spring. Having felt the venture successful, we returned and one of the pheasants was prepared for our evening meal.

Claiming a return of my illness, I excused myself from partaking and satisfied myself with some fish broth and noodles. I do not feel that I possibly could have partaken of the pheasant whose brutal and untimely death I had witnessed that afternoon.

The next day I remained in bed, so I did not have to participate in a second expedition, again claiming that my illness had returned.

More pheasant were executed that day as well as a small fox whose winter coat was coveted by my hostess for a Western style wrap. It completed the set of five necessary for the construction of the garment. The next day we were scheduled to leave and in the morning were conveyed without further incident to the ship where we embarked for our return home.

We had traveled only a short distance when a storm blew through the Strait causing our craft to move simultaneously in all directions at once. I became exceedingly ill and remained so for the rest of the voyage. Upon arriving at the shore of blessed Honshu, I was unable to travel any further and took refuge in a local hotel, built in the Western style with a roof that didn't leak and a large white porcelain tub in which I immersed myself for approximately three hours.

The next morning I awoke terribly ill and had to remain three more days for fear of my health deteriorating. Watanabe Bonze remained with me while his family returned home.

Feeling a little better on the fourth day, I visited my friend the British doctor, Dr. Winston Caine, and his brother John, a non-conformist missionary. The good Dr. Caine then dosed me with a concoction of calomel and other un-known ingredients.

When I returned to my hotel I discovered that my return home had been delayed two more days by the effect of the medication. Finally, reaching my own dwelling, weak and exhausted and still suffering from 'le gripe' (a cold) and perhaps incipient pneumonia, I retired immediately to my futon and the care of my own servants.

As soon as I had sufficiently recovered, I had a Goma per-formed in thanksgiving and seriously vowed never to travel extensively again.

Pilgrimage to a Mountain Temple
Translated from Dr. Usui's notes

Two years after the disastrous trip to Hokkaido, Watanabe Bonze asked me to accompany him on a pilgrimage, again in fall, to a small temple where one of his worthy ancestors had served as Bonze. As the Imperial Corps of Engineers assisted by the Germans and Americans had built a railroad that would take us within 12 miles of our destination, it seemed that it might be a safe endeavor.

And as time heals, I had forgotten some of the more painful memories of Hokkaido. And since we would be traveling south rather than north, and since the weather was pleas-antly warm, I felt that it might not be as painful an experi-ence as my previous trip. Also, in the general area there were a number of local herbs grown and I wished to acquire their seeds, cuttings, or roots for my own pharmacy garden.

Therefore, one bright warm Sunday afternoon, Watanabe, two of his sons, his manservant, wife and her maid boarded the marvelous contraption, this triumph of Western engi-neering, and set forth on our journey. There were splendid views of the mountains and the coast road. As we rose in elevation, the outside temperature became crisp and the air beautifully clear. On reaching our transfer point, our hotel had properly provided carriages and we were whisked away in great comfort.

The next morning carriages were provided again which conveyed us the twelve miles to the temple, where our nightmare began. We arrived to a fine dinner and settled ourselves in for our four-day stay at a nearby inn.

That evening the snow came and for two days it continued to snow. We were informed that it was impossible to convey us to the monastery and we would have to remain at the inn until the storm had passed

Because the storm was a surprise and most unseasonable, I was assured, no wood had been laid in and there was very little charcoal. Fortunately I had brought my woolen kimono and sat wrapped in it with a quilt over my lap on a frame over a brazier for almost two days. Finally, the weather cleared and we proceeded to the temple where a Goma was performed and Watanabe visited the ashes of his illustrious ancestor. After having tea with the abbot, we respectfully retired to board our carriages, whereupon, while boarding I slipped on the icy step and tore a ligament in my hip and thigh. That night was spent in misery and the twelve-mile ride to the railhead was a torture.

The ride on the railroad which had been pleasant on our earlier excursion was a torture, but fortunately on arrival was mitigated by the fact that at my insistence, Watanabe had wired for a horse drawn ambulance to meet us and I was conveyed home in relative comfort. It took me approximately three weeks to recover and at that time I resolved that the only pilgrimages I would make would be to my own garden.

Visiting Buddha at Kamakura

Translated from Dr. Usui's notes

Spring had come early and since it was the 700th anniversary of the dedication of the Kamakura Tendai Temple, I chose to attend the celebration. I am happy that I did.

This time we traveled in early summer and by carriage. As we were early for the celebration, we were able to obtain good accommodations at an inn with an illustrious 800-year old history. The futons were delightful and the food most marvelous. The ceremonial invocations of the founders of the lineage and Amida Buddha were glorious and colorful. As the Emperor himself attended, there was grand music and I was able to catch a glimpse of His Divinity as the Son of Heaven walked from his carriage into the Imperial entrance to the Temple.

Over 5000 living creatures were freed and the celebration continued for eight days. During that time I was transported in mind and spirit to the Western Pure Land. During my entire stay, due to the wonder of the occasion, I heard not one word of discord and no violence of any kind occurred. It made clear to me that if humankind could live for seven days in such harmony and in such beauty, that there was more than a possibility that we could abide forever in that way. Before this time I had not really doubted, but had questions that universal enlightenment was indeed possible.

After my stay at Kamakura in such beauty, joy, harmony, and tranquillity, my questions were put to rest. I do believe it is possible that this land of suffering and pain can be transformed into a Pure Land with universal charity, kindness, and equanimity being the Rule of Law.

When we are faced as humans with such splendor, as went into the preparation for the ceremony and which made it seem as if we were in the presence of the very Enlightened Ones, our own demeanor undergoes a transformation. Kindness, generosity, and open-heartedness tend to replace meanness, rudeness, anger, and hatred.

At the ceremony I saw one of the highest nobles in the land lift up a beggar child so the child might behold a procession of monks. I saw the wealthy open their purses to the poor and unfortunate. And I saw soldiers act with courtesy and kindness, even to the poorest and lowliest.

It seemed to me that the energy of enlightenment streamed from the great statue of Amida and from the precincts of the Temple, permeating and transforming everyone and everything that it touched. But it brought to mind, at least to me, that this did not need to happen only on a single occasion. The reason that it happened was simply that we expected it to; and similarly that every day this enlightened energy is in the world if we will only take time to be aware of its presence.

There is no place that it is absent from, no place that is impenetrable to it, except the human heart which, most of the time, blocks it out. I have resolved to seek it each day and to encourage others, my friends, students, and patients, to look for it and to allow it to permeate their very being, allowing it to transform suffering into joy, pain and sorrow into happiness, and darkness of the soul into the light of wisdom.

I am so happy I made the trip and was able to bring back with me this realization: that the knowledge and compassion of Buddha is not limited to the Temple ground at Kamakura, nor is it only present during the great festivals, nor need it be looked for in a temple, nor is it enclosed in a ceremony, but it is a living guiding presence for his compassionate gaze and is always turned upon us. This land too can be transformed by our actions and our aspirations into the Great Pure Land of the Western Paradise and further I realized that Amida is just as present here as he is there. It is only our own stupidity that prevents us from realizing this. In fact all the Buddhas and Bodhisattvas, protectors, and servants, are all as present here as they are in their Pure Lands.

Their enlightened energy permeates all things but it is up to us to perceive it, take hold of it, make use of it, and apply it in our and OTHERS' daily lives.

24

BUTTON, BUTTON,
WHO'S UNBUTTONED?

Remember the first time you used chopsticks or tried to eat a meal squatting on your haunches, or tried some other strange Oriental custom, such as an Indian curry, not to mention attempting Origami, flower arranging or a tea ceremony? Then just imagine the problems Japanese had in mastering the strange Western customs introduced into Japan in Dr. Usui's day. Although this chapter is humorous in the extreme and, obviously Dr. Usui found its subject matter so; it nevertheless gives a certain insight into Japanese culture at this particular time in history. The Japanese having just discovered Western culture, as Westerners had just discovered Oriental culture, show however that the Japanese took this very seriously. Just as in the West, particularly England and America, Oriental furnishings, dress in the form of kimonos and silk smoking jackets, lacquered tables and Oriental bric-a-brac, and so on had become fashionable in the West, Western clothing had become fashionable in the East. But of course neither the Japanese nor the Chinese had thoroughly mastered either the multitudinous fasteners or customs connected with Western dress. This short amusing and somewhat poignant chapter taken from a lecture given by Dr. Usui to his students thoroughly illustrates this fact.

On Western Table Manners And Other Assorted Oddities
Translated from Dr. Usui's notes

We have been talking today about various Western customs, particularly the manners used while dining. Now, I wish to speak about the various table implements.

We civilized people are satisfied with one simple set of chopsticks and a small knife, this is not so with Westerners. You have all been staring fixedly at this basket covered with a napkin I have brought out and are wondering what it contains.

Perhaps an anatomical specimen, a new medical implement, or some root or herb. It contains none of these. Rather I have brought a portion; one 'setting' as it is known, of Western eating implements, part of a set presented to my father by the American consul, Mr. Townsend Harris. I am going to present them to you in sequence as they are used during the meal.

How such a simple activity as eating, and the attendant ritual could have developed is far beyond my comprehension. Particularly when Western food is generally presented in such an unaesthetic way, all thrown together on one plate with no regard to its appearance, and in such an overcooked state in the case of greens, vegetables, and seafood; and such an undercooked state in regards to any animal meats. However they do come from the other side of the world, so perhaps it can be understood that their cooking habits, as are their bathing habits, are exactly opposite and diametrically opposed to ours.

So I will begin.

This tiny 3-pronged implement is known as a 'cocktail fork'. It is used to search for the small corpses of overcooked sea creatures, which have been hidden within the glutinous red sauce made from tomatoes. One might find also, pieces of the Western onion, if one were to search carefully. It is their custom to serve this dish at the beginning of the meal.

Next this large flat spoon is known as a 'soup spoon'. It is used only during the soup course. It is not ever used at any other time, nor is it used to serve you other dishes.

It is not to be confused with the larger serving spoons which are placed beside various other dishes which are presented upon the table, and are only used to serve that particular dish. One must eat one's entire bowl of soup with this spoon including all of its liquid.

It is most inappropriate to prod around in the soup with one of the various kinds of forks. It is also extremely inappropriate to lift your soup bowl from the table and place it in your lap when eating, but one must carefully move its contents from bowl to lip while it remains firmly resting upon the table. One must be exceedingly careful during this operation that none of its liquid contents drips on one's clothes. This is considered socially unacceptable.

That is apparently why one must cover the upper portion of one's body with the white linen napkin provided for that purpose. This is usually tucked immediately below one's collar button by one of the corners, but not below the second button of the shirt. It is allowed to hang down in a diamond pattern covering one's shirt, waistcoat, and coat, the opposite end coming to a point at the level of your genitals.

Another custom is to simply place it on your lap, and women seem to do this more often. This of course leaves your shirt, waistcoat, and coat perilously exposed. I might mention at this time that I have seen a piece of sauced meat fall down between the breast cleavage of a lady diner who had the napkin placed on her lap. It is inappropriate to assist her in retrieving the lost remnant of food.

When you have finished eating most of your soup, it is most inappropriate for you, as any civilized person would, to lift the bowl from the table and drink the rest of its liquid. One should allow the unretrievable by spoon portion to remain in the bottom of the bowl. It is considered inappropriate by Westerners to belch. I might also add that it is considered inappropriate to produce sucking and slurping sounds when consuming the soup or any other portions of the meal.

Now we go on to bread and butter. This small flat knife is referred to as a 'butter knife'. It is the implement wherewith you apply butter to bread. Now for those of you who are unfamiliar with butter, I will say a few words about it.

It is a fatty oleaginous substance, rather like a thinner version of candle tallow. It always seems to be in a state halfway between liquid and solid, but is relished by Westerners, and used in their cooking.

It is extracted from cow's milk that is allowed to turn and subjected to some mysterious process known as 'churning'. The finished product is then heavily salted and used as a condiment with bread. One dips one's knife and then spreads the top portion of the bread, placing it upon the small plate provided. This plate can be readily identified by the fact that the butter knife is usually placed within it on the table.

Now, this smaller of the two large forks is known as the 'salad fork' and is used in consuming the raw greens and vegetables which are generally the next course, and quite frankly the only palatable part of a Western meal in my opinion. They are usually ruined, however, by the Western custom of hiding their natural flavor and texture under an oily sauce that is sometimes seasoned, sometimes not.

This next fork is the 'dinner fork'. This is used to consume the meat and the accompanying overcooked vegetables. In most cases you will be served beef which is their favorite. It is generally baked or fried. In the case of the British it is boiled. At the German consulate I have been frequently served baked pork, which was excellent. The British serve lamb and sometimes goat when lamb is unavailable. Occasionally a baked fowl is served, or in the case of an American, chicken dipped in flour and fried and is somewhat reminiscent of tempura, though the delicacy of tempura is decidedly lacking.

Sometimes a 'stew' is served; this consists of boiling meat of whatever kind with the vegetables and the meat's juices into what appears to be an unappetizing mass; however, many of these, though unappetizing in appearance, are actually quite delicious and the meat contained therein is thoroughly cooked. For some reason the wealthier families never seem to serve this, which is a disappointment to me as it is one of their least unappetizing dishes.

Now when eating with Americans, one of the dishes likely to be served is known as 'corn on the cob'. This is one of their only foods that may be eaten with the hands. However, it is not held directly but usually two small silver spikes are provided. One carefully inserts one of these in each end of the cob and then smears it with butter, using not the butter knife but the dinner knife, and then one chews the corn from its cob rather like a horse eating an apple. Although I find this Western vegetable quite tasty, the manner in which it is consumed I find slightly disgusting. Sometimes it is removed from its cob by the thoughtful cook, which I consider a most civilized way of preparation.

This last 'desert fork' is for your desert, which almost inevitably is a pie made from apples or other fruits. A pudding occasionally replaces it. A pudding is a most unfortunate kind of food made from flavored, sweetened, cooked starch. As generally it is semi-liquid, it is consumed with a spoon known as a 'desert spoon.'

The last item here is the 'teaspoon'. It is used only to stir sugar and milk into your tea or coffee and for no other purpose whatever. It is very inappropriate to use it or any other spoon to consume your meal other than the soup or pudding. The fork is used entirely for this purpose, assisted by the knife.

Before attending a Western feast I suggest that you attend one of the many schools of Western customs that are now popping up all over the Tokyo area.

As to the matter of Western clothing: The first concept you must hold in mind is that unlike Japanese, Chinese, or Koreans, who prefer loose and comfortable clothing, appropriate to the season, Westerners for some reason, perhaps the concept of suffering in Christianity, prefer tight, uncomfortable clothing, which in summer is terribly inappropriate.

Westerners even in summer tend to layer themselves in exceedingly heavy garments which then become soaked with their perspiration and always exude an extremely unpleasant odor. This is exacerbated by their usual refusal to bathe.

Now, the first garment you must be familiar with is the underwear. This usually consists of what is called a vest, then one has the underpants. In summer these are both made of linen or cotton and are worn next to the skin. The underpants have a slit sometimes held by a button in the front to facilitate urination. When dressing, it is important to appropriately position the slit. In winter a second layer of underwear is worn. This is usually woolen or at least flannel and covers the entire body leaving only the feet, hands, neck, and head exposed. It buttons up the front and has a large flap in back, the purpose of which should be apparent.

Unlike an unfortunate young man I know, when not used for a specific purpose the flap should be firmly buttoned in place. The young man to whom I am referring thought it was perhaps kind of a decoration and allowed it to hang from the top of his pants.

I have found that Western woolen underwear is one of their finer cultural achievements. As I generally suffer from cold in winter, fall and early spring, I find these to be a convenient and marvelous garment with one exception. The wool instantly irritates the skin wherever it touches, causes itching, and in my case, even chafing and even infection. Perhaps this is the cause of the Westerners general bellicose nature and ill temper, and one of the reasons that they are so prone to boils and carbuncles.

I solved this problem however by having a small interlining made of silk. When I suggested this to a foreign friend however, he indicated he felt it terribly feminine and would not make use of it. I truly fail to see why comfort should have a gender. I most certainly would not wear an obi or have my hair, at least what remains of it, lacquered and pinned; however, as a matter of clothing I most certainly cannot understand why one cloth must relate to one gender and another to another.

This certainly lacks logic in my mind. Apparently it is appropriate for Western females to wear silk next to the skin and make use of woolen outer garments, while Western men inevitably wear wool next to the skin and silk outer garments occasionally. But to return to my original subject.

This most important item of Western clothing is the button. When dressing one must make sure that all of the holes provided for the buttons line up equally on the garment, then they all must be buttoned, not even one being left open. Now if at some point while in public you discover a button that is open, one does not fasten it in public.

I will tell you the story of another young man I know. Not realizing that adjustments to clothing, particularly buttons, are inappropriate, this young man at a dinner party noticed that one of the eight buttons on his trousers was unfortunately unbuttoned. He found that to remedy this situation it was necessary to unfasten all the buttons above, and since it was the very first button, this allowed the entire front of the trousers to gape open. Noticing the expression of horror on the women's faces and the shocked disgust on the faces of the men present, he hastily rebuttoned only to find that it was unaligned. This of course necessitated a reopening and closing of the front trouser gap. Later during the party one of the men took him aside and explained the etiquette.

He of course was terribly mortified by his unfortunate error and quickly excused himself in embarrassment and left the gathering.

You will notice that in Western shirts there is no top button and two holes. This is for the insertion of the collar button. This also holds the collar in place in front. There is also a hole located to the back, directly opposite and a small double button is inserted through this hole and the hole provided in the collar to give stability. The back double button is usually unadorned, whether made of metal, ivory, whatever.

The front button is usually gold and sometimes adorned with a gem. This one is always worn in the front and never in the back. The cuffs of the shirt sometimes are provided with their own button, sometimes not. In the latter case, a stud is used to hold the cuffs together.

If it is a so-called French cuff, two studs are not used, but the cuff is folded back and the stud inserted through all four holes. When I was a young man I unfortunately made this mistake, and purchased two sets of cuff studs, I was exceedingly proud that I had found matching ones, then it was explained to me by one of the missionaries that this is not the way in which a shirt is worn.

Now for the tie. The tie is a Western connivance, as well as the collar for that matter, designed particularly to cause discomfort to its wearer. The tie I have decided is symbolic of a hangman's noose and is worn most likely to remind the wearer to obey all laws. The tie must be tied in a particular kind of knot.

One is called 'four-in-hand' and the other is a 'Windsor'. There are some others I understand, but I have not mastered them yet.

Now as a matter of button shoes, it is not possible for either a man or a woman to button their shoes without the use of the device known as a buttonhook. The implement is inserted through the buttonhole and then the button is pulled through the hole. One, of course, particularly if there are a number of buttons, must align the button with its corresponding hole. This, of course, can be exceedingly difficult if one is not experienced or if you are in the dark.

Also it is not necessary or proper to remove one's shoes or boots when entering a Western home or office. A few Westerners such as Mr. Townsend Harris, the American Consul General, and a number of the German and Dutch have actually had leather shoes with elastic in the sides made especially for them while they are stationed in our country.

Of course it would be impossible for Japanese to continually wear button shoes, since our customs dictate that shoes must be removed before stepping on a tatami; if we were to visit friends, much more time would be taken by removing and putting on our footwear than with the visit itself.

Both the European and Americans have a number of different boots for different purposes. There are riding boots and cavalry boots, and the so-called Mexican or cowboy boot. They require special implements to care for them and also to get oneself in and out of them. I do not suggest that any of you attempt to wear them.

Now the last bit of footwear I am going to mention are 'laced shoes'. Their closure is achieved with lacing made from string or leather thongs. They are very similar to old armor lacing and function in the same manner. It is important, however, that they remain tied properly in what is known as a bowknot. It is most inappropriate to walk about with the lacing untied; it can also be quite dangerous, especially when ascending or descending stairs.

Lastly but most important, it is extremely important that the shoes, boots, or any kind of footwear be properly brushed and polished. Those who do not attend to their footwear are looked upon as slovenly and lazy. One of their sayings that I have heard quoted frequently is that 'you can tell a man by his shoes'.

As to caring for Western clothing, woolen clothing must always be washed in cold water. If wool is immersed in hot water, when drying, it reduces to almost half its size, but not in an even or regular manner. Outer woolen garments usually are not washed but brushed. One gentleman told me that he had actually worn his suit for four years without having it cleaned, and I believed him, as one could detect his approach if the wind were right for at least three city blocks.

I have found that my woolen suits are much improved by frequently having my servants wash them in cold water with mild liquid soap, then during the rinsing they add a few drops of Indian Sandalwood oil, camellia oil, or lavender oil. This gives them a pleasant note and hides the animal smell of the wool, or in the case of tweed, that disgusting burned odor.

If one owns a Western suit, one must own a clothes brush and a flat iron. The suit is flat ironed when wrinkled and brushed for all other purposes. One's white shirt must be white, it also must be starched, and wrinkle free. Starch is a substance apparently of vegetable origin that is dissolved in water and then both collars and shirtfronts are soaked in it before flat ironing.

I leave these operations to my servants and if any of you have a wife, mother, or servant who is desirous of learning this mysterious process I will gladly arrange with my servants to give them instruction at the appropriate time.

The last item of dress I intend to mention is the hat. Unlike ours, Western headwear is rather simple, at least for men. I will tell you now I know nothing of women's headwear customs, for our women usually go hatless except in the sun. Western women are always seen in extremely flamboyant creations that certainly enter the realm of the bizarre. The simplest is known as a bonnet and ties under the chin. This of course makes it difficult for them to speak and one must listen carefully to a woman who speaks to you if she is wearing a bonnet.

Some of these creations are decorated with plumes, flowers, or even very life-like wax fruits. I have heard a story, though I was not present, of an unfortunate young man who when at a garden party thought a woman was a servant and her hat was being used to serve fruit, and to her upset and horror tried to detach a small life-like pear as she passed. Women hold these items in place with small, pointed weapons known as hatpins.

I know that you would not think of these items as weapons or that this would be the appropriate place for a woman to carry a weapon, but it is true. I myself with my very eyes have seen a low class Western prostitute remove one of these small daggers and put to flight a rascal sailor who was angry with her for some reason or another. She prodded him a number of times with one that was over 8 inches long, causing him to scream, run, and fall into a latrine ditch, whereupon she let out one of those raucous Western screeches which among them passes as laughter and then went her way.

I should also mention that both the umbrellas carried by men and parasols carried by women are generally carried at all times summer or winter and are also equipped with a sharpened steel point. I have seen two young Western ladies fend off a Malay thief with the points of their parasols and also on one other occasion I have seen three prostitutes come close to bludgeoning a Filipino seaman to death with a combination of parasol and handbags.

I must also mention that it is extremely inappropriate for men to use hatpins to hold their hat in place. My father tells me that shortly after the fall of the shogunate and the restoration of our beloved Emperor, that the renowned Minister of the Right who was naturally possessed at that time of an elaborate court hairdo carefully placed a Western felt hat on top and held it in place with ornate carved hat pins. This caused much amused comment among the Americans with whom he was meeting.

Hats must be properly brushed and shaped. This is usually done by steaming, but I do not suggest that you do this yourself. The first time that I steamed a hat I believe that I must have done it a bit too much for it disintegrated in my hands. Among Western servants and shopkeepers there is a division of men who specialize in this process which is known by the Western word 'blocking'. So when dealing with one's hat, one needs to go to a 'blocker'.

Silk and formal hats must be treated in a specific way that I do not understand. Western men's hats are very important to them and one must never make derogatory or rude comments about them, as among the court nobles and the old military government, they seem to be symbols of rank or social standing; or even perhaps relate to the region from which the foreigner comes, especially among 'Texans', the hat is extremely important and no matter how bizarre to our eyes, must not be laughed at.

The military people of course also wear hats, as do their naval officers and seamen. The Europeans seem to be much more elaborate and even somewhat bizarre and the Americans somewhat simple and plain.

The last thing I will mention about hats is that it is important when being seated in a Western parlor to notice whether or not someone's hat has been placed in a chair. This does seem to be somewhat their custom but a simple glance before you sit will save considerable embarrassment to yourself and upset to the hat's owner. Also I will mention here it is one of their taboos to place a hat on a bed in a hotel room. They believe it can bring misfortune and even death.

Next I wish to mention gloves. Both Western men and women make use of gloves. Before shaking hands it is appropriate to remove the glove on the right hand and hold it in the left, in the case of a male. When shaking hands their women never remove their gloves and generally when a women offers her hand one doesn't shake it, one bows and brushes one's lips over the top of the glove. This is usually the only time I have ever seen a Westerner bow to another, other than the British who always bow to their superiors when their superior is of noble rank. The superior usually does not acknowledge, and never returns the bow, although among Japanese this would be exceedingly arrogant and impolite. It is not so among them.

Germans bow slightly to one another and particularly to women while making an audible clicking sound with their boot heels. Frenchmen when taking a woman's hand usually linger much longer than other nationalities and it is not considered improper. I have noticed among the French that their politeness, courtesy, and good humor, has almost developed to a point of being civilized. They also appear to bathe more frequently and also use scented colognes to mask their odors. Their food, unlike the British, American or Germans, is extremely well-seasoned and usually presented in a pleasing way.

Now unlike among us, it is most inappropriate among Westerners, especially among women, to belch or pass gas in a social setting. One also does not announce the need to perform a bodily function; one asks in a whisper the location of the 'necessary room' and slips quietly away to belch, pass gas, or perform other bodily functions.

Now a mention about the 'water closet'. One will find generally placed squares of newspaper or a large book in the necessary room. These are not provided for reading but serve the same function as our waxed rice paper to clean oneself. The colognes and so on set out in a Western necessary room belong to your host or hostess and are not provided for your use. It is inappropriate to make use of them. Soap and towels, however, are provided for your use and one expects that you would make use of them.

As I have said earlier it is inappropriate to remove your shoes when entering their homes, but one must thoroughly wipe mud or excrement from one's shoes or boots before entering their homes. You will notice that at the entrance of their homes, a mat or piece of carpet is provided and sometimes even a broom. It is extremely important to perform this act, as some of their carpets are very expensive and can be seriously damaged by neglect of this custom, although it usually will not be mentioned to you out of politeness.

The last piece of male apparel I will discuss is the gun and gun belt. Other than military people wear it under the garment, and at any social gathering one divests oneself before entering upon a social occasion. In Yokohama particularly it is the custom that every male wear this bit of apparel while on the street. It apparently is a symbol of their manhood as our swords used to be a symbol of ours. I have noticed that some of our young men have started wearing this particular item of apparel, but one really should not wear it at any social gathering. If you own one it is best to leave it at home.

Now, there is one custom I will mention before closing, and that is their inter-sexual dancing customs. Unlike our custom that men dance with men and women with women, the custom among Westerners other than their sailors is to dance with the opposite sex. Numerous taboos and manners are associated with this custom, and I do not suggest that you even attempt it unless you have taken particular instruction from one of their servant class who is referred to as a 'dance master'. At one point in my life I attempted to learn this and found it to be so complex that I gave up the endeavor.

The particular dance master had a number of female servants with whom we were partnered. Their dancing requires that the partner be touched in places the Japanese would consider inappropriate with a stranger, not to mention the nausea caused while being in close proximity to the odors of a Westerner whilst whirling in their waltz movements.

Well, enough for today. If any of you have any particular questions, please feel free to consult with me privately at an appropriate time, some other day.

25

THE TRAGEDY AT OTSU

Dr. Usui lived during interesting times. It is not coincidental that he participated in at least one historic event of his time.
Here Dr. Usui gives an account of his participation in the events
at Otsu in 1890. Included following this account is another
short excerpt from his writings which at the same time referred
to the events of 1890 and supply us with important information on the practice and uses of Reiki as well.

The Visit of the Tsarevitch
Translated from Dr. Usui's notes

In the ill-fated and inauspicious summer of 1890, I traveled
with my friend Watanabe and my father for a visit to the
shores of Lake Biwa and the town of Otsu. Six months
before, my father had secured rooms at an historic Inn, not
knowing that during the ensuing summer, there would be
a visit by the Russian Tsarevitch Nicholas. Looking back on
those events, I am wondering if they perhaps presaged the
unfortunate conflict with Russia in 1904 and 1905, after
Nicholas had ascended the throne of all of Russia.

The first thing that occurred was that the manager of the Inn tried to repurchase our reservations, but to his dismay, even though he offered twice their value, we were adamant on staying our ten days. Otsu was extremely crowded due to Nicholas' presence. The town was filled with enough police to fight a small war, both secret and public.

There were numerous gaping Westerners from all over the country, as well as that class of Japanese who will travel far to see a tailed frog or a two-headed bovine. The attraction of a foreign dignitary has never moved me. But to some people whose lives must be so boring as to be almost intolerable, anything will be a reason for travel simply to break the monotony of their lives.

We found it disagreeable and inconvenient as the prices in most shops had tripled or quadrupled during the Russians' visit. Also various parts of town and even the lakeshore itself were quarantined whenever the Russians were present.

All the criminals, drifters and con men had been rounded up and expelled before our arrival and much care was taken to improve the already beautiful aspect of Otsu. Over my protests on the day of the Imperial procession I accompanied my father and Watanabe to a street corner to view the Russians. It was fortunate that I did. The procession was led by troops of our own Imperial guard followed by the very large Russians in full dress uniform and their band. This was followed by another group of Russians wearing blue, who were apparently their Imperial guard, then carriages containing our Imperial officials and local notables, and then the carriage of the Russians.

When the carriage was approximately forty yards from me, one of the police left his station and with a sword struck at the Crown Prince's head. The unfortunate and deluded man was named Tsuda Sanzo. One of the rickshaw pullers saw the blow coming and was able to somewhat deflect it. Two of the Russians jumped from the carriage and began to struggle with the assassin. Two other rickshaw pullers grabbed the assassin's legs and the group wrestled him to the ground.

The Crown Prince's plumed military headgear had been knocked aside and blood was pouring down his face from a cut on his scalp. My instincts immediately took over and I rushed toward the stricken noble. A number of police immediately restrained me but my continued shouting that I was a doctor calmed their fears that I was perhaps another assailant and they allowed me through. I noticed that he was barely conscious and had an extremely elevated pulse and respiratory rate. He was carried by his own guard into the lobby of a nearby hotel and I was hustled along.

A room was immediately provided and the Tsarevitch was taken there. I accompanied him, followed by number of Imperial officials, as well as the police with their revolvers drawn. He was placed upon the bed. I was then able to loosen his jacket and give him a thorough examination.

The cut though shallow, was bleeding profusely, and I tore hasty bandages from a sheet provided me by the management and cleaned the wound. My father had rushed back to our Inn and delivered my medicine bag about ten minutes later. I was quite fearful for the foreigner's life, as his pupils were unequal and he was perspiring profusely, though still only semi-conscious.

I feared that a subdural hematoma might be forming, as the blow had been struck on his left side and he was experiencing small tremors and spasms in his arm and the leg on the right. I am not a head surgeon, but I feared that surgery might be necessary to relieve the pressure, however, at that moment I called upon Medicine King Buddha and was told what to do. I placed both hands on the left side of his head and spread my perception inside of the injury. I noticed the formation of a small hemotoma, and from my Hara directed the energy through my hands and visualized the dissolution of the hemotoma.

To my perception and amazement it dissolved almost immediately and the sub-cranial bleeding ceased. At the same moment both his heartbeat and respiration slowed and he began to moan. In about five minutes he was fully awake and complaining of the pain the wound was causing him. There was a collective sigh of relief from both the Russians and the Imperial officials present.

The Crown Prince called for brandy but I forbade it; instead I called for green tea and administered a small dosage of morphine to assist in alleviating the pain. I was then informed that two trains had left Tokyo, one containing the Imperial envoy Kitashiwakawa and numerous other Imperial officials. The other contained the Emperor's Imperial physician and the entire staff of the Tokyo Imperial Medical University. They arrived a number of hours later and he was examined by all.

It was determined simply that he had suffered a mild concussion from the blow and feeling that further explanation of his condition would be fruitless, I concurred. I was profusely thanked by both the Imperial physician and the Imperial envoy and sent on my way.

The next day I was invited to the Imperial Russian presence and thanked by the Crown Prince himself who presented me with a small dagger and 1000 gold rubles for my fee. I attempted to decline the offer saying how embarrassed I was that such a horrible thing had occurred in my country.

He, in a very friendly but nevertheless imperious manner, refused my refusal to accept and told me that it was only a small way to express his gratitude. I then accepted and inquired if he needed anything in the way of medical or other attention. He informed me that he was being overly cared for and truly nothing else was needed or in fact would be welcome. We chatted for a few more moments on inconsequential things such as the weather and the beauty of Lake Biwa and I politely withdrew.

I was immediately grabbed by the police commandant and escorted to the room of the Imperial envoy Kitashiwakawa who expressed the Emperor's personal thanks for my quick attention to the Crown Prince and indicated that he would be in contact with me after I had returned to Tokyo.

Subsequently, a few weeks after my return, I was summoned by two of the Imperial bodyguards and accompanied into his presence.

After I was accompanied to his audience room, he expressed his gratitude and then to my complete and utter shock the Emperor himself entered dressed casually in Western garments and personally himself expressed his gratitude. Whereupon I was presented with a small tea service from the Nara period and three embroidered silk kimonos, one for myself and one for my mother and father, a small letter signed by the Emperor himself and a purse containing 5000 British sovereigns. This money combined with the Crown Prince's gift I used to found my small clinic a little later.

After taking tea and refreshment with the Emperor and envoy, the Emperor withdrew and I was offered a position on the staff of the Imperial Medical College. I explained to minister Kitashiwakawa that there were certain aspects about my medical practice which were traditional rather than modern and this might cause a conflict with the other staff and professors. Though pressing me a few times to accept, the envoy was relieved at my refusal.

I am sure that I had been thoroughly investigated before this audience and that mention perhaps had been made of my traditional inclinations toward healing which would not have been generally accepted by the Medical University staff. After much polite small talk I was dismissed and readily withdrew. I was shown to one of the Imperial carriages and returned home.

Unfortunately, just as I was leaving the Imperial grounds, my stomach, responding to the excitement and awe of having met the Emperor in person, insisted on emptying its contents to the politely concealed amusement of my guards. They did comment however, that should they have had an audience, they probably would have done the same thing, but most likely in the Imperial presence. Mentally I thanked all the Buddhas and Kami that that had not occurred in my case.

A few weeks later a number of members of the Imperial envoy on Kitashiwakawa's staff consulted me and later a number of other notables from the Court as well as their families. This greatly gratified me.

After the attempted assassination, our country had a great outpouring of sympathy and apology which was most graciously accepted by the Crown Prince whose sympathy for the Emperor's grief was even reported in the Russian press. I was most pleased at my small part in the affair. I am also happy that the Crown Prince recovered quickly without further incident or any disablement.

Now that all the treaty arrangements have been concluded and the politeness of our ministers has led to far fewer territorial gains than we expected, I cannot help my mind from turning back to that fateful summer of 1890 when the Crown Prince was attacked near Lake Biwa in Otsu. It saddens me to think that this incident could have been perhaps the seed that led to this conflict, or that if I had not been present to aid the Tsarevitch, another might have been on the throne of Russia and this conflict might not have occurred and much suffering would have been prevented both on the Russian and on our own side.

Although necessary sometimes, I cannot help but feel that war is a terrible waste of both the national treasury and of precious human life. Yet at the same time I cannot but help to feel that it is most proper to defend oneself from aggression by a proclaimed and vicious enemy.

This may seem to many of you, my students, as a contradiction and against the Buddhist way, but it is not, as much more suffering would occur if a nation or people remained passive and allowed themselves to be vanquished and conquered by a cruel aggressor. You may think this odd of me to say, but it is not, for if we were to allow such things to happen, the very teaching of the Buddha could perish. Examine the Islamic conquests that so devastated the Buddhist kingdoms of Northern India or of the many unfortunate things that have occurred to the native cultures in Africa and Polynesia when the first Christian missionaries arrived, and then the Christian soldiers, and then the Christian governors, and finally the merchants. The people were then exploited in a most cruel and unsuitable manner.

My maid has just returned from Hawaii and told me of the terrifying conditions among our people there. I also see the very unfortunate conditions in our silk and textile factories that are inspired by the greed and lack of humaneness that we have learned from the Westerners about treatment of employees. I shall continue to speak out against this and I am urging many of you to give medical aid and succor to such unfortunate female workers and also to speak out to the Imperial government about these abuses.

During the last two years, during the war with Russia, I have ministered to many of our returning soldiers and sailors and it proves to me the efficacy of the system of Reiki. Of the soldiers and sailors treated by myself, I have administered Reiki to each one, and they have recovered much quicker than those treated by my colleagues. Cases that were given up by them as moribund and beyond help have made a complete recovery.

One young man had suffered a shrapnel wound to his lower abdomen, severing both the ascending colon and several loops of his small intestine. Before we were able to receive him, both peritonitis and general septicemia had developed. He was given only hours to live. I performed some surgery, which at the time I thought to be useless, and administrated a hefty dose of morphine to ease his passing. I then administered Reiki with Mizu-Hari in hopes that it might assist.

On my visit the next day, I had expected that he would have gone forward to his next life, yet I discovered him conscious, coherent, and almost fever free, and having refused his morning dosage of morphine, told me he was almost without pain. Since he was moving around a bit, I insisted that the morphine be given, lest he tear some of the delicate internal stitching I and the other surgeon had made. But the surgical incision itself seemed infection free and his fever had almost entirely abated. No longer were there any symptoms of septicemia, although a few symptoms of the peritonitis persisted.

The next day on my visit however, they too had subsided and he was actually joking with one of his recovering comrades.

Five days later I happily discharged him to the care of his wife and parents. I have visited his home twice since and the young officer seems to be in excellent health and has been assigned some light duties in the Osaka garrison.

This is true of a Major I also had treated, whose liver had almost been severed from his body by a Russian bayonet thrust. Even though some surgery had been used to effect a repair, until I administered the Reiki with Mizu-Hari, the hepatic bleeding had not stopped. It immediately ceased after the administration of Reiki and his recovery was speedy and most uneventful.

It seems that all the patients I have treated in this manner have had a most uneventful and speedy recovery, far swifter than that of my colleagues, and that those who have not recovered, all have had a peaceful passing as they were all resting clearly on the support of Medicine King Buddha, engulfed by his compassion.

Thus, I must conclude that Reiki is of extremely great benefit in all forms of disease, injury, and accident when administered with the right attitude, with compassion and equanimity. Therefore, I can only urge you to make use of it whatever the circumstance and whatever the injury, illness, or accident that has occurred.

This brings something else to mind, which though it does not truly fit in with this discourse, I feel I need to mention.

Approximately two weeks ago, a young man known to my mother was executed for his attempt upon the life of an Imperial magistrate. The young man had deludedly accepted the doctrine of the Russian malcontent Kropotkin and believed that anarchy was the only acceptable political system. He had killed the official and severely wounded the bodyguard. His sister and mother had pleaded with my mother asking that I go and speak with him. To please my mother and my new wife, I agreed.

When I entered the miscreant's cell he was in both arm and leg chains and exceedingly bitter. I could make no headway against his bitterness so I returned home downcast and almost broken hearted, moved by his suffering.

That night I had a dream, or perhaps a memory of some past life, where I had been a prisoner in chains and feeling very bitter against the government and my captors. Then Medicine King Buddha accompanied by Amida came into my cell and Medicine King Buddha performed Reiki upon me. I had a change of heart and when executed the next day, immediately entered the presence of Amida in his Western Paradise.

I awoke and immediately visualized the unfortunate captive before me and performed Reiki upon him. The next day I returned to the prison and had my second interview with the captive. He was totally receptive to my conversation and though he had been Shinto, took refuge in the Three Precious Ones in my presence and I communicated to him the Nambutsu (Amida's mantra). A few days later he was executed and I was present. He had a calm peaceful countenance and died with the Nambutsu on his lips.

I have had to conclude that not only does the administration of Reiki heal physical injuries and disease, but also can heal spiritual injuries and illness and soften the mind of individuals and alleviate suffering in that way. I have been experimenting with this since my experience and find it to be true.

Yesterday our neighbor's wife and mother were engaged in a major conflict in his absence. Their household servants were equally divided. Sounds of breaking crockery, tearing shoji screens, and blood-chilling curses were issuing forth from their dwelling.

The conflict was so audible that neighbors even four and five houses away had begun to gather and a constable had been summoned, but ineffectually stood around wringing his hands, deciding whether or not to call for reinforcements. I thought this an excellent time to experiment by sending them both Reiki and to the servants as well. I immediately went into meditation, focused, opened my Tori, and sent forth healing and peaceful energies. Within moments a change could be felt and within a few minutes the noise had stopped. My mother and a neighbor from across the way gained admittance to the shambles of our neighbor's dwelling, only to find the wife and the mother in law embracing and weeping when moments ago both had been ready to sever the other's jugular vein.

The constable entered and after giving a short dissertation on domestic harmony departed with his head and limbs still connected to his body, which I am sure five minutes earlier would not have been the case if he had intruded.

One of my students told me, when I mentioned this to him at dinner this evening, that earlier in the week a small fire had broken out in his uncle's residential quarter while he was visiting there. He confessed that at the time, even though it had not been a part of his instructions, he let the fire draw Reiki, hoping that it could be alleviated before greater damage was done. Even though the fire had been raging terribly at the time, it immediately began to subside.

I am wondering if perhaps this is not a useful activity. If so, then a practitioner should be attached to every fire brigade. This might be most beneficial and might increase their poor efficiency in controlling conflagrations.

Now, I do not want to discourage experimentation (regarding the inner system), but at the same time I wish to caution you to use preliminary meditation and follow the instructions I have given to the letter before attempting such experimentation. This is both to protect you and make certain that unfortunate incidents do not occur. I am so certain that the compassion of Medicine King Buddha and the other supernatural entities will cover any such situation, that when invoked the result can only be positive.

For as we walk in their compassion so they will walk with us and guide our steps on the right path and guide our hands to the correct task.

Part III

The Contribution of
Dr. Watanabe

26

ABOUT WATANABE KIOSHI ITAMI

Dr. Watanabe Kioshi Itami was Dr. Usui's principal student and protege, and the son of his spiritual mentor, Watanabe Bonze, the Shingon priest. It would be improper for me to exclude from any book on Medicine Dharma Reiki some of the material by Dr. Watanabe.

Very different from Dr. Usui, Dr. Watanabe approaches things in his own unique, and in a much more left-brained manner. First, he was the empirical scientist; secondly the student devoted to his master.

Since most of Dr. Watanabe's notes are technical in nature and it would be inappropriate to include them in this introductory volume, I nevertheless feel it most appropriate to include this material, as well as two meditations that point to the essence of Men Chhos or Medicine Dharma Reiki.

However, I am beginning this section on Dr. Watanabe with a short selection from Dr. Usui that contains advice apparently given only to his student Watanabe.

Advice from Dr. Usui to His Student, Dr. Watanabe

Translated from Dr. Usui's notes

The chief cause of illness is unhappiness; the primary cause of health is happiness. When treating a patient, it is important to remember this, because if you don't, then you cannot successfully treat your patient. Speak to your patients, ascertain their living conditions, ascertain why they are unhappy, and exactly what has caused this unhappiness. Teach them to view unhappiness as impermanent and changing and instruct them to let the unhappiness pass right through; in fact, or give them specific advice and instructions on how to eliminate their particular unhappiness.

Many women have come to me with a variety of severe conditions and various other simple illnesses that obviously spring from the activities of their husbands or mothers-in-law. Many cases of cancer that I have examined and have treated successfully, or have attempted to treat but not successfully, are simply caused by unhappiness. The person is fearful of opening their belly or inserting a knife in their throat, yet their own body, through the production of cancer or another ailment succeeds where their own valor has failed.

Therefore, when treating a patient, you must convince them that they have a purpose to continue their existence, for without a purpose, even if you are able to help them successfully cure their present illness, a future illness will develop in its place and carry them away.

In each patient that you treat, you must awaken in them a purpose to survive. Set them on the track of the living and even the severest case will miraculously recover. I am not saying that this is the only treatment that should be administered. Of course, there are many allopathic treatments from the Western countries, America and Europe, and herbs from China along with moxibustion.

Incidentally, the reason that moxibustion works in many cases, I have discovered, is that often the person is unhappy because of a real or imagined past infraction of a social code or morality, or for whatever reason, they feel that they need to be punished. Moxibustion certainly punishes. I don't believe that moxibustion has any effect at all on the channels or the flow of energy in the channels. I believe, however, that it has a profound effect on the being, a very profound effect. And that profound effect may be that it is sufficient punishment to relieve the guilt that causes the unhappiness, which in turn has caused the illness.

I can relate a very odd story that is an example of this. A man I once treated had a melanoma on his foot that was growing. There was nothing that we could do, because the melanoma had spread into surrounding tissue and had metastasized into other parts of the body. We simply gave him five to six months. After the first month with this awareness the unfortunate soul developed an extremely painful gall bladder due to a number of stones. I, as the surgeon, removed the gall bladder. He had suffered extensively and due to his weakened condition due to his melanoma, his recovery rate from surgery rate was slow and painful.

Yet, he recovered and what else began to happen, is that the melanoma began to disappear throughout his body. He had created his karma; his mind, his guilt had created the melanoma to make him suffer. However, his gall bladder made him suffer. I removed the gall bladder. Evidently in his Mind Stream, by the removal of the gall bladder and the subsequent pain, he felt that his suffering was finished and complete and therefore, the cancer disappeared. It was amazing.

I once had a woman patient who suffered extreme sciatica due to a calciferous extrusion near the emergence point of the sciatic nerve. She suffered horribly and was in constant pain. I gave her opium. I even instructed her to smoke it. Having smoked one day, she began to iron her husband's pants and burned her hand severely.

She felt almost no pain because of the level of opium in her body. Yet the pain appeared later along with the ugliness of the burn on her hand. Amazingly, this healed approximately a month later after much suffering, but after that month, she also found that the calciferous extrusion had been absorbed back into her body and was no longer afflicting the sciatic nerve. So, the one painful burn and the subsequent needed month of recovery was enough also to help her recover from her other illness.

27

DR. WATANABE'S PARTING LETTER TO HIS STUDENTS

Translated from Dr. Watanabe's papers

I am writing this letter for you, my students, at this very crucial time in the history of our country. We are engaged in war with America and her Asian and European allies. We will of course be victorious, as Japan has never suffered defeat in any military conflict.

I have just returned from Nanking where our armies have been victorious. Japan's destiny, I am sure, is to be a guide to Asia, economically, culturally, and spiritually. Yet I cannot but weep at the suffering that war, in general, causes humankind.

What bothers me the most, is that both Japan and China are countries which early on in our history were privileged to receive the teachings of the Buddha, which urges us to prevent suffering, both in our realm and in the lower realms and to work for the happiness of all beings. I recently traveled, before my return to Manchukuo, where I found the troops of His Im-

perial Majesty the Manchurian Emperor and those of our Heavenly Lord enjoying brotherly camaraderie. I was presented to the Emperor in his modest but graciously appointed apartments and examined him for chronic tonsillitis.

He is of an age and also bears responsibilities for his people where the usual procedure of a tonsillectomy would not be appropriate. I prescribed the usual remedies and a change in diet and used Reiki both on his afflicted part, the throat, and his body in general. I am concerned for him because he is somewhat debilitated by his responsibilities, yet I am encouraged at his attitude and spirit, and the marvelous cooperation which our people and his are engaging in at the present time.

Our Emperor has said that he is like a younger brother and he himself said to me that he views our Divine Emperor as an elder brother or a wise uncle. The Manchurian people are extremely hospitable and have welcomed me. They are sorely lacking in trained medical personnel as all the European doctors fled except a couple of Germans, when we ratified our treaty. The Germans, though kind and diligent, are hard pressed and I found myself working 16 and 18 hour days both in treating our and their troops and civilians and at the same time, training their and our military orderlies and nurses in more modern procedures.

Therefore I am most glad to be back in Japan and taking a deserved rest before departing for the Philippines, which is my next assignment, as all of you know.

But I look at our progress in Manchukuo and our fraternal relationship with the Manchurian people and truly wonder why, we cannot alls f us, all the nations of the world, maintain this kind of relationohip. It would seem to me to be far less expensive both in lives, suffering and Yen, if nations could develop among themselves the kind of relationship that we have developed here with the Manchurian people. It is a partnership where aid is given from both sides and instead of the surly unwelcoming populace that our people have found in the South, it is a joyous and I am sure, a productive relationship that is occurring in the North.

I do wonder, especially during the dark hours of the night, why we humans cannot develop cooperation among ourselves and so question why war, as a solution to geopolitical problems, is necessary. Things would be so much better for all human beings and there would be so much less suffering, if we could learn that cooperation instead of confrontation is a far better means for people and nations to solve their problems.

But I digress. What I wish to do in this epistle is record for you, my students, a few of my experiences that I have not spoken about to you, concerning our new discipline. Although I am certain that we will be victorious in this conflict, nevertheless a number of times during my stay in Southern China, I found my life in danger and although I am a non-combatant physician, things do happen in war and it is not unknown for physicians to be killed by unfortunate accidents or their karma of being in the wrong place at the wrong time. Therefore, since I would not like to take a chance that you be deprived of some of my experiences due to an unfortunate accident, I have chosen to write this letter and to deposit it with the material left to me by Usui and the sacred texts upon which our discipline is based.

I do not have a premonition of my own death, if some of you fear this, but all of you know me to be a prudent man and therefore I am allowing prudence to dictate my actions in this case. Please do not worry for me, as I feel there is no cause. I am only being my usual cautious self and I would not like this unfortunate war to deprive you of my experience and the wisdom that I have gained therefrom.

When my father first introduced me to Usui I was a very young man. I did not desire to become a priest like my father, but desired to become a great military man like the Samurai of old and accomplish great things for my country and Emperor. However, in the person of Usui I found a different kind of warrior, one who engaged wholeheartedly in the war against human suffering. He inspired me and, thus, I chose the profession of physician, rather than soldier, although I ironically find myself in the position of a soldier-physician. Perhaps Buddha ordained in his wisdom that my juvenile wishes for military glory be fulfilled in this way. I do not know, but do find it somewhat amusing. But back to my younger years.

At that time Usui was engaging in research on our system of Reiki and was promulgating its teaching and methodology. Although I truly believe and have no doubt of the existence of the Buddhas and our Kamis, I have always been a scientific man, and at the time decided that my mission in life along with healing would be to discover the scientific explanation for the supernatural forces for I did not then, nor do I now, believe in the supernatural. I do believe, however, that mankind has not yet the wisdom and has not discovered the forces that we term supernatural. I believe that they are only natural forces, which we in our ignorance have not yet come to understand.

In the ancient days, our ancestors felt that lightning and rain came directly from a Kami, instead of the electrical forces created in the atmosphere by the rotation of our planet and its warming and cooling. Now this is where the European scientist would stop, but my question is, what are the forces that move our planet and are responsible for the divine order that we see in the universe?

As to the Buddhas, just because we cannot see, smell, hear or taste them in the usual way, does not mean that they do not exist. Right now sitting in my parlor in Tokyo I cannot see

Mukden, but because I have visited it, I am certain it is there. I have not seen, touched, tasted, or heard America, but just because I have not, doesn't mean it is not there. I have had experiences of American prisoners captured in Mukden and met a few Americans before the war. They had to come from some place. As we all know, they are very different from us, and even the Ainu aborigines.

So following this logic, many priests are around, my father included, and they had to come from some place, and so did their belief system. I do not believe that such a noble doctrine as the Dharma could have been thought up by an ordinary unenlightened human; therefore it had to be the work of an enlightened being. And if that being was enlightened, the methodology that would transform him from an ordinary warlike human concerned with everyday life, bickering with his wife, arguing with his associates, worrying about his appearance and how people related to him, to an enlightened being had to come from somewhere.

So using logic as my tool, just like the Americans, I have to conclude that it had to come from somewhere, and considering the general human condition on this planet, it had to have originated outside of our human sphere of existence.

Now as to Kamis, I have never seen, felt, nor touched one; I think I have sensed them on occasion, but that may just be a fantasy. But for thousands of years our people have believed in their existence and have built shrines and made offering to them.

As a physician, I have seen many instances where all of my scientific knowledge of medicine would have failed in preventing the death or further suffering of an individual. I have further seen prayers offered by pious and believing relatives to have caused miracles to occur. Particularly in one case of cancer, one case of cerebral edema, and one case of streptococcal *septicemia; in each case the patient was moribund and suffering, the relatives invoked a Kami and in a very short time a complete cure was affected.*

I do believe that these powerful beings can intervene in human affairs, have done so in the past and will do so in the future. But I also believe that they are best left to their own affairs, and that we as humans should solve our own problems and not depend on the Kamis for our every need. I am sure they have their own responsibilities and unless we are totally defeated by a situation, they should be left to their own affairs.

I truly cannot imagine that they wish to hear every trivial problem that an aging peasant widow would bring before them. The Buddhas, on the other hand, because of their enlightened intention do wish us well and like kind parents seek the benefit of their children. I have seen this time and time again. But to continue:

When I was a young man studying medicine and then having entered practice, I truly wished to find a scientific explanation for all phenomena. Though a devout Buddhist and believer in the Kamis, I sought an explanation and still do, for their existence and scientific law that would cover their actions. As I said before, I encountered Usui at an early age and was most taken with his practice of Reiki. I found that the patients with the same ailment who received only scientific medical treatment recovered far more slowly than those who received both. And that those who received no scientific treatment but only Reiki also recovered. I found this especially so on my recent visit to Manchukuo. At one point our supplies had not arrived and there were a number of wounded. I stitched and sewed and removed lead projectiles from their bodies. I had no morphine or other medication for pain and very little ether and no chloroform whatever. Yet I found that the administration of

Reiki and the use of some of the advanced practices were almost as effective as any drug.

And I found the patients recovered remarkably well. Now you might say that they would have without the Reiki and perhaps so. But two other doctors were working with me and many of their patients did not. They were amazed at the quietude of mind that my patients had and that mine speedily recovered where theirs did not or lingered. They said I had the true calling of a physician, which is true.

Yet I taught the lay practice for non-Buddhists to them and gave them initiation. Their patients began to improve, as well as mine. I even taught one of the Germans in Mukden, Dr. von Ronnie, my system. He had previously been a student of Rudolph Steiner and therefore his mind was open to the benefits of the system. Not so the other. His "spirituality" came directly from the Nazis and he scoffed and rejected anything to do with our system, labeling it merely an Oriental superstition.

I felt sorry about this, because his patients were deprived of the relief that Reiki might have given them, but also I felt sorrow at the condition his soul must have been in, to have had such a barrenness of spirituality and no support other than Hitler and the Reich to lean on.

Now to return to my original thought, when at first the system was taught to me, I do admit that I had many doubts, having just finished my very scientific training in medicine. Yet in order to humor my father and his and my friend Usui, I chose to practice it. When I saw the results, I became convinced of its efficacy.

Now all of you know that I am a sober individual, not given much to the use of sake, or given at all to flights of fancy. Unlike many of my colleagues I do not make use of my medical drugs to alter my consciousness; only two times in my entire life *has morphine sulfate been injected into my body. Once by Dr. Usui himself as an anodyne after he had removed my infected appendix, the other time when I had a fall as a young man, injuring my neck. Even though from that injury I sometimes suffer extremely painful and lasting headaches, I use no other medication than aspirin or sodium salicylate as an anodyne. I could make use of methyl morphine phosphate (codeine) or morphine itself. I do not.*

I have never made use of paregoric or tincture of atropos belladonna, other than when suffering from extreme dysentery, and then only for the duration of the illness and only in its prescribed beneficial dosage, and not as do Japanese mediums, combined with other vegetable drugs, to produce so-called supernatural visions. Nor is it my habit as it is with many of my Japanese colleagues and more so the European physicians I worked with, to either ingest or inject myself with morphine sulfate before surgery to banish fatigue or to give detachment. I believe this is a dangerous practice both in regards to the physician and the patient.

I wanted to reiterate these things before going on and to add that when the following events occurred, I was fresh out of my medical training and at the same time zealously scientific and at the height of my period of skepticism.

It was decided, in the summer of 1924, that I was ready to receive empowerment into the Mizu-Hari and be taught more advanced techniques. For a number of years I had been practicing the first levels of the teaching with some success and had developed a trust, though not without skepticism and a little hesitation, in the validity of my training. But you can't doubt success, especially when it occurs through your own hands.

With much Shingon panoply and ritual, Usui, assisted by my father, bestowed the empowerment of the Mizu-Hari upon me. I will apologize and use the excuse that I was a young man, but at least two times during this majestic and moving ritual, I had to severely bite my lip to keep from breaking into uproarious laughter. I was a young doctor trained in the most advanced techniques of medical science engaging in ancient Buddhist ritual which would have brought sneers from most of my colleagues.

However, I was profoundly moved and not just to laughter. I began to see at that time the majesty of our own national religious tradition and that of the wider aspect of Buddhism. When the ceremony was over, I felt that a beneficial change had occurred both in my spiritual consciousness and my attitude and outlook on the physical world. Yet I was still the young and slightly iconoclastic scientific physician. That was about to change.

As on graduation, I had ceased living in my father's home and had taken rooms in the Northern Prefecture of Tokyo prior to seeking a wife; I was alone that evening. Though it was not necessary that evening to perform the consecration of the Mizu-Hari, I would be required to the next day. Like a child presented with a new toy sword, I decided it wouldn't hurt if I went ahead. In fact, I thought it might be a virtuous act and perhaps make up for the undeserved amusement that had earlier occurred.

Setting up my altar and invoking the name of my kind and beloved mentor, Usui, I performed the ritual. Nothing whatever occurred. I felt somewhat disappointed. I went to the kitchen to prepare myself a cup of tea as my servant had retired for the evening and was sleeping at home. I returned to my bedroom shrine, sat down, and began to think about what I had just done and its implications both in the physical and on the spiritual planes.

All of a sudden I began to feel great warmth in my Hara. It spread throughout my body and I experienced such a sense of

physical and spiritual well being as I have never experienced before. I closed my eyes for a few minutes and reveled in the feeling, which was almost sexual. I shook off the feeling and opened my eyes in preparation to rise. I then noticed that although when I had sat down I had extinguished my lamp, the room was well lighted with a soft golden glow that was emanating from my flask of Mizu-Hari.

At first I thought there was fire outside the building and ran to the window and flung it open. But I only saw a few lights in my neighbors' homes and experienced the usual night sounds. I returned to my altar and the glow was still there and it was unquestionably emanating from my bottle. I felt the bottle gingerly but it felt cool, smooth, and slightly damp. After a few moments of reflection on this unusual event, I poured a little bit of the Mizu-Hari into my hand.

It felt like water. I ventured to taste it. It tasted like water with a slight salty taste that obviously had come from my palms that were profusely sweating at this time. I sat down and pondered. I obviously was not suffering a hallucination. My mental condition at this time could not have been better. I felt it could not be a hallucination as the room was being illuminated by it. I picked up my copy of Gray's Anatomy, opened to a random page and read about the cellatersic and other bone processes with which it is associated. I sat back down and pinched myself in a number of places to make certain I was not dreaming. I was not.

I stood and paced the room for a while and the light remained. I felt overwhelmingly tired and went to my futon. I immediately fell asleep and woke refreshed in the morning.

Now I need to mention here that when I injured my neck as a child I also fractured my left elbow. It had not healed properly and I was not able to fully extend my left arm. The first thing I noticed when I woke was that I could fully extend my left arm. I then thought to myself what a wonderful dream I had had. That was before I saw the Gray's Anatomy open on my writing table. I had not taken my clothes off the night before.

I hurriedly grabbed a coat and rushed to my father's home. I found my father and Usui having breakfast and they invited me to join them.

Later, my father told me I had the look of one who had been chased through the woods by a troop of Samurai Kami. I related my story of my experience to them both. They listened seriously and then Usui commented, 'Yes, I have noticed that to happen frequently with me.'

We talked the rest of the day. I had lunch, then supper, then returned home. It was getting dark and I rather carefully entered my bedroom shrine to see if the bottle was still glowing. I was somewhat disappointed but greatly relieved that it was not.

My rational mind began to take over. My father and Usui had tricked me. They had introduced a luminous substance such as Calcium sulfate or a phosphorescent compound of some kind into my bottle. I knew that even if the bottle had been washed, that there would be remains of the compound. So I chuckled, did the consecration again, made some prayers especially to Fudo that evening, and retired.

The next morning found me early at the University Chemistry Laboratory, analyzing the contents. And what did I find? Water, with a consistent profile as to its place or origin, a spring on Mt. Heiei. On microscopic examination, however, there was a difference. Although the water had not been boiled or any antiseptic added, there was absolutely no evidence of the usual bacteria or other plant life usually found in such water.

I could only conclude that the ceremony of the Mizu-Hari infuses ordinary spring water with an energy that is beneficial to sentient beings. I have concluded that this energy is present throughout the universe and is a physical thing, that had we the technology and instrumentation, it could be perceived and measured, as electricity or X-ray radiation, or as the energy emitted from the element Radium, or from Uranium; that through the activity of the mind and the power of ritual, had become concentrated in my water bottle.

We all know that when an X-ray tube is powered, its filament heating its cathode and current applied to its anode, both energy in the form of visible light and in the form of the higher spectrum X-ray radiation is emitted. Although we cannot see the X-ray energy, it is present, and many physicians have found out that overexposure can cause serious cellular damage to their hands.

I believe this Universal Life Essence is somehow concentrated in the human Hara and also in the Mizu-Hari bottle. The apparatus that concentrates it, are the bottle, the ritual, and the human mind. It is something our ancestors discovered and have passed down to us.

The symbols seem to be focal points to concentrate, direct and utilize the energies. That there is a rational, and scientific explanation for this, I have no doubt. When Madame Curie beheld the blue glow of radium, I am relatively sure she did not attribute it to a supernatural origin, but at her time had no explanation for the phenomena. The science of her day had not advanced to the same degree that it has in our time. She however recognized it as another chemical element.

When I beheld the glow from the Mizu-Hari, I am sure I felt very much as Madame Curie had felt. I had discovered something new. I feel that, just as in Madame Curie's day when there was no explanation for the energy emitted from radium, I feel that there is a reasonable, scientific explanation for this energy, but that our science has not progressed, as her science had not progressed in her day, to reveal the explanation to us.

Now mind entered into this. And immediately many of us feel on shaky ground, but as a physician I know that mind affects the body in a very real and apparent way. Dr. Freud has proven this and there are so many other examples that I do not need at all, to in any way reiterate them.

Now if the mind can affect the energies of the body, I have no doubt that on a very subtle level, it can also affect the energies around us, and when moving from point to point in a structured ritual, it can bring about a specified result. As I have become older and I hope, a little more wise and meditative, I begin to wonder that if all physical ailment, from toothache to cancer, cannot be wholly attributed to the workings of our mind, even accident; for have you not met an individual that accidents constantly befall, though apparently through no fault of his or her own. And again as the Buddhas teach that it is karma that affects the mind in such a way as to bring about illness and mishap. As I grow older I have come to more and more accept this as an universal certainty. Thus, the scientific explanation for Reiki begins to unfold in a clearly defined way.

Therefore, as medical science applies physical knowledge to heal the body, so Reiki makes use of spiritual science, in an as yet unmeasurable phenomena, to achieve the same end. For this reason, I urge all of you to whom I am writing, for a moment to suspend your disbelief, if you have any, and look at the other science that as yet has no rational explanation for its phenomena, but not dismiss it out of hand as 'ancestral superstition', but to look to it as a phenomena that science has yet to explain. Simply look at it as Madame Curie looked at her radium and simply look at spirituality and spiritual science only as another phenomenon that science has yet to find an explanation for.

Radium was not claptrap and superstition although before Madame Curie proved it, many scientists denied its existence. Consider the professional censure that she and Pierre underwent and the almost impossible conditions they worked under to prove their theory. Therefore, do not dismiss phenomena that you cannot explain out of hand as silliness and superstition; rather simply view it as unexplained and seek to find the explanation.

This is what I wish to tell you. I am departing soon for the Philippines where I will be working as a physician for the military government. I hope that when the war has passed, I will be with all of you again and we can together endeavor to cooperate and discover new scientific truths as we have in the past.

I know that during this conflict, all of you will focus on putting your best efforts forward, especially in this trying time, as I am doing, to faithfully serve Emperor and country and to bring the benefits of our knowledge and civilization to less fortunate peoples.

At first I doubted the wisdom of this, yet seeing the squalid and diseased condition and the utter filth that much of the world lives in, I can only feel that our way of life will be a great improvement and of great future benefit to the recipients of our civilization. Therefore I urge you all to do your best to bring victory to our Divine Emperor and those who faithfully serve him in our glorious military. Then when the conflict is over, to continue in the struggle against human ignorance and disease.

Banzai! Tora! Tora! Tora!

I am sending each of you a copy of this letter and I am

writing the copy by my own hand so that if my duties require of me to give my life for homeland and Emperor, you will have something of mine as a memento I am also depositing a copy for safekeeping along with the scripture and notes that Usui passed to me, along with my earlier notes in the Temple of my father's friend. You will also find there, in the case of my death, in the small red lacquer box, my will for the disposition of my property, along with my grandmother's antique chopsticks. I wish that they be given to my sister, should I not return.

With the utmost respect to all of you, my beloved and wise students.

Watanabe

28

TWO MEDITATIONS TO SUPPORT THE PRACTICE OF REIKI
As Suggested by Dr. Watanabe

The following two meditations point to the essence of Men Chhos or Medicine Dharma Reiki. I do not believe that one is required to have taken formal refuge to the Buddha, the Dharma and the Sangha to practice these. I do believe that they will be most beneficial to the practitioner of lay Reiki or even to the practitioner of other healing systems.

Compassion and Equanimity
Translated from Dr. Watanabe's notes

Begin to focus on and see all of the suffering that is experienced by all beings. Look around your own environment and notice your lack of satisfaction in your work, and also the lack of harmony in the home. Also notice the hunger, famine, thirst, injury and disease in the world. All of these things lead to abject unhappiness and misery. Anger being inflicted and suffered by others, not getting what one wants out of life, an unjust superior, or insubordinate inferiors, plowings and conspiracies, implacable enemies, wars and fighting, shootings and drowning and unforeseen accidents. Broken limbs, severed members, and gashes inflicted by sharp weapons. Drought, hail and inclement weather, not enough of this and not enough of that; all of these are what beings experience. Stronger animals devouring the weaker, water buffalo horses and dray animals, serving in ignorant servitude. We see these every day.

The farmer's hands are blistered and the fisherman becomes entangled in his net and is pulled overboard and drowned. The merchant defrauds the poor and the banker gathers money. The Emperor and the Prime Minister sit in their palaces, but no matter how exalted they are; they have their sufferings as well which they cannot escape. The burden of government weighs heavy upon them and the responsibility for our lives. These are the sufferings of the human and animal realms.

Is there no escape from this ever turning and grinding wheel? Carefully put yourself in the place with your mind of each of these beings. Visualize yourself as an Emperor, a water buffalo, the prey animal of another, a farmer or peasant, shopkeeper, or courtesan. In your mind experience their suffering and, thus, gain understanding of them. From this understanding will then arise compassion and from compassion will arise the path of your duty. And by following the path of your duty and comprehending it, will come enlightenment.

The compassion of the Buddha extends to all sentient beings in all six realms of existence, and that compassion must ever be in the mind of the physician, nurse, or ward aid. Without that compassion we are even lower than beings of the animal realm, for animals even show compassion to one another. Have you never observed an animal standing by its dying mate or an animal gently licking the wounds of its wounded friend? Have you never observed the faithfulness of your dog or the maternal love of your cat for her kittens.

Oh, that we could be that cat and look upon all beings as our children or to be that dog demonstrating our faithfulness to all beings and looking upon them as our master.

We are healers and therefore the servants of all, binding wounds, soothing pain, and administering comfort and healing. Compassion is the virtue we must develop within ourselves and foster, for without compassion, empathy, and sympathy, we cannot begin to heal, for it is the intention of our hearts rather than the action of our hands or the words which issue from our lips, that give us the true ability to bestow healing and alleviate suffering.

Meditation on Usui-Sama, Our Revered Teacher
Translated from Dr. Watanabe's notes

Like a kind father and nurturing mother, a brother who protects and a sister who cherishes, like the Emperor whose commands must be obeyed, and like a lantern lighting one's path, like a slave who fulfills every request made by you, like a friend with whom you share every confidence, like water cleansing your obscuration, like fire refining your defilement. Like a sword cutting through the knot of your ignorance and stupidity, like a dagger penetrating the dullness of your mind, like rice satisfying your hunger, like wind cooling your temper, like earth ever supporting you, like space vast, pervading all and incomprehensible, so is Usui, so is my teacher.

Like a whip goading me to accomplishment, like a doctor alleviating my pain, like a geisha bringing me joy, like a port giving me haven, like sake raising my spirits, like the ocean without limit is his wisdom, like a sail moving the vessel of my *life onward, like a stone ever immovable in knowledge, like a mountain unifying earth and sky, like a lake placid and tranquil, like the Buddha, source of all, so is my teacher, so is Usui.*

Sensei, grant that I may ever hold in mind these thoughts and your wisdom. Let me never stray from the training and precepts you have taught me. Let me never be turned aside from the purpose you have imparted to me, by the thought and cares of everyday life. Grant that I may become a servant and physician to all beings and, thus, emulate the course of your life.

29

CLOSING REMARKS

The journey with Dr. Usui and Dr. Watanabe continues to reveal a new and yet very ancient path of healing first introduced by Shakyamuni Buddha and now called Men Chhos or Medicine Dharma Reiki. Included in this book is all of the introductory information that is so far available (so far translated and edited), which can be shared with non-initiates.

It constitutes only about one quarter of the material so far translated, which then constitutes about one third of the material actually available (not yet translated). It is not my intent and never will be, to hide or hold back any material, but the traditions and restrictions of Tantric Buddhism make it necessary to exclude much of the material from the general public.

As a Buddhist Lama I have thoroughly examined the translated material and can see clearly that it is in no way contradictory to traditional Buddhist teachings. It does not contain any unusual twists and turns, and is in accord with the most orthodox guidelines of both Japanese and Tibetan Vajrayana Buddhism. The structure we have created to convey the teaching is not some unusual Japanese offshoot of Shinto and Buddhism, but an organization for the teaching and propagation of Dr. Usui's inner system of Buddhist practices for healing, which in essence is what Men Chhos or Medicine Dharma Reiki is.

We have purposely not incorporated teachings from any other system or method of healing, such as Babylonian, Egyptian, Celtic, Kahuna, or Native American teachings. There was also no attempt made to add Western psychology to our views of the system. I have attempted to present it as Dr. Usui himself presented it, with explanations of the foundation of Buddhist healing and of some Oriental customs.

In this dark time of the Kali Yuga, the age of degeneration, when societies are failing, the elements are in turmoil, and resources in the environment are being exhausted, when I believe that social changes of catastrophic proportions are eminent, perhaps will occur even in the next few years, I believe that Men Chhos Reiki is one of the methodologies of healing that can provide balance, comfort, and support during these troubled times.

The greatly compassionate mind of Medicine King Buddha has recognized these upcoming challenges and made provision for the support of peoples of right intentioned heart and mind during this turmoil. I feel that it is my duty and the duty of our Senseis to do our utmost to promulgate and spread these teachings throughout the world.

Therefore, I have endeavored to write this little book and to include some of the wisdom, knowledge, and techniques that Dr. Usui revealed for us. It is my sincere hope that you can make use of the information contained herein and will add Dr. Usui's and Dr. Watanabe's wisdom, not to mention that contained in the Tantra, to the sum of human knowledge, that it be used for the benefit of all and the harm of none.

I wish to close with a prayer recorded by Dr. Watanabe and attributed by him to Dr. Usui, whom we are told recited it together with his students at the end of each of his teaching sessions.

Closing Prayer

Translated from Dr. Usui's notes

NAMO

Mahavairochana, Universal Radiance of Enlightened Mind,
In union with the Clear Light Essence of Wisdom;
Medicine King Buddha, healing emanation of the Universal Mind
And Amida, Lord of the Boundless Light,
Throughout the entire three thousand fold universe.
May your radiance spread, illumining the darkness of ignorance,
Alleviating pain and suffering and bringing comfort and solace.
Send us forth, Oh Lords that we may be your messengers and servants
To the suffering and sorrowful.
Spreading the universal radiance of your compassion and comfort
To everyone everywhere,
That it may abide throughout the Three Times.

Part IV

Appendices

Appendix A

THE TIBETAN CONNECTION
Translated from Dr. Usui's notes

We know that the Tibetans hold many secrets and have preserved portions of the Dharma that have been lost to the rest of the Buddhist world. Of course, this is because in their mountain land, they were able to abide in peace and escape wars and fighting that have so plagued both China and Japan. In this wondrous place of peace and contemplation the Tibetan people have been enabled to put aside mundane matters and cultivate only the enlightened mind. That is why I am seeking to obtain Tibetan material, especially any material from the great medical college at Lhasa.

I believe that some of my missives may have reached the Grand Lama but I do not know this for certain. I am simply going to have to wait until my friend in India communicates with me again. I have certitude that secret texts exist which have not been promulgated in the rest of the world, and I am hoping to acquire some of these so that I may utilize their contents in my endeavors.

I would so love to travel to that place which most certainly must resemble Amida's Paradise of Great Bliss and drink from the incomprehensibly deep well of their spiritual wisdom in person, but age and infirmity prevents the realization of this desire at least in this lifetime.

So I must depend upon my friends and co-searchers for truth, who are utilizing the trade connections of the Indian merchants through Shigatse to Lhasa. So far, nothing has come out, but I am sending to India now 100 Gold British sovereigns, and promising them to any merchant who can bring my friends valid medical texts written authentically in the old Sanskrit or even in Tibetan characters. Our circle here has decided among us, that we will not accept texts in Chinese, as they may be adaptations or perhaps non-authentic apocrypha, or even, considering the greedy propensities of certain individuals, outright forgeries.

So for the present time, we must remain patient and wait, hoping our prayers and expectations will be fulfilled by the infinite kindness and compassion of Medicine King, for I am sure our intentions and aims are beneficial.

Appendix B

THE TITLE OF THE "TANTRA OF THE LIGHTNING FLASH"

Translated from Dr. Usui's notes

One of my students asked me why the "Tantra" is called "The Lightning Flash", or what is the actual name of the Tantra? I will say a few words about it for the record.

The title of the Tantra, "The Thunderbolt" or "Lightning Flash", relates to many things, so I am going to explain this title in the way that it ought to be explained, which is within itself a teaching.

You may remember that Vajrapani was previously known as the Indian God Indra. After becoming Buddhist he became Vajrapani. In Japan, he is called Wei-To. He is the great power of all the Buddhas. His name is Chana Dorje in Tibetan, in Japanese Wei-To, the holder of the thunderbolt; this is the thunderbolt of enlightenment.

The name of the Tantra, "The Lightning Flash", the Thunderbolt, is significant in that it relates to the healing power that is contained within Vajrapani, who is the power and the application of Medicine Buddha. It is very important to understand this relationship. It is the lightning flash that flashes across the sky, brilliant, blinding, immediately dispelling all darkness - the darkness of ignorance, the darkness of obscuration, the darkness of suffering, the darkness of disease. The "Lightning Flash" brings light so that beings can find their way through the maze of the darkness, and perceive reality as it is.

This darkness is the darkness of delusion that has spread across the entire three thousand-fold universe. The lightning bolt that flashes across the sky is the lightning bolt of the illuminating wisdom and power of all the Buddhas. As it flashes across the sky, it dispels that darkness: The darkness of those who have lost their way, who are fumbling about in the darkness of ignorance and delusion, not understanding the true nature of reality and not understanding the true nature of themselves. This is why the "Tantra" is called "The Thunderbolt" or "Lightning Flash" which was thrown by Indra, and later as Vajrapani, the thunderbolt of the Vajra Family; the thunderbolt, the diamond of enlightenment, immovable, unchangeable.

It is all this and it is even more. The Tantric teaching contained within, dispels the darkness of suffering, this darkness of delusion, this darkness of ignorance, and it leads to the knowledge of Self and knowledge as to the reality of the true structure of the Three Thousand Fold Universe. It illumines the true nature of one's own true Self, and one's own Mind, and the true structure of the universe and of Buddha Nature.

All of this is contained in this "Tantra", "The Lightning Flash", the Lightning Bolt. It dispels darkness; it dispels illness; it dispels all of this suffering. That is why the "Tantra" is named, "The Tantra of the Lightning Bolt", the "Tantra of the

Thunderbolt", the "Tantra of the Lightning Flash". That is why it is named in this way, because these are the things that it dispels. It dispels illness, it dispels suffering. In dispelling ignorance, it reveals the nature of one's own mind, and the reality, the true reality, which is inseparable from the universe, but is hidden by the darkness of delusion.

This is why the "Tantra" is named as such. And this is the purpose of the "Tantra", and this is all I have to say on this subject.

The word for "thunderbolt" is Vajra in Sanskrit, Dorje in Tibetan. It has many connotations, like 'diamond', 'immovable', 'unshakable', 'unchangeable', 'lightning bolt' or 'flash' (usually implying the lightning striking something). The word is used frequently in Buddhism to indicate the effects on one's psyche of the realization within oneself of the deeper teachings; Vajra and Dorje also refer to the male organ; in Tibet, Dorje is frequently used as a given name for a male child.

Appendix C

MORAL PRECEPTS OF MEDICINE DHARMA REIKI

Devoutly revere the Buddha, the Law, and the Teachers.
Do not forget the power of meditation.

Devoutly practice the mantra.
Do not engage in superflous disciplines.

Devoutly trust the Law of Compassion.
Do not denounce the creed of others.

Devoutly promote the sense of equality.
Do not arouse discriminatory feelings.

Devoutly awaken the sense of compassion.
Do not forget the suffering of others.

Devoutly cultivate an amicable disposition.
Do not display an angry countenance.

Devoutly preserve a humble manner.
Do not arouse the spirit of arrogance.

Devoutly visualize the source of defilement.
Do not develop a sense of attachment.

Devoutly study the Law of Evanescence.
Do not arouse a sense of greed.

Devoutly examine your own faults.
Do not make comment on the faults of others.

Devoutly go on trying to influence others.
Do not forget your own proper business.

Devoutly follow the Path of Enlightenment.
Do not mix with frivolous pleasure seekers.

Devoutly follow the teacher's guidance.
Do not indulge in your own desires.

Aided by these precepts to the end of the world, exert yourself and do not be negligent. The activities of body, speech, and mind have as their ultimate end a single devotion to Buddha.

Appendix D

THE FIVE MEIJI PRINCIPLES
Adopted by Dr. Usui for the Practitioners of Lay Reiki

1. Don't get angry today.
2. Don't worry today.
3. Be grateful today.
4. Work hard today (meditative practice).
5. Be kind to others today.

Appendix E

GLOSSARY

Amitabha: Buddha of 'Boundless Light', one of the most important of the Mahayana representations of Perfect Enlightenment. Amitabha is the patron of the 'Western Paradise' of Sukhavati; enjoys particular popularity in Japan where he is known as Amida. Amitabha is the Buddha of the 'Pure Land' school and the famous Lotus Sutra.

Bhaishajya Guru: Commonly known as Medicine King Buddha; of central importance to the practice of Medicine Dharma Reiki and the teachings of the Tantra of the Lightning Flash. His name translates as 'Master of Healing' or 'Master of (All) Remedies'. In many of his vows, Medicine King Buddha pledges to aid beings, who hear his name. Further described in the Sutras are nine instances, in which sincere recitation or concentration upon Bhaishajya Guru's name has a potent, saving force. By calling on Medicine King Buddha, and by intending wholesome change, one can have a spiritual rebirth and gain freedom from the fetters of one's concepts and emotions. Among the many tools learned in Medicine Dharma Reiki there is, for example, a special invocation of Medicine Buddha and

Vajrapani, to be done over a number of days, when life is threatened by incurable disease. Dr. Usui used this ceremony with great success in his clinic during the terrible flu epidemic, which swept the world in 1918-19.

Bodhisattva: A 'Buddha in training'; one who has not achieved as yet a fully enlightened state and may be 'in the body' (currently alive on this earth) or 'out of the body'. Buddha Shakyamuni's disciples are called 'Bodhisattvas', and are also known as 'the sacred Sangha'. There are said, variously, to be either 10 or 13 stages or levels in the career of a Bodhisattva, leading to full Buddhahood.

Buddha: A fully enlightened Being, embodied or not. Examples: *Shakyamuni Buddha*, as one we know historically as having been on this earth embodied; and *Amitabha Buddha*, one who lived as a man on this earth in a previous pre-historical time and achieved Buddhahood and stays in an unembodied form with close connections to current events because of his vow to help all sentient beings to likewise achieve Buddhahood.

Buddhism: Buddhism is not really a religion. It is a philosophy or way of life. Shakyamuni when asked if he was a God and his teaching a religion said definitely: 'No'. He said that he did not come into the world to teach religion, but to teach humankind how to live at peace with themselves and with others, and how to fulfill their purpose and achieve enlightenment.

Dharma: Basically, the teachings of the Buddha. Also, a way of life based on these teachings, in harmony with natural or universal law.

Dharmakaya: (also see *Sambhogakaya* and *Nirmanakaya*): The aspect of a Buddha that goes beyond form and formlessness, free of duality; the True Nature common to all Enlightened Ones. The *Dharmakaya* is emptiness and its realization beyond the limits of time and space; pure transcending awareness.

Earth Touching Gesture: When Shakyamuni sat in full lotus posture under the Bodhi Tree and was making his difficult struggle to gain enlightenment, he was constantly besieged by temptations of many kinds, particularly by the 'head demon' Mara. When Shakyamuni achieved his final realization and his body began to emanate light, Mara appeared before him and taunted him that it was just his imagination, enlightenment was not reached. Shakyamuni reached out his right hand, touched the earth below him with the tips of his fingers and swore by the earth, which he sat on, and that the earth itself should testify that he had gained enlightenment. Therefore, his paintings and images are shown with his hand extended in the Earth Touching Gesture.

Five Buddha Families: The Five Buddha Families represent a division of the cosmos into five categories or functions, each headed by an ethereal, but 'real' Buddha who is able and willing to help. They are:

BUDDHA FAMILY, in the center of the Mandala, represented by Mahavairochana Buddha, color white;

VAJRA FAMILY, in the eastern direction of the Mandala, represented by Buddha Akshobhya, color black or mid-night blue;

RATNA OR JEWEL FAMILY, in the southern direction of the Mandala, represented by Buddha Ratnasambhava, color golden yellow;

PADMA OR LOTUS FAMILY, in the western direction of the Mandala, represented by Buddha Amitabha, color red;

KARMA FAMILY, in the northern direction of the Mandala, represented by Buddha Amoghasiddhi, color green.

This present world era and its development are under the direction and responsibility of Amitabha, the Buddha of Boundless Light, and the Lord of Discriminating Awareness. If you wish to learn more about Buddha Amitabha, you may contact Lama Yeshe at one of the addresses given in the back of the book.

Hinayana: (see Theravada)

Karma: A complex term. Karma does not just infer a simplistic view that all 'wrongdoings' must be paid for in unpleasant retribution from some (non-existent) God like 'Lord of Karma'. First of all, 'wrong' and 'right' often depend on whose view is being expressed. What is 'wrong' according to one person may very well be 'right' according to another. Karma simply means 'action', and that every action executed by a mind stream identified with the action, will cause a reaction. The 'Lords of Karma' only reside inside of us, in what Carl Jung called the 'collective unconscious' or what in Buddhism is referred to as mind stream: the continuity that flows through multitudinous incarnations. We are our own 'Lords of Karma' and we ourselves bring about situations that eventually, over the period of all of our lifetimes, will mature our inner being so that it will be naturally compassionate and loving. This is why Fritz Perls, the founder of Gestalt Therapy called the Buddha 'the first and greatest psychologist there ever was.'

Kukai: Born on the island of Shukoku in 774 A.D.; died 835 in Tokyo. Kukai was posthumously awarded the title of 'Kobo Daishi' by the Japanese Emperor. He received the empowerments and texts of many teachings from Master Huiko, the 7th Patriarch of Shingon Buddhism while at Ch'ang An monastery in Mainland China. In 805 A.D. he returned to Japan and brought the teachings with him, including the Tantra of the Lightning Flash. In 809, he received permission to reside at Jingoji Temple, where he initiated the teachings and practice of Shingon Buddhism, a major Vajrayana (Tantric) Buddhist school in Japan. He is known as the 8th Patriarch of Shingon, and as a crucial link in the Lightning Flash lineage, is also an important figure in Medicine Dharma Reiki.

Mahayana: (see also *Theravada* and *Vajrayana*) The 'Great Vehicle', one of the two main branches of Buddhism, the other being the Hinayana or 'Lesser Vehicle'. The Vajrayana, or 'Diamond Vehicle', is actually a part of the Mahayana branch of the Dharma, as all Vajrayana lineages have as their foundations in the Mahayana teachings on emptiness and compassion. In the Mahayana tradition, the practitioner focuses on the Bodhisattva path, to gain enlightenment for the sake of all beings, and to forsake Nirvana until even the last being has been liberated from the suffering of Samsara.

Mandala: 'Circle and circumference', a symbolic representation of cosmic forces in two-or three-dimensional form.

Medicine Buddha: see *Bhaishajya Guru*.

Medicine Dharma Reiki: A system of healing using various techniques and tools, such as:

Mizu-Hari, or blessed and empowered water;
An entire pharmacopoeia, also using gemstones
to charge the elixirs;
oils, such as sesame oil;
laying on of hands;
individual prayer and meditation;
communal rituals and special prayer ceremonies;
Mantras and visualizations.

All these tools and practices are part of a set of Buddhist teachings, which were handed down in a scripture, called the Tantra of the Lightning Flash Which Heals the Body And

Illumines the Mind. This scripture is based on a teaching, given by Buddha Shakyamuni to two physician brothers at Deer Park in Sarnath. It was handed down in a long lineage from Northern India, via China (and Tibet), and came to Japan in 805 A.D. when Kukai established Shingon Buddhism in the Land of the Sun Goddess. Beginning in 1896, Dr. Usui developed Medicine Dharma Reiki from a copy of the Tantra, which he had found in an antique bookstore. The system is deeply rooted in Vajrayana Buddhist practices, and for its transmission, relays heavily on the use of empowerments.

Men Chhos Reiki: The Tibetan word for Medicine Dharma Reiki.

Mizu-Hari: Blessed and empowered water usually retained on the altar of a Medicine Dharma Reiki practitioner; used in hands-on healing of serious conditions.

Nirmanakaya: The embodiment of Buddhahood on the physical plane, i.e., taking on a physical body. The vehicle of the 'Great Compassion' of a Buddha, projected into the world for the benefit of sentient beings. In the Nirmanakaya aspect, the Buddha's purpose on earth is to teach the Dharma.

Nirvana: Absolute realization; the inexpressible reality of Oneness, which is always present, and only needs to be recognized. According to the Mahayana and Vajrayana tradition, Nirvana is not separate from Samsara, as they are both empty in nature.

Pali Canon: The collection of scriptures of the Theravadin school of Buddhism. According to the Theravadins, this collection contains the actual words of the Buddha.

Pure Land of Sukhavati: Also known in Tibetan as Dewachen. This is the Pure Land established by Buddha Amitabha to which 'lost and wandering souls', and others may be sent or brought so that they may enjoy peace and safety, receive instruction, and achieve understanding and spiritual growth. When dying, people may focus on Amitabha and his Great Compassion. If they do, they will swiftly be carried to Dewachen, and find companionship and a teacher, and all their needs will be met. People who undergo a traumatic sudden or violent death remain very often unaware of their own passing, and are, thus, 'stuck between worlds'. They do not know how to get out of their condition. Knowledgeable Shingon bonzes or Tibetan Lamas can call attendants (entities that in the West are called 'angels') who can guide these beings into the safe haven of Sukhavati, the 'Western Paradise' of Buddha Amitabha.

Reiki: A technique of spiritual healing and self-healing, a gentle routine for easing pain and promoting general well-being so that the body can heal itself. Like Medicine Dharma Reiki, Dr. Usui devised the lay practice of hands-on Reiki on the basis of his study and experiences with the practices of the Tantra of the Lightning Flash. Reiki was popularized worldwide through the lineage of Dr. Hayashi and Hawayo Takata. Dr. Usui referred to it as the 'pacification', or the 'soothing hands'.

Rice Congee: A soft-cooked rice dish, not quite soupy, sweetened with honey and spices. Among the Tibetans, even today a similar dish (no doubt a derivative), of rice cooked very soft, beaten with finely chopped raw ginger, and finely cut white cheese is considered very curative of any digestive problems, and is the usual staple for the sick. Incidentally, it is delicious.

Sambhogakaya: The pure enjoyment aspect of a Buddha, also represents the aspect of communication. Much like the Nirmanakaya can be compared to physical embodiment, Sambhogakaya can be compared to the level of experience in the etheric or finer energy body. The way in which a Buddha manifests in a Pure Land, like Amitabha in the Western Paradise.

Samsara: The wheel of birth, death and rebirth; the six realms of existence. All existence within the cycle of Samsara is characterized by suffering and impermanence, no matter how splendid and glorious it may appear temporarily. All existence within Samsara is due to a basic misunderstanding as to what is real and what is not. According to the Madhyamika School of non-duality, Samsara and Nirvana are both devoid of any reality as they are mere concepts of the mind.

Sangha: see also under Three Precious Jewels: The community of monks, nuns, novices and lay practitioners. People of like mind and heart, who follow the teachings (Dharma) of the Enlightened One.

Shakyamuni: 'The silent Sage of the clan of the Shakyas'; epithet for Siddhartha Gautama, the source of the sacred Dharma in our era.

Shingon: The 'School of the Pure Word', or Mantra. A Japanese form of the 'Diamond Vehicle', or Vajrayana. Esoteric Japanese Buddhism, founded by Kukai, the 'Kobo Daishi' (774-835 A.D.). According to Shingon Buddhism each and every human being is endowed with the 'Three Secrets' of body, speech and mind, and is thereby inherently gifted with the qualities needed to attain full and complete enlightenment. Shingon practitioners believe that Buddha Mahavairochana is the source of their lineage. Initiation into the different Mandalas is a necessary prerequisite to fully grasp the nature of his teachings. The two main teachings of the Shingon tradition are represented by the Garbhadhatu- and Vajradhatu-Mandala.

Sutras: The words of the Buddha, memorized by Ananda, usually starting out with the words, 'Thus have I heard...' The

Sutras comprise the basic body of the Buddha's teaching. All Sutras were originally compiled in either Sanskrit or Pali, and later translated into Tibetan and Chinese and other languages. Some Sutras stress the importance of devotion and surrender to the Buddha, either through focusing on the miraculous feats by the Enlightened One, or by praising the teachings of the Middle Path of non-duality. There are also Sutras that are of a more philosophical intent, focusing on direct inquiry into the nature of reality.

Tantras: The Buddhist teachings of an esoteric nature, including magical and ritual texts; secret teachings entrusted to only those few that the Buddha felt would not misuse them by causing harm to others. Some medical texts from Medicine King Buddha were also listed as Tantras and were only passed down in direct transmission from teacher to student, sometimes without being written down. The Tantra of the Lighting Flash is a good case in point.

Theravada (see also under *Hinayana*): The 'School of the Elders', at present the predominant form of the Dharma in Southeast Asia in Sri Lanka, Burma (Myanmar), Thailand, Cambodia and Laos. The fundamental teachings of the Buddha, such as the 'Four Noble Truths', the 'Noble Eightfold Path', and the 'Doctrine of Interdependent Arising'. Because the Theravada School emphasizes individual liberation, based on personal effort, it is much criticized in some Mahayana scriptures for lack of compassion. According to the Mahayana view, the quest for enlightenment needs to include the motivation to be of benefit to others as well as oneself. The basic teachings of the Hinayana approach of the Theravadins, however, play an important role in the Mahayana tradition. They are as much a cornerstone of the Dharma as are the purely Mahayana doctrines of the 'emptiness of all apparent phenomena' and the Bodhisattva path.

Three Bodies: 'Trikaya' in Sanskrit: Dharmakaya, Sambhogakaya and Nirmanakaya. The Three Bodies of a Buddha are representations of the same enlightened presence, viewed from different vantagepoints and emphasizing different aspects of Enlightenment. Dharmakaya represents the truth of what is, also called 'Thatness'. Sambhogakaya and Nirmanakaya can be best viewed as supports, which help to communicate the absolute.

Three Precious Jewels: The Buddha, the Dharma and the Sangha. The Buddha is Shakyamuni, our First teacher (in this world era). The Buddha manifests in the mind stream of the practitioner in the form of a Lama or teacher, who represents the Buddha. The Dharma is his teachings, which gives us the knowledge necessary for enlightenment. The Sangha (or 'Noble Assembly') is (1) the personal followers of Shakyamuni, who gained enlightenment in his lifetime or shortly thereafter; and (2) the members of the present day congregation of Buddhists, who support each other in achieving emotional stability in the challenging illusion of Samsara.

Three Times: Past, present and future.

Three Thousand Fold Universe: The universe times three thousand, multiplied by three thousand more. Supposedly the number of universes there are. Frequently used to indicate a number so large as to be unknowable and uncountable.

Three Vehicles: Hinayana, Mahayana and Vajrayana.

Two Purposes: The benefit of self and others.

Usui, Mikao: Dr. Usui Mikao, born August 19th, 1862 in the Osaka district of Japan at the Usui family home where the family had lived for eleven generations; died March 9th, 1926 after the last of several strokes. The family was of minor aristocracy, to quote the good doctor, and supported the Meiji restoration. The Usui family were Tendai Buddhists, but after Dr. Usui Mikao had recovered from his near death experience induced by a bout of cholera, he became a close friend of a Shingon bonze by the name of Watanabe. Thereafter he joined the Shingon School of Japanese Tantric Buddhism. Dr. Usui's development of the Reiki healing practice occurred within the parameters of Shingon Buddhism, except for the lay practice which he devised and taught so that those who are not followers of the Dharma might also enjoy the blessings of spiritual healing.

Vajrapani: A Tenth Stage Bodhisattva; the guardian of the secret Tantras.

Vajrayana: The 'Diamond Vehicle', a further development of the Mahayana approach in which compassion and working for the benefit of others is intensified. The direct or swift path that enables one to gain enlightenment for the benefit of all beings in only one lifetime.

Vinaya: A definite set of rules of life and conduct for monks and nuns as formulated in the Pratimoksha Vows.

Watanabe, Dr. Kioshi Itami: Heart student of Dr. Usui in the inner Tantric teachings; son of Watanabe bonze, who served as Dr. Usui's spiritual mentor. Dr. Usui left his papers, the manuscript of the Tantra of the Lightning Flash, his office files and patient records with Dr. Watanabe when he realized that he was dying. He instructed Dr. Watanabe to see to it that they were preserved at all costs, as they would be needed in the future.

Wisdom Being: The consciousness that occasionally 'puts on the physical overcoat' of the physical body and creates the appearance of experiencing Samsara.

BIBLIOGRAPHY

Birnbaum, Raoul: *The Healing Buddha*, Boulder, 1979

Gyaltrul Rinpoche: *Generating the Deity*, Ithaca, 1996

Hakeda, Yoshito S.: *Kukai — Major Works, With An Account of his Life and Study of his Thought*, New York, 1972

Shifu Nagabodhi Tomi: *The Bodhisattva Warriors*, York Beach, 1994

Snodgrass, Adrian: *The Matrix and Diamond World Mandalas in Shingon Buddhism*, 1988

Stevens, John: *Sacred Calligraphy of the East*, Boston & Shaftesbury, 1988

Tsogyal, Yeshe: *The Lotus-Born, The Life Story of Padmasambhava*, Boston & Shaftesbury, 1993

Yamasaki, Taiko: *Shingon and Japanese Esoteric Buddhism*, Boston & London, 1988

Information contained in Dr. Usui's and Dr. Watanabe's notes and papers and in the different manuscripts of the text and commentaries of the "Tantra of the Lightning Flash", as well as other contents in the famous lacquer box, purchased by Lama Yehe's father in 1946, are not completely translated and not available to the public at this time. Further publications are planned for a later date as gradually more of the information becomes available.

ABOUT THE AUTHOR

Dr. Richard Blackwell is a Buddhist Lama and retired clinical psychologist. Lama Yeshe, as he is also called, is completing the translation and editing of the Usui material as well as a number of never before translated Tibetan Buddhist texts on healing and related subjects. His hobbies include growing unusual medicinal plants. Before his ordination as a Buddhist Lama, he served in the military in an intelligence-gathering capacity and directed a mental health and substance abuse program in the private sector. He designed a number of mental health and substance abuse programs for small hospitals. He refused any copyright remuneration for such material, believing that such material should be available for the public good. He presently conducts *Men Chhos Reiki* seminars in the US and teaches *Men Chhos Reiki* on a one to one basis in his home. *Medicine Dharma Reiki* is his first book.

Contact Addresses: For more information regarding upcoming seminars, or questions about *Medicine Dharma Reiki* write to:

Dr. Richard Blackwell, (Lama Yeshe) Spiritual Director
Men Chhos Rei Kei© International Inc.
P.O. BOX 907,
Edgewater Maryland, 21037 U.S.A

Your e-mail can be sent to: Teresa Fulp, MCRK Coordinator medicinedharma@yahoo.com. The following two web-sites give access to more information about Lama Yeshe, Medicine Dharma Reiki and classes held by his students world wide: www.paulahoran.com and www.healing-touch.co.uk

FULL CIRCLE publishes books on inspirational subjects, religion, philosophy, and natural health. The objective is to help make an attitudinal shift towards a more peaceful, loving, non-combative, non-threatening, compassionate and healing world.

FULL CIRCLE continues its commitment towards creating a peaceful and harmonious world and towards rekindling the joyous, divine nature of the human spirit.

Our fine books are available at all leading bookstores across the country.

FULL CIRCLE PUBLISHING

Registered Office

18-19, Dilshad Garden, G.T. Road, Delhi 110 095
Tel: 228 2467, 229 7792 • Fax: 228 2332

Editorial Office

J-40, Jorbagh Lane, New Delhi 110 003.
Tel : 461 5138, 462 0063, 465 3930. Fax: 464 5795

Bookstores

5B, Khan Market, New Delhi 110 003
Tel: 465 5641, 465 5642